CLARK CO. LIBRARY

ENGLISH LANGUAGE SERIES

Creating Texts: An Introduction to the Study of Composition

ENGLISH LANGUAGE SERIES
General Editor: Randolph Quirk

ADVERBS AND MODALITY IN ENGLISH
Leo Hoye

CREATING TEXTS: AN INTRODUCTION TO THE STUDY OF
COMPOSITION
Walter Nash and David Stacey

THE ENGLISH INFINITIVE
Patrick J. Duffley

RHYTHMIC PHRASING IN ENGLISH VERSE
Richard D. Cureton

GOOD ENGLISH AND THE GRAMMARIAN
Sidney Greenbaum

THE LANGUAGE OF HUMOUR
Walter Nash

THE RHYTHMS OF ENGLISH POETRY
Derek Attridge

STYLE IN FICTION
Geoffrey N. Leech and Michael H. Short

AN INTRODUCTION TO MODERN ENGLISH
WORD-FORMATION
Valerie Adams

COHESION IN ENGLISH
M.A.K. Halliday and Ruqaiya Hasan

A LINGUISTIC GUIDE TO ENGLISH POETRY
Geoffrey N. Leech

INVESTIGATING ENGLISH STYLE
David Crystal and Derek Davy

Creating Texts:
An Introduction to the
Study of Composition

WALTER NASH and DAVID STACEY

Longman
London and New York

Addison Wesley Longman Limited
Edinburgh Gate
Harlow, Essex CM20 2JE, England
and Associated Companies throughout the world

Published in the United States of America
by Addison Wesley Longman Inc., New York

First published 1980
This edition published 1997

ISBN 0 582 24486-2 Paper

British Library Cataloguing-in-Publication Data
A catalogue record for this book is
available from the British Library

Library of Congress Cataloging-in-Publication Data
Nash, Walter.
   Creating texts : an introduction to the study of composition /
Walter Nash and David Stacey.
      p.   cm. – (English language series : 20)
   Includes bibliographical references and index.
   ISBN 0–582–24486–2
   1. English language–Rhetoric.   I. Stacey, David, 1955–
II. Title.   III. Series.
PE1408.N22   1997   96–44575
808 '.042–dc21   CIP

Set by 33 in Bembo
Produced through Longman Malaysia, CLP

Contents

Preface   vii
Acknowledgements   ix

1   BEGINNING AT SOME BEGINNINGS   1

2   HOW READING TEACHES WRITING   19

3   ABOUT PARAGRAPHS   39

4   CHARLEY'S TALE, OR THE GAPS BETWEEN
    SENTENCES   58

5   SENTENCES: PENNING AND PARSING   82

6   PLAUSIBLE WORDS IN POSSIBLE PLACES   110

7   OBJECTS AND VARIETIES: DESCRIPTION AS ACTIVE
    PARTICIPATION   129

8   DISCOURSE AS DIALOGUE: WRITING ON THE
    INTERNET: E-MAIL, DISCUSSION LISTS AND
    NEWSGROUPS   149

9   PROJECTS, THEMES AND DIVERSIONS   182
    A. Compositions, free and bound   183
    B. Creative Analyses   195

C. Rewritings and Interventions   219

BIBLIOGRAPHY   226

Indices   234

Preface

This book has a simple brief: to be of practical value to anyone faced with the task once called 'putting pen to paper', latterly recognised as 'typing a document' and possibly to be known in future as 'uploading a text'. Its subject is the technique of what the British call *composition* and the Americans *rhetoric*. It dwells on the writing of sentences, considers the structure of paragraphs, and invites reflection on broader questions of composition – in personal correspondence, journals, essays, academic articles, fictions.

In describing these matters, it draws variously upon concepts of traditional grammar and rhetoric and the modern conventions of the Internet. At one point, lost for an adequately descriptive title, one of us had a humorous impulse to imitate TV kitchenspeak or handymantalk and call the work 'Here's one we made earlier: how to cook up a style' or 'Build your own text: a Do-It-Yourself guide'. These formulations, however ineligible as titles, do in fact express quite well what is going on in the book. Our view is that you can learn something about writing by studying closely how other people have done it; further, that writing is *societal*, its stylistic varieties depending on contexts, communities and relationships. You build as those skilled in the craft have built; you cook for your invited guests.

In much of the book, the reader is treated as a member of the college class, a more or less passive observer of what is demonstrated, although there are many useful and entertaining projects to be derived from the first eight chapters. It is in the final section, called 'Projects, Themes and Diversions' that readers are invited to come into their own as writers. These exercises, we would insist, are no more than indications of what might be done.

Books are seldom written without a great deal of auxiliary support and nurturing. In this connection our warmest thanks are due to Dakota Hamilton and Helen Hunter, to which *blest pair of Sirens* the book is dedicated; and thanks also to Neomi Lugmayer, for her timely loan, in a far country and a remote place, of the typewriter Samsung Agonistes, without which we would have missed deadlines. On this occasion the keyboard proved to be mightier than the ballpoint.

WN   DES

Acknowledgements

We are indebted to John L. Rouse, Ian York, Janet Aber, Shea Bennett for permission to quote their 'email' addresses and extracts from their discussions on the Internet 'In defence of Nigel' in *rec.arts.tv.uk.eastenders*; and to Arlene Rinaldi to quote information about 'The Net User Guidelines and Netiquette', John Buckman to quote him and information about the Walter Shelby Group and Jacob Haller for his quote on Jazz'L.

For Cody and Taff
who keep us in touch with the context

One

Beginning at some beginnings

Let us suppose that you are about to write, at the request of your insurance company (Brightside Brokers), a brief factual description of what happened when your motor vehicle was rear-ended at the intersection of Rollinghome Road and Wanderlust Way, one fine afternoon in July. You are of course wholly innocent of any responsibility for this deplorable event, which occurred while you were singing along to some old Leonard Cohen tapes and patiently waiting for the traffic lights to change. All you know is that a big car came up behind you and removed your rear bumper, your stop lights, and most of your baggage compartment, including your fairly usable spare tyre and those pretty flowering baskets you were carrying home from the garden centre. It is a miracle that you are not going round in an orthopaedic collar. As you recall the event your grief and rage are truly indescribable, but never mind, if a description is what they want at Brightside Brokers Inc., a description is what they are going to get. So you describe:

> I'm sitting at a stop light on Rollinghome Road, doing no harm to anyone, when suddenly BANG this mindless oaf or to put it more accurately this lobotomized gorilla chooses to ram his BMW up my tailpipe. Right there in broad daylight, visibility perfect, the street empty. He demolishes my back end, this yuppie hooligan. *Totals* my fuchsias, he does, and has the gall to ask me what of it? Then, would you believe it, he accuses me of *rolling back*, the unprincipled hound, yes, *rolling back* – at 20 m.p.h.! – into his squeaky-clean corporate sales-chariot. Can

you believe that? Do I have witnesses, you ask – well, yes, I have a witness, I have a myopic pensioner being taken for a walk by his long-haired dachshund, which, I am happy to say, paused to lift its little leg against the BMW, proving beyond a doubt the intelligence and discriminatory powers of this breed of animal. That man, or possibly that dog, could if invited testify to the accuracy of my narrative.

Now having at this point experienced the first fiery outbreak of the compositional impulse – the *calor cogitationis* as Quintilian calls it – you stop to read over your work, with a possible view to improving a turn of phrase here, sharpening a point there, even, it may be, adding one or two tasty insults to what is already a reeking dish of contumely. You are quite pleased with it. You consider it not half bad. You show it, looking for approval, to your spouse, or your partner, or your sibling, or your best friend, and you are surprised and a little hurt when they tell you that, fine though your description undoubtedly is, it will not get you too far with the steely-eyed cynics at Brightside Brokers. Much more in this vein and you might find yourself paying for your own repairs. What is required, they gently remind you, is a brief description of the facts; not of how it feels to have had those outraged feelings; not of how satisfying it is to nurture feelings until facts disappear; just a little cool description of the facts themselves.

At first you sulk, because nobody likes to abandon a fine ebullient piece of writing, but eventually you are persuaded to attempt an impersonal, coldly objective account, in conventional documentary style, of what really happened at the intersection of Rollinghome Road and Wanderlust Way on that afternoon in July. This turns out to be surprisingly hard. It is always easier to give expressive rein to your personality than it is to come down to little brass tacks. You struggle with the problem, however, and after several drafts manage something along the following lines:

> The accident occurred on Friday, 22 July, at 3 p.m. approximately, at the intersection of Rollinghome Road and Wanderlust Way. (See the enclosed sketch-map.) My vehicle, a 1957 sand-coloured Bono-de-Luxe convertible, reg. nr. OUR A1, was waiting at the traffic lights in Rollinghome Road South, when it was struck from behind by a silver-grey BMW saloon car, reg. nr. BEAST 666. I estimate that the BMW was travelling

at 10–12 m.p.h. when the collision occurred. It appeared that the driver had failed to apply his brakes in good time. Visibility was good, and the road surface dry. The impact was so hard as to result in appreciable damage to the rear of my vehicle. (See the enclosed mechanic's report.) The collision was witnessed by a passing pedestrian, Mr J. P. Shufflewell, a retired minister of religion, whose address I append.

This you show to your friendly adviser, who reads it through with nods and grunts and eventually suggests that you should add the words 'with the gear shift in neutral and the parking brake engaged' after 'waiting at the traffic lights in Rollinghome Road South'. You make this addition partly for the sake of domestic peace, and partly because you see the wisdom of representing yourself as one who follows good driving practice to the uttermost letter of virtue. Of course your purpose is to present a reliably objective account, but even so there are ways, without actually *loading* the piece, of conveying to the insurance assessor how blameless you are and how culpably negligent the other driver has been. 'It appeared that the driver had failed to apply the brakes in good time', you say. *Appeared*? You wouldn't really know, would you? Butter wouldn't melt in your mouth, would it? You wouldn't like to imply that he was asleep, would you, or drunk, or reaching into his back pocket for a sachet containing a narcoleptic substance, or just suffering one of those blinding lapses of memory he has kept concealed from his general practitioner? You will only say that when he slammed into your rear end it *appeared* that he had failed to 'apply' the brakes – and let the experts at Brightside see what they make of that. It is devious dealing, but the conventions of this kind of writing allow for it. Then again, 'the road surface was dry'. This is in case the other fellow, in his account, comes up with the well-known slippery tarmacadam ploy, or invents an oil slick, or happens to remember a sudden squall of intensively localised rain breaking precisely over his car. You forestall him with your laconic assertion, 'the road surface [was] dry'. Good stuff. It will probably save your no-claims bonus. Peace descends on your heart as you fold the form into its pre-paid envelope. These things, you tell your domestic consultant, should only be written after a period of mature reflection. And you are right. Never be in a hurry to put pen finally to paper; you may presently be obliged to put paper finally into waste basket.

Such experiences, however, may tell us something about the craft of writing. If nothing else, they teach us to write *appropriately*, using – or exploring, sometimes expanding – conventions of form and style most likely to achieve an envisaged purpose: making a report, arguing a case, appealing to an audience, telling a story. All such purposes are essentially social, or, as we shall say, *societal*. A society is an intricate thing, a complex of institutions, hierarchies, kinships, practices, assumptions about behaviour, powerfully influential not only as they exist in themselves, but also as they are perceived in the mind of the individual. We each have a diffuse mental impression of our society, a kind of internalised map/guide in accordance with which, whether consciously or unconsciously, we think and act *societally*. Writing itself thus becomes in many ways a societal practice, though beginners in prose, and college aspirants to poetic stardom, dislike the proposition that writings exist and take shape in societies. Asked why they write, they will often say 'to express myself', learning only by grudging degrees that 'self-expression', if not exactly a will-o'-the wisp, is always a light to be followed circumspectly. In any case, nobody who writes formally, in full sentences and completed texts, can write for 'myself' and 'myself' alone. Even diarists do not write wholly for 'themselves', unless, perhaps, like Samuel Pepys, they resort to a secret code; as long as they write in plain English (or any 'natural' language), they write for someone, for 'the other me', the postulated audience. They write *as if* this diary-making, for all its privacy, were nonetheless a societal act.

Let us nevertheless allow that of all forms of text, the diary is the most *personal*. It is even, to use an out-of-town word, solipsistic. Your diary will allow you to please yourself in many ways. You need not be able to spell, or construct grammatically correct sentences, or use a standard vocabulary, or proceed logically in connected stages, or indeed do so many of the things a societally-governed text will demand of you. The diary puts no constraints upon you. It leaves you to scribble, to fumble, to stumble, just as you please and just as the words come out; and for that very reason the keeping of a diary may be an excellent school of unhampered facility and assurance in writing.

The case is greatly altered, however, when you have to write a letter of application for a job, say, or an academic essay. It will be a vain endeavour, and a foolish one, if you write 'Having seen your advertisement in *The Times* newspaper for a linguist with special reference to Spanish, seek no further *señoras y señores*! for I am *el supremo* when it comes to languages and such'; or if your paper on the disposition of the fleets at Trafalgar begins 'Horatio Nelson, England's number one sea-dog, had an ace plan to whack the French'. You will get no job and you will be graded C minus, because you are technically incompetent and too dull (or conceited, or deranged) to understand the proposed *function* of the piece of writing on which you are engaged. Society is, let us repeat, complex. It has its hierarchies, its accepted attitudes, its permissible relationships, its notions of normality, its patterns of conduct, its prescriptions for correct behaviour. With all this, it has its institutionalised activities, and to each of these certain conventions are assigned: there are conventions of writing for letters of application, for submissions to insurance companies and other commercial bodies, for laboratory reports, for conference papers, for many of the functions we associate with our map of society. Such writings are thus functionally framed, and in them we express our societal selves only by accepting the functional conventions. That fictive fellow whose car was rear-ended at the corner of Rollinghome Road made the initial mistake of supposing that in writing to his insurer he could come directly to the societal heart of the matter − that he had been *wronged*, in a world that accommodates *complaints* and proffers *remedies*; he had to be persuaded that his personal feelings and his societal position could only be expressed by working through the appropriate functional channels. Had he been setting out to write a novel − to *invent* that scene and those characters − he would have been at liberty to reject the conventions that direct the writing of a simple report; though even the novelist, seemingly so free to roam the societal field, is not altogether free from functional constraints.

There are, it would seem, three stations on the route through the beginnings of writing: call them *person*, *convention*, and *society*. The route is circular. Map it in this way. Draw a circle, and then at the six o'clock position locate a point marked person. At ten o'clock locate **convention**, and then at two o'clock place **society**. (The diagrams on p. 8 illustrate this.) For some kinds of writing, the route runs clockwise. When 'I' set about writing an academic paper or a report, for example, my first reference is to the functional conventions of my task, as modelled by papers and reports beyond number. My paper then takes its place in the societal repertoire, as a representative of a certain kind of institution. 'I', as a member of society, defer to the force of that institutional repertoire – I read academic papers or reports, and am personally affected by them; they stimulate my thought, they change my ideas, they shift the landscape, or 'mindscape', of my observations and memories. The case then is not so much 'I express myself by writing' as 'I am expressed *by* many writings, including my own'; and so the route comes full circle.

That, however, is only one of three possible routes. We must all be aware of writings that do not take as their first step the imitation of conventional models, but rather seek to express without impediment the relationship – the negotiations and explorations, if those words are preferred – of a person within a society at large. When 'I' sit down to write a story, I take no functional guide, no formula – or if I do, I must risk the scorn of literary critics, who will expect me to disguise the mechanisms of writing. There *are* formulae in fiction, to be sure, and – to complicate matters – fiction may, as part of its fictionalising, parody or mimic the conventions of purely functional writing; but still the fact remains that for the fiction writer, or, in general, the 'art writer', the compositional route runs anti-clockwise, through a contemplation of societal actions, suppositions and relationships which may then beget imitations of some functional styles. Consider again the accident on Rollinghome Road. If 'I' want to make out an insurance report in due form and order, I write 'clockwise'. If I want to let off steam and damn all careless drivers in expensive automobiles – but still present the semblance of an insurance report – I write 'anti-clockwise'. This is the route I will later follow if I want to recover the experience in a short story. The creative act goes widdershins, in risky opposition to the normal round ('risky' because there is usually no middling result between total success and utter disaster; the conventions are a safeguard which is removed as soon as one tries to write non-conventionally).

Now there remains a third possibility, when the route runs both clockwise and anti-clockwise. Take a case. 'I' embark on my paper for the Journal of Philological Conundrums. 'In this paper', I write,

'I propose to address some aspects of the study of English pronunciation in the eighteenth century.' So far, so good, for the language of this opening is wholly conventional, following a well-established model. Dozens of papers begin in that way. The Journal likes them that way. Contributors like them that way; it makes them feel secure. But as the writing proceeds, as my paper bids fair to fill its societal place among the massed exhibits of scholarly deliberation, I am struck by the thought that this is dismally boring – not necessarily that the topic itself is boring, but that this way of composition is inert, mute, unsinewed, and wholly devoid of companionable appeal. I accept that writing should instruct, but I feel the force of another societal notion, that writing should cajole, please and persuade. So, when the time for a second draft comes round, it is possible that I will attempt a different strategy for my opening. I begin, perhaps, like this: 'Did Samuel Johnson distinguish a *sewer* from a *shore*? How did they pronounce *tea* in Queen Anne's day? Why did Dean Swift rhyme *vermin* with *garment*? These are not uninteresting questions.' Quite probably the editor of the Journal of Philological Conundrums, a conservative soul, will reject my paper, or return it with a request that I re-draft it in the good old conventional-functional style that has kept the Journal going for the last fifty years. What I have written is more like a *causerie* or an essayistic book review than a 'serious' academic article. But in the event of his accepting it, I will have made a breakthrough of a kind. My revision of the customary form is potentially *innovative*; by insisting on my societal role, I will have pointed to the possibility of modifying the functional conventions. The *innovative*, the *creative*, and the mainly *functional* make up what is described in the diagram on p. 8 as the 'three-ring circus' of writing. It is easy enough to perform, and to train others, in the conventional round; much less easy to perform, and virtually impossible to take on a trainer's role, in the creative ring; and in the circus of innovative feats it is desperately easy to fall and come off limping.

Writing, like other phenomena, exhibits the refusal of things in general to be assigned to places in particular; there are all sorts of blends, borrowings, mixtures, hybrids, making it difficult to establish, in the abstract, what modes of writing are to be called 'functional', clockwise-running, and what species are unmistakably

THE THREE-RING CIRCUS
P = 'personal'; C = 'conventional'; S = 'societal'

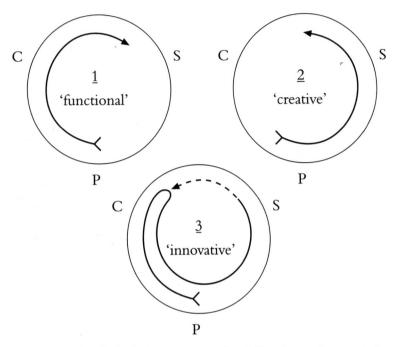

Ring 1, **Functional**: Clockwise route; personality yields to convention, convention enters into societal practice and norms. Type: the report, the instructional text.

Ring 2, **Creative**:   Anti-clockwise route; personality explores the societal frame directly, with no conventional interface. Type: the story, the literary essay.

Ring 3, **Innovative**: Switchover route, clockwise/counter-clockwise; personality rejects convention and runs a 'societal' course, challenging the conventional and possibly modifying or enlarging its norms. Type: the 'popularising' textbook; some kinds of humour and satire.

'creative'. Fictions, obviously, are creative, and so are literary essays – those that come under the title, or stigma, of *belles-lettres* – and the commentary columns of the freelance journalist, and some kinds of scholarly work, for example histories and biographies, and personal memoirs, and, not infrequently, books designed to 'popularise' an academic subject. But documentary exercises – official letters, applications, complaints, claims – are functional; as are encyclopaedia entries, general instructions, formal reports, minutes, editorials (some), abstracts, papers in learned journals. Some of these 'functional' types can be handled creatively, and hence innovatively; some – but not all. An innovative tax return is not to be contemplated, and committee chairpersons will not be amused if the minutes run creatively counter-clockwise. ('Right on, Madam Chair! Greetings, people! Well, didn't we have a *wicked* meeting last week?') But editors and complainants, for example, have been known to turn the occasional circus trick, and even professors in their learned writings, studiously avoiding the first person pronoun and cultivating the passive voice, will sometimes mount a creative rebellion against customary forms. It becomes, in the end, a question of judgement, taste, and the willingness to take risks – none of which properties can be conveyed or taught or even hinted at in any but the most specific contexts.

Then let us look specifically at beginnings. Here are some examples of beginnings in books, in essays, in newspaper columns, in learned papers. The first task, without benefit of source-references, is to identify them for what they are, or, to be tediously accurate, the sort of thing they apparently purport to be. They are set out in random order:

1. In this article I want to argue for a multi-levelled approach to the linguistic study of literary irony. Previous studies have tended to discern the presence of irony in a text chiefly by reference to the levels of syntax and the semantics of speech act analysis. Although such approaches are valuable, greater descriptive adequacy might be achieved if fuller reference were made to the linguistic level of *lexis* and more particularly, to the inter-penetration of different linguistic levels.
2. Here in the airport lounge, how becalmed we voyagers are, all spellbound and dreambound! How equable this climate – this mild, well-regulated air, untouched by frost or torrid heat, or the bite of chilling wind! Suspended between Somewhere and Elsewhere, we bask in the light of Anywhere. It is a place where fantasies luxuriate.
3. There has been a revolution in the nation's health over the

last century. Better sanitation, improved diet, better health care and greater prosperity have all contributed to an immense improvement. People today live longer, healthier lives. And still we are making progress.

4.   Most of the people I like, or love, or can barely stand are between the ages of forty-five and sixty-five, give or take a year or two at either end, and only about three of them are capable any longer of achieving what was once casually called, and is now wistfully called, a good night's rest. For ours is the age of the four 'A's: anxiety, apprehension, agonizing, and aspirin.

5. This book is intended to impart the fundamentals of harpsichord playing. It will tell you some basic facts about the instrument, the technique of making music with it, and the vast classical and contemporary repertoire composed for the harpsichord. It will explain the essentials of performance practice and musical style for the classical repertoire. And it will offer guidance for further study through additional reading.

6. Language is so closely bound up with our everyday experience that we seldom stop to think of the roles it plays. In a well-known passage in his *Lives of the English Poets*, Dr Johnson says that 'Language is the dress of thought', and it has become commonplace to quote this in support of the view that conscious thought is behind all language, and that language is primarily used to 'dress up' thoughts and send them on their way: give *substance* to thoughts.

7.   If a prosperous modern man, with a high hat and a frock coat, were to solemnly pledge himself before all his clerks and friends to count the leaves on every third tree in Holland Walk, to hop up to the City on one leg every Thursday, to repeat the whole of Mill's *Liberty* seventy-six times, to collect three hundred dandelions in fields belonging to any one of the name of Brown, to remain for thirty-one hours holding his left ear in his right hand, to sing the names of all his aunts in order of age on the top of an omnibus, or make any such unusual undertaking, we should immediately conclude that the man was mad, or, as it is sometimes expressed, was 'an artist in life'.

8. The first time I ever felt a girl inside her blouse was because of a book. A novel I bought in a drugstore. In it a sympathetic character of about my age felt a girl inside her blouse, something I had thought just wasn't done (or, more to the point, allowed)

by a decent young person. The girl responded, literally, the same way the girl in the novel did, eagerly. So that's one thing I owe to reading.

9. Theodore Dreiser was the ninth child of a poor godfearing family of Terre Haute, Indiana. His father's harsh bigotry made his background something to escape from as soon as he could, leaving him with a distaste for organised religion. Dreiser managed a year at the University of Indiana and then obtained a job on the Chicago *Globe* as a reporter. He also worked in St Louis and Pittsburgh and arrived in New York in 1894.

10. They had a house of crystal pillars on the planet Mars by the edge of an empty sea, and every morning you could see Mrs K eating the golden fruits that grew from the crystal walls, or cleaning the house with handfuls of magnetic dust which, taking all dirt with it, blew away on the hot wind. Afternoons, when the fossil sea was warm and motionless, and the wine trees stood stiff in the yard, and the little distant Martian bone town was all enclosed, and no one drifted out their doors, you could see Mr K himself in his room, reading from a metal book with raised hieroglyphs over which he brushed his hands, as one might play a harp.

It should not be too difficult for a reader unacquainted with these pieces to assign them to one or other of the general categories, 'functional' or 'creative'. The 'functional' pieces are numbers 1 (an academic article), 3 (a government pamphlet), 5 (a manual of instruction), 6 (a textbook for the general reader), and 9 (an entry from a reference book). Numbers 1 and 5 (the academic article and the manual of instruction) are doggedly functional in their insistence on a pattern of procedure. The writer of the article begins by stating his intention, or what he 'wants' to do, indicates what previous studies in the field have done, and goes on to suggest what ought now to be done. This is basic stuff, the run of the clockwise mill. The harpsichordist, too, comes briskly down to functional routines, with (a) a statement of general intention, (b) an indication of the kinds of facts that will be found in the book, (c) a promise to explain instrumental techniques, and (d) an offer of guidance for further study. After 'intended' (compare 'this book is intended' with 'in this article I want') important words are 'impart', 'tell', 'explain' and 'offer'. Also important are 'fundamentals', 'basic facts', 'essentials of performance', and 'guidance for further study'. Through these words and phrases, allocated to sentences in a stepwise progression (on 'steps', see Chapter 3), the writer spells out his preliminary announcement, which is I WISH / TO COMMUNICATE / SOMETHING. The other examples are perhaps more subtle, but still they present discernible patterns of step-by-step exposition and argument. Passages like number 6 (on language) and number 9 (about Theodore Dreiser) typify the compositional methods that students must regularly encounter in their library readings, and may eventually take as stylistic models for their own assignment themes and term essays.

These extracts begin with 'topic sentences' − declarative sentences announcing a theme for discussion − and proceed immediately to develop the topic. But the development in each case is not quite as plain and straightforward as the 'intentional' declarations ('I want to argue', 'This book is intended to impart') of numbers 1 and 5. An element of judgement or predisposition is smuggled in. 'We seldom stop to think' and 'it is commonplace' suggest that the authors of this textbook may be about to modify somewhat the authoritative claims of that 'well-known passage'. ('Well-known' is a loaded word; it apologises for resorting to the obvious example, and at the same time convicts the readers of ignorance if they happen not to know it.) In the Dreiser passage, the 'harsh bigotry' of the second sentence immediately prompts a reassessment of 'godfearing' in the first; a normally positive (or at least neutrally descriptive term) takes on a pejorative colouring. Such instances demonstrate how texts may perform their clockwise functions and yet accommodate, creatively, some counter-movement of feeling and subjectivity.

The creative mischief − the insistence on working anti-clockwise − is wholly apparent in numbers 2, 4, 7, 8, and 10. Numbers 4 and 7 are openings of essays, by James Thurber ('The Watchers of the Night') and G. K. Chesterton ('A Defence of Rash Vows'). The juxtaposition of Thurber, rehearsing the trials of the elderly, and a government pamphlet (number 3) telling us all how lucky we are to be living longer under a benign and provident administration, makes a piquant contrast: the one so cussed, so quirky, so humorous, ultimately so despairing, the other so bland, so assured, so strenuously optimistic. The pamphlet text insists, step by step, on the orderliness of things. Step one, we enjoy better health care; step two, we live longer; step three, and lo, still we are making progress. So the clock ticks, as its function requires. Thurber, with grim joy, demolishes any such perception of humanity's improving state and tidy progress. With him, all is contradictory and incongruous and approximate – the people he loves or can barely stand, who are aged somewhere between forty-five or earlier and sixty-five or later, cannot achieve (note, *achieve*, not *enjoy*) what *might* be called, casually or wistfully, a good night's rest. All this he puts into the well-designed confusion of his first sentence. Then comes the second sentence, with a striking stylistic change, to the incisive manner of the platform speaker declaring his topic – 'ours is the age of the four 'A's'.

Sentence-length is the strength and creative astonishment of Chesterton's opening. Here is a single sentence, some 130 words long, built round a stack of infinitive clauses, with propositions absurd enough to keep the reader in a pleasurable state of uncertainty as to what is going on, but at length representing, quite simply, an expansion of the statement 'If a man were to do such-and-such we would think him mad'. It is a virtuoso performance. It could hardly be called a 'topic sentence', for it does not announce a topic. Indeed, it goes to a great deal of trouble to postpone any such announcement. What it does is pull the reader into the circus tent. It is a spiel, a come-on, an inducement: an 'inductive sentence'. Roll up, roll up, roll up, it says, hurry along now, the show is about to begin.

This craft of creative inducement is also illustrated by passage number 8, the opening of an essay by the American columnist Roy Blount Jr. The essay, entitled 'You can move your lips', deals enthusiastically but quite straightforwardly – moving methodically around from topic to topic – with the pleasures and properties of the printed word. Only the first paragraph runs cheerfully and saucily counter-clockwise, a mischievous inducement to the reader to be a little shocked, a little amused, and to read on. As a rhetorical device this is not at all uncommon. Getting the reader puzzled and persuaded is the whole point of passage number 2, for example. What could this be? The opening of a story? A piece of advertising copy, or a travel brochure? It is in fact something of a cheat, for it is the beginning of a textbook, on *Language in Popular Fiction*. If it were doing its functional stuff in stuffily functioning style, the book might begin 'The purpose of this study is . . . from a certain standpoint ... in the first place ... next ... finally, with the aim of ... ', or with some comparably clockwise routine. It does not begin like that because its author was seized with the playful notion of framing the whole book, chapter by chapter, in the metaphor of flight, beginning in an airport lounge in Britain and concluding on a runway in the USA. The writer in this instance was one of the authors of the present text. His counter-clockwise proceeding was at first dubiously received by the publisher, who had expected something more closely conforming to academic convention – but who eventually yielded to the idea. Thus an innovatory brainwave or casual creative wheeze estab-lished in due course a functional procedure for the writing of the book: each chapter was committed to beginning with a note on the progress of the flight, and the conducting metaphor then became as formal as counting one–two–three-and-finally. This might be a warning to innovators: your liberating acts can become, at length, your shackles.

Passage number 10 is, of course, a piece of fiction, and could hardly be mistaken for anything else; it is the beginning of Ray Bradbury's story 'February 1999: Ylla'. Here is pure fantasy, with those wine trees in the garden, and the fruit-bearing crystal walls, and the magnetic dust that whisks away the dirt. But what, after all, gives the fantasy room to play freely, is a societal perception. A husband and wife, a house by the sea, a garden, books, the household chores – these are quite ordinary assumptions about things as they are, things as we know them. It is the lexicon that makes them things as they aren't. How ordinary it would seem if the story began 'They had a house built of quarry-stone, in Cornwall, on a cliff overlooking the sea, and every morning you could see Mrs K cleaning the house with the attachments on her Hoover ...'. And yet that ordinariness, that banality, is the *societal frame*, so to speak, or *underlay*, of the story; the story-teller's craft here lies in the innovative power of a lexicon that imposes on the details of the familiar and banal the excitement of the new and extraordinary. We enter Bradbury's tale with a sense of the marvellous, powerful enough to distract us from the knowledge that the recipe for marvels is there within us, in our societal awareness of everyday things.

These are other people's beginnings, which the student of

composition may learn, mark, and profitably analyse without finding a complete answer to that dreadfully recurrent question, 'How should *I* begin – *this* time?' It is probably of no comfort to the apprentice to be told that everybody quails, every time, at the prospect of making a start, but so it is. Once upon a time there was the cool demand of the paper under the writer's fist, the pen poised and fidgeting, ready to scratch its way into the first sentence. A little later in technological time there was that intimidating white sheet rolled into the typewriter platen, blatantly staring at the operator, waiting for something to happen. Now most recently we have word processors: no paper to stare us out, but a screen for easy recording and deleting, and a host of keystroke functions encouragingly to hand, small manipulative games to distract us from the fact that something ought to be taking shape: but nothing does. The would-be writer then engages in what psychologists might call a displacement activity: going for a walk, playing the piano, washing the dishes, performing some personal or household task of cleaning and regulating: and still it seems that the problem will not budge. The beginning has yet to be begun.

In fact, the 'displacement activity', whatever it may be, can serve a very useful purpose. It makes time for a necessary premeditation on the text. One must decide not only what is to go into the text, and in what running order, but also in what spirit, or in what varying degrees, of showing and showmanship. There is a hidden decision, not so explicit as 'what is this about?' or 'what sequence shall I follow?'. It is an intuitive assessment of the anticipated *stance* of the writing – as 'direct', or 'oblique', or 'humorous', or 'sober', or 'ironic', or 'elegiac'. The question, following 'what is it about?' and 'what is the sequence of topics?', is 'how do I want to play this?', and it is not an easy question to answer with confidence. It is well if it can be settled in the main while the dishes are a-washing, or during the walk, or while Haydn dances his elegant minuet. Leaving it open until after writing has begun means leaving too much to chance and risking a stylistic chaos. And good three-ring circuses, though lively, are not chaotic.

Take your walk, therefore, trim your beard, braid your hair, clip the privet, turn out your wardrobe, or simply sit and stare – but not for too long. Two minutes is scant time for fruitful meditation; two weeks is on the long side, and will sink you in melancholy; two hours will probably do for a warm-up, if you have any useful ideas in your head. Then settle down with the tools of your trade and oblige yourself – one, two, three, go – to begin. There are those who counsel a slow compositional tempo at the start, until the rhythm is settled, the diction determined, the length and cohesion of the sentences regulated. Others recommend instant speed – to set off in scribbling tempo until the first impetus runs out, and then to make corrections and adjustments. This is largely a matter of temperamental preference. What is important in either event is to frame that first sentence. Write it. Now.

The sentence that issues from that moment of resolution will correspond to one of four types: declarative, interrogative, directive, exclamatory. Declaratives make statements ('Theodore Dreiser was born in Terre Haute, Indiana'). Interrogatives put questions ('Who was Aldus Manutius, and why is he important?). Directives convey forms of command or recommendation ('Consider the following facts', 'Let us thank heaven for rainy winters', 'The tourist in France should carry a *Guide Michelin*'); and exclamations simply exclaim ('Here in the airport lounge, how becalmed we voyagers are!', 'What nonsense, these Sunday trading regulations!'). Of these, the declarative sentence is, as computer manuals might put it, the default option. Most compositions begin with a declarative sentence; in strictly functional texts, it is the automatic choice. Imagine your accident report beginning 'Where did it happen? How? By whose agency? And what was the weather? Sirs, you may well ask', or 'Look here. Take this down. Ignore all circumstances but these', or even 'I say! What an absolute disgrace! Responsibility my foot!' Such openings are not available to you in that instance, as long as you want to stay at the functional end of the three-ring circus. You are bound to begin declaratively. In non-fictions you are generally so bound, though that need not always cramp your style, since declaratives can assume a variety of grammatical forms, presenting different 'orientations' to the matter in hand. (Compare, for example 'The fate of the Confederacy was finally sealed by the fall of Vicksburg' with 'It was the fall of Vicksburg that sealed, finally, the fate of the Confederacy', or 'Finally, with the fall of Vicksburg, the fate of the Confederacy was sealed.') But discussion of the varieties of declarative sentence structure must be postponed to another chapter.

Questions, directives, and exclamations may be of some importance in the psychology of writing, as representatives of the precompositional dialogue that most writers conduct with themselves. 'What is the importance of making marmalade?' I ask myself. 'To whom is it of interest?' 'How should it be treated?' I might very well commit those questions directly to paper, designedly choosing a 'non-default' form, but that would possibly set the wrong stylistic tone. Without too much trouble, I transform my questions into a declarative sentence: 'The preparation of marmalade is a matter of considerable importance to all lovers of conserves, and one that must be approached without false preconceptions.' Or perhaps my inner dialogue is of the directive kind: 'We should all eat more cabbage. Let's make it exciting. Here's how.' This can become 'Today's recipe suggests ways of making your oh-so-necessary fibre intake tastier and tangier'. (In academic style this would read: 'In this article I propose firstly to examine the dietary significance of cabbage, and secondly to define parameters of consumer acceptability.') The dialogue with oneself might even consist of exclamations – 'Oysters! Yuck! The food of love for some, but not for me!' – leading to 'Oysters, repellent to many, are an acquired taste, their aphrodisiac reputation notwithstanding'.

Then how do we begin? After a period of preliminary brooding, a meditation on the general character of the proposed text, we come to the moment of putting down the first sentence -possibly without much difficulty, because a typical pattern is readily available, or perhaps after a brief episode of self-communing expressed in questions or directives (e.g. 'What am I doing?' and 'Look at this'). When that first sentence – usually a declarative – is on the page, or screen, and when the writer is satisfied that its structure matches its intended role as an introduction to the subject and an orientation to the reader, then the business of composition can proceed. But that is where the labour and the fret really begin, for whereas any fool (almost) can write a sentence, it takes experience and a little judgement to put two sentences together and then add a third, with meaningful consequences. There are surely many ways of acquiring judgement through experience; but one feasible method is by selecting and studying appropriate models of writing. We do not learn to write in a theoretical vacuum, following an abstract system. Our progress in composition is a consequence of *noticing*, of half-consciously recording, then imitating and developing, things done in passages of prose that please us or at least appear to be effective in their proposed function. What remains beyond that is the effort to confirm intuition, to elevate *noticing* into *knowledge*.

Two

How reading teaches writing

We read with varying degrees of attentiveness: sometimes with a rapid scanning that seeks to do no more than pick out salient pieces of information; sometimes more carefully, to retrieve meanings and deeper meanings; sometimes most exactingly, to capture the relationship between the semantics and the aesthetic values – in general, the content and the form – of the text. In each of these instances, the reading is for the benefit of reading itself, to enhance the skill of the reader, to raise the power of *understanding*. But reading can also work for the benefit of the reader as potential writer. Not consciously, as a rule, but somewhere along the peripheries of attention, we take note of how things are written. Compositional devices become apparent – the structure of a paragraph, the connecting of sentence to sentence, the management of transitions, the variations of sentence-length and sentence-type, the emergence of patterns of vocabulary, the configurations of metaphor. It is not strictly necessary to read 'great literature' or 'the best writers' to become versed in these matters. Functional prose (the 'clockwise' kind) often has much to teach, because compositional devices are brought more or less emphatically to the reader's attention, whereas the lessons are not so easily learned from imaginative ('counter-clockwise') composition, in which writers are often at pains to camouflage or 'recess' their methods of shaping a text. But almost any text will serve for instruction, provided that it is sensible and coherent and not predominantly technical or specialist. (This should eliminate legal documents, hire purchase agreements, insurance policies, car maintenance manuals and computer user guides, all of which serve purposes of *definition* rather than *composition*). Let us take a few examples of different kinds of composition, and try to perceive, as we read them, what lessons they may have to teach us as writers.

A

Begin with one of the commonest of compositional scenarios – the investigator addressing himself methodically to the business of expounding his subject:

> There are experimental ways of investigating stereotypes. One of the most obvious is to ask a group of people what traits characterise the Germans, the Italians, the Americans and so forth. Results of such studies on the whole agree fairly well with what might have been expected; there is considerable agreement between different people in any one nation regarding the most characteristic traits of other nations. There is even agreement between different nations; for instance, the Americans and the English agree with respect to other groups, and even, though less markedly, themselves.
>
> (H. Eysenck, *Uses and Abuses of Psychology*)

At first sight not a very remarkable demonstration of the craft of running clockwise, this functional prose nevertheless has lessons to teach. Principally, it turns on two kinds of device, one textual and one semantic. The textual devices are the words and phrases implying or overtly signalling the *cohesion*, that is, the connectedness of the text, as it runs from sentence to sentence. The semantic devices are the expressions that qualify, delimit, or in some way 'hedge' parts of the wording of the text. 'Linkers' and 'hedges' might indeed be convenient labels for these small tricks of the expository trade. Underlining some words in key phrases will bring out the textual linkages in Eysenck's exposition: 'There are experimental *ways* . . .', he begins. He then starts to enumerate the *ways*: '*One* of the most obvious . . .' leading to '*such* studies'. He predicates: the results of *such* studies '*agree* fairly well . . .', and repeats 'there is considerable *agreement* . . .' and 'There is even *agreement* . . .'. Further, he cites an example: '*for instance*, the Americans and the English *agree* . . .'. Some of these linkers are grammatical words, or tags ('one', 'such', 'for instance') having a *deictic* function. 'Deixis' means 'pointing'; in every text there are demonstratives, pro-forms (verbal 'stand-ins'), expressions that enumerate or exemplify, words that refer to other words in the text, not directly signifying the world outside it. So the *such* of 'such studies' points backward, comprehensively assuming the whole of a long preceding clause, 'to ask a group of people what traits characterise the Germans, the Italians, the Americans, and so forth'. (*Such* then includes 'and so forth', referring specifically to an unspecific formulation).

Other linking expressions are *lexical*: they are, that is to say, dictionary words forming repetitive patterns; either the word itself is repeated, or there are synonyms forming clusters of allied meaning. In this passage, the obvious instance of lexical cohesion is in the repetition of *agree, agreement*. Less prominent, perhaps, is the patterning of *different people . . . other groups*, and *other nations . . . different nations*. Less prominent still may be the connection between 'ways of *investigating*' and 'such *studies*'. The lexicon of a text is two-dimensional. It has an evident surface and a not-so-evident depth, and these dimensions are related to the writer's wish either to demonstrate by flat repetition, or to work more covertly through the nuances of synonymy and paraphrase.

'Hedges' are often bound up with linkers – for example in *one of the most obvious*. Not *one* alone – 'one' being the linking word – but *of the most obvious* because the writer wishes to concede that this is not the only way, that it is indeed a fairly obvious way, and hopes that we will not think him guilty of thinking otherwise. It is his way of glancing over his shoulder at the stalking critic. 'Mind your back' could be a motto for all writers in the expository-academic kind; minding one's back is a scholarly practice sometimes referred to as *rigour*. (And sometimes derided as *rigor mortis*.) However, it will be enough to call this cautious practice 'hedging'. A hedge may be an adverb or an adverbial phrase (hedges frequently take this form – NB 'frequently', which is itself a hedge, put up lest readers should assume 'always'); but adjectives will also serve to fend off hostile critics. Typical hedges in this passage are 'on the whole', '*fairly* well', '*considerable* agreement' 'even, *though less markedly*'. The sentence reading 'Results of such studies on the whole agree fairly well with what might have been expected' is a good example of prudent hedging; it means 'Investigating stereotypes in this way yields results best described as stereotypical', or 'The results of such studies are typical of the results of such studies'.

It is all too easy to smile at the academic habit of hedging, but in fact there are very few instances of argumentative or expository prose, 'academic' or otherwise, which have no recourse to the protective hedge. Newspaper editors and political speech-writers, no less than professors, have an interest in seeming to be wholly assured of more things than they can actually be certain of when push – in the appropriate circumstances – comes to shove. Hedging becomes a habit enabling busy expositors to turn out useful boilerplate. We write with many qualifications, if possible laying out the text to an enumerative pattern of 'ones' and 'twos' and 'furthermores'. Our psychologist demonstrates the routine. Here is another short piece by the same author:

> Two further points may be mentioned next in connection with our discussion of the phenomena characterising hypnosis, although they are only indirectly related to this topic. One is the question of whether people can be induced to commit criminal acts under hypnosis; the other is how many people are capable of being hypnotised.
>
> (Eysenck, *Sense and Nonsense in Psychology*)

The hedges are not quite so obvious there, although the cautious modality of '*may* be mentioned', and the qualification of '*only indirectly* related' suggest the usual scholarly unwillingness to be downright and abandon prudence. The enumerative design, however, is quite prominent: 'Two further points . . .' – 'one is . . .' – 'the other is'. What is exemplified here is a common pattern of exposition, so common as to suggest that any tolerably attentive reader might infer and mentally store a working formula, perhaps something along the following lines:

> There are *two* ways, *provisionally*, of diddling a dum. *One*, *probably* the simpler, is to begin the diddle on the North side and work Southward, avoiding the distortion, *if any*, of the hi-de-ho. *The other*, used by some *but by no means all* experienced dum-diddlers, is to proceed from South to North. A *third* method, of diddling the dum from East to West, and *in certain circumstances* vice-versa, lies beyond the scope of the present discussion, which will be confined, *in the main*, to dum-diddling of the first kind, with *some* reference to *the principal* findings of *relatively* advanced research into diddling technology.

Writers of abstracts and first paragraphs of papers to be published in the *Journal of Theoretical Impulses*, may care to have this formula in mind, and to collect, from their own reading, variants on the technique of marking a sequence ('first', 'secondly', 'in addition', 'finally') together with synonyms and similitudes for 'provisionally', 'relatively', 'by no means all', 'in certain circumstances' and other tokens of qualified certitude.

B

Now here is a piece of exposition – 'exposition' signifying the laying-out of a topic, the setting-up of the market stall – that presents to the reader something more subtle, more *ingratiating*, than the blunt professional-functional prose of passage A:

> Like all his generation, Louis XVI was brought up to worry about happiness. His grandfather, Louis XV, had redesigned
> Versailles round its pursuit and had a natural aptitude for its indulgence. But for his young successor, happiness was hard work, and being king of France put it virtually out of reach. Gradually enveloped by anxiety, he would later recall just two occasions when the business of being king actually made him
> happy. The first was his coronation in June 1775; the second, his visit to Cherbourg in June 1786. On the first occasion he wrapped himself in the mantle of arcane royal mystery; on the second he revealed himself as modern man: scientist, sailor and engineer. To onlookers on both occasions, the paradoxes of the royal personality were cause for comment, perhaps even for concern. But it was part of Louis' innocence that he never perceived a problem.
>
> (S. Schama, *Citizens, A Chronicle of the French Revolution*)

Like passage A, this is the opening of a topic; in fact, the beginning of a chapter in a scholarly text with a strong appeal to a literary public, telling the story of events in France at the end of the eighteenth century. It is in most ways quite unlike Hans Eysenck's routine excursus into themes in experimental psychology, and yet there is one incidental point of stylistic kinship. The device of enumeration plays some part here as the structure of the text develops: *just two occasions . . . the first . . . the second . . . on both occasions*. Yet in this instance the device seems to play a part less prominent than its role in passages of textbook exposition or abstracting, such as the extracts from Eysenck quoted above. Why is this? Is it because the process of enumerating *propositions* is inherently and necessarily more emphatic than that of outlining *circumstances*? Enough, perhaps, to note that story-tellers, like social scientists, may count, but count in different ways, to different effect.

Certainly, the general structure of Simon Schama's historical narrative is not governed by numbers. It develops in a much less tightly scheduled way. In broad outline, the extract quoted above can be divided into two parts, the first including the three sentences from 'Like all his generation' to 'virtually out of reach'. In those three sentences, the vital agent of cohesion – of perceived progression and connection from sentence to sentence – is the possessive adjective *his*, in 'his generation', 'his grandfather', 'his young successor'. The reference of this word shifts progressively from sentence to sentence. In the first sentence *his* refers to Louis XVI's generation; in the second, to Louis XVI's grandfather, Louis XV; and in the third, to the 'young successor' of Louis XVI's grandfather, that is, to Louis XVI himself. This is historical narrative in miniature, and it all turns on the *deixis*, or demonstrative scope, of the possessive *his*.

So the passage begins, with the announcement of a topic, in three sentences linked by a simple scheme of connections (the repetitions of 'his'). The second phase of construction is marked by the sentence beginning 'Gradually enveloped by anxiety'. That phrase, that semi-detached adjectival phrase, is most important for its position at the head of the sentence, where it creates a focus of attention on the transition from the opening statement of a general theme to a quoting of particular examples, which are introduced by means of the enumerative structure mentioned above (i.e. 'two occasions ... the first ... the second ... on the first ... on the second ... on both occasions') .

This prose turns, then, on quite simple structural devices, not emphatically prominent or powerful, at least on a first reading. Semantically, the procedure to which this ordinary structure is adapted is that of *stating the topic* followed by *exemplifying the topic*. The power of the exemplification is contained in the richness of the lexicon, in a multivalent vocabulary. Certain phrases assume a controlling figurative importance: 'the business of being king', 'the mantle of arcane royal mystery', 'the paradoxes of the royal personality'. In these phrases there are – to invent a term – 'nodal nouns', representing symbolically the very argument that Schama is developing, a reflection on the nature of kingship. On the one hand, being a king can be treated as a *business*; but on the other, royalty may be regarded as an arcane *mystery*; and while either one attitude or the other may sustain a monarch in the conduct of his realm, having both together presents a *paradox* for his uneasy subjects.

At key points in its construction, this extract presents words either in a slightly unfamiliar, teasing light, or as players in a special set of semantic relationships. Take a phrase already noticed, the phrase introducing a transition from topic-stating to exemplifying: 'Gradually enveloped by anxiety'. Is there not something remarkable about *enveloped*? Not 'overcome', or 'possessed', or 'haunted', or 'consumed', or any of the words suggested by a casual trawl through acceptable clichés, but *enveloped*? As in 'enveloped in mist', or 'enveloped in a cloak'? Then consider the two cited occasions of Louis' happiness. On the one, he has *wrapped himself* in *the mantle* of arcane royal mystery. ('Arcane' signifying 'deeply hidden', with an additional nuance of 'ancient', 'time-honoured'.) But on the other, he is said to have *revealed himself* as 'modern man'. These wordings express figuratively (the figure being that of costume and concealment) the 'paradoxes of the royal personality'. Here is the king who sometimes 'wraps himself' in his historical and ritual costume, and sometimes puts that dress aside to 'reveal himself' in up-to-date and practical character. 'Gradually', however, he is 'enveloped' by anxiety, the ultimate wrapping, a guise not to be put off.

The first and last sentences of this extract similarly tease the reader with veiled assumptions, about words and meanings and about the validity of statements. Take the opening: 'Like all his generation, Louis XVI was brought up to worry about happiness.' This is presented as a piece of straightforward information, but only a little reflection suggests that it is far from straightforward. It is not an assertion in the same category as 'Like his father before him, Louis XVI wore knee-breeches', or possibly 'Like many of his generation, Louis XVI had rather bad teeth', or even 'Like most of his generation, Louis XVI believed in God', all of which are statements open, more or less, to factual verification or falsification. This opening, in this wording, is a non-verifiable *judgement* about a habit of mind, attributed not only to Louis in person, but to all his contemporaries. We might paraphrase the sentence, much less attractively: 'Towards the end of the eighteenth century, the pursuit of happiness became a matter of intellectual concern to many eminent people, including the French king Louis XVI.' That is still not entirely 'factual' or 'informative' (there is an opinion lurking in there somewhere), but simply by substituting *many* for 'all' and *eminent people* for 'generation' it removes some of the boldness of unqualified judgement. (It might be said, indeed, to be an exercise in hedging – even 'towards' has the fuzziness of a hedge.) 'Intellectual concern', furthermore, is a good deal more diffuse, less particular, less personal, than *worry*. *Brought up to worry about happiness* humorously raises the image of a whole generation of Frenchmen being sedulously schooled, by parents, nursemaids, tutors, in the practice of uneasiness – not about salvation or the social order or the economic state of the realm, all things amenable to instruction and provision, but about that most elusive and unreckonable thing, happiness. Schama's first sentence, his topic sentence, is in fact a humorous paradox. His tremendous subject begins with a joke: Louis XVI, that mixed-up monarch, was *brought up* to be unhappy about not being happy.

  The last sentence in our extract (which, however, is not the last sentence of the paragraph in the original) presents, similarly, a little essay in judgement, a 'loading' of the account: 'But it was part of Louis' innocence that he never perceived a problem.' This has something of the teasing force of an aphorism. If 'worrying about happiness' obliquely reminds us of the exordium of the Declaration of Independence – Schama actually uses the word *pursuit* in his second sentence – this pronouncement on Louis' 'innocence' suggests the eighteenth century liking for a lapidary turn of phrase. ('Lapidary' meaning carved in stone – originally, in a tombstone, by way of testimonial.) Aphorisms deal in absolutes, in 'all' and 'every' and 'no' and 'none' and 'never'; wit rarely hits the target, aphoristically, with 'some' and 'a few' and 'occasionally'. So Louis, it is affirmed, *never* perceived a 'problem' – never, that is to say, perceived the 'paradox' of his own nature; and that impercipience is part of his 'innocence' – which begins to look like a synonym for 'stupidity'. This clever writer puts a tricky spin on that innocent word 'innocence'. Who was responsible, if any individual was responsible, for the march of events leading up to the Revolution? Not the king – he was innocent; meaning, catastrophically incapable of knowing a hawk from a handsaw.

One of the things we learn from a reading of this passage is the importance of vocabulary in carrying and colouring an argument. The 'right word' is 'right' not only for its immediate value in a particular phrase, but also for its diffused significance, its place in a linkage and expansion of meanings observable over quite long stretches of text. To 'observable' we should perhaps add 'though not immediately'. An author's words, intuitively chosen, the result of some inner process of evaluating and predicting, in their turn work gradually on the reader's own intuitions. As messages pass from writer to reader, much happens beneath the surface of recognition and comprehension. Periodically, however, the surface is broken with those confident declarations, those aphorisms that seize the reader's conscious attention, formulating overtly certain instructions – *think this! be of this opinion!* – that the words of the text at large are murmuring surreptitiously. What we can learn from this extract, if we are duly watchful, is how to develop intimations in support of declarations, or how to make 'you might think' lead on to 'this is the case', or how to generate the smoke that breaks out into fire.

C

The strength of some passages lies in the repetition and extension of certain constructions: in syntax as the circus act. Here, for instance, is a comic exposition of a familiar theme, our struggle to achieve neatness against the slovenly pull of daily existence:

> In the last 20 years or so, life has got progressively more orientated towards Neatpots and against Shamblers. This is very confusing because very few people are complete Neatpots – totally organised, finicky, dexterous, tidy, obedient, disciplined, their desks (if they are desk people) clear at the end of each day; and very few are complete Shamblers, setting off on random journeys, wearing odd socks, forgetting to put their clocks back or forward, losing tickets, unable to fold a newspaper in a

crowded train – and, of course, having chaotic desks.

Most normal people oscillate between these two poles. The pressures of life force them into an increasingly Shambler attitude, then one day the Neatpot side ups and says 'enough of this'. They clear their desks, they sew up the hole in the coat lining where the ticket keeps slipping through, they even get all that ghastly rubbish of sweet papers, odd gloves, forlorn little springs, Band-aids, crayons and small foreign coins from under the back seat of the car.

(P. Jennings, 'Shamblers and Neatpots', in *I Must Have Imagined It*)

Note, to begin with, the structural set-up – a quite familiar one, since this opening is merely a disguised variant of the enumerative method, as in 'There are two ways of being what you are, namely X and Y', or 'In this article I propose to examine common propensities to X, on the one hand, and to Y on the other.' In Paul Jennings' humorous version of the functional routine, X and Y are Shamblers and Neatpots. (Note how the names themselves have a descriptive value, implying judgements; we recognise immediately the fussy virtue of the Neatpot, the fallible humanity of the Shambler.) 'Most people oscillate between these two poles', the author declares at the beginning of his second paragraph, by which time he is able to assume that the 'two poles' are established as recognised facts of character and behaviour, observable in *most people*. (This is next door to *everybody*, to the inclusive certainty of an aphorism – 'Humanity consists of two species, the neat and the slovenly'.)

To propose a basic duality in this way is a device common to serious and comic exposition. Scholars may use it to propound and test a thesis. Humorists use it with almost wearisome regularity as a sleight of caricature, a short-cut to the grotesque: in their world, things ordinary in themselves become extraordinary by juxtaposition with other things, also ordinary in themselves. What is important is not so much the primary device (i.e. the proposed either/or of Shamblers and Neatpots), as the means by which the device is extended until absurdity supervenes. In this case, the means-to-absurdity is the inspired rambling of those ever-lengthening lists of words, phrases, and clauses, moving towards final definition without ever quite getting there. Thus in the first paragraph:

very few people are complete Neatpots – totally organised, finicky, dexterous, tidy, obedient, disciplined, their desks (if they are desk people) clear at the end of each day;

and very few are complete Shamblers, setting off on random journeys, wearing odd socks, forgetting to put their clocks back or forward, losing tickets, unable to fold a newspaper in a crowded train – and, of course, having chaotic desks.

Writing in lists might be a cumbersome business, a trial for the reader, especially if the list extends beyond three items. Triads are quite common: the founding fathers of the American Republic, for example, staked their claim to 'life, liberty, and the pursuit of happiness', a phrase memorable both for its sentiment and its rhythmic cadence. Had they seen fit, just at that point in their manifesto, to make a comprehensive claim for life, liberty, the pursuit of happiness, equality before the law, relief from excessive taxation, freedom of religious observance, primary education for all and liability to military service under certain circumstances, their phrasing would have lost something of its lasting power over the imaginations of readers far and wide, not to say its *pizazz*. But all the items in that imagined list are in some way related; there is a *homogeneity* of topic – everything refers to aspects of the state and its functioning. Some principle of organisation evidently governs that kind of list, the commonplace inventory. Now suppose that some frivolous founding fathers out there in a parallel existence – a sci-fi world running in tandem with our own – were unable to resist the temptations of a *miscellaneous*, disorganised list of items apparently cropping up in random reference to this, that and – by the way – the other: eg. 'life, liberty, lying in bed on Saturday mornings, old sour mash whisky, Mrs Hancock, the pursuit of happiness, and all that jazz'. The list would immediately become interesting, and potentially funny. The length of a 'homogeneous' list eventually makes for tedium, wears away any pointedness in the composition; but the items in a miscellaneous list occur unpredictably, in casual and lively collision, and then the length of the list is no longer tedious. The reader remains attentive, wondering what on earth is going to come next. Jennings, as a smart humorist, naturally favours randomness in his listings. See him again in his second paragraph, repeating the trick, designing associations of disparates:

They clear their desks, they sew up the hole in the coat lining where the ticket keeps slipping through, they even get all that ghastly rubbish of sweet papers, odd gloves, forlorn little springs, Band-aids, crayons and small foreign coins from under the back seat of the car.

What emerges from that is not only a delight in miscellany, but also a free experimentation with the varying lengths of the items constructing the list. They become longer, to the point of unwieldiness, defying uniformities of rhythm. (Read the sentence aloud – note how the 'beat' keeps changing.) They become clauses, incorporating other clauses, incorporating chains of words and phrases. What Jennings does here is to make a disorderly comedy out of a mode of construction that seriously presupposes order-liness. He disrupts the shopping list, subverts the inventory; and that one rhetorical device sustains his humour through two paragraphs.

D

This stratagem, of picking out and exploiting a particular pattern or structure, works well in the rhetoric of humour, and even better in polemic, where, for example, the so-called 'rhetorical question' is a favoured resource. Here it occurs with extraordinary repetitive intensity, taking rhetoric to the edge of reasonableness:

What do you do with a kid who can't read, even though he's fifteen-years-old? Recommend him for special reading classes, sure. And what do you do when those special reading classes are loaded to the roof, packed because there are kids who can't read in abundance, and you have to take only those who can't read the worst, dumping them on to a teacher who's already overloaded and who doesn't want to teach a remedial class to begin with?

What do you do with that poor ignorant jerk? Do you call on him in class, knowing damn well that he hasn't read the assignment because he doesn't know how to read? Or do you ignore him? Or do you ask him to stop by after school, knowing he would prefer playing stickball to learning how to read, and knowing he considers himself liberated the moment the bell sounds at the end of the eighth period?

(E. Hunter, *The Blackboard Jungle*)

The text from which this extract is taken continues in this vein for a page or more. Interrogatives rule, OK? This writer refuses to take the default option (as we have called it – see p. 16 above). His questions frame all the points that might otherwise be made in the 'declarative' mode of a 'functional', 'clockwise' account of Some Problems in the Teaching of Remedial Reading. Perhaps like this:

A teacher may have to cope with the learning difficulties of a child who, at the age of fifteen, still cannot read. The obvious measure is to refer such a child to a special reading class. That, however, hardly solves the problem. Special reading classes are full of pupils with severe reading difficulties. The children sent to them are the poorest of poor readers, and those charged with teaching them are burdened by the weight of numbers as well as by their own unwillingness to take remedial classes.

The problem of dealing with an illiterate fifteen-year-old is intractable. Since he cannot read, he will be unable to do his homework, and there will be little point in asking him to speak up in class. The teacher has, perhaps, two options. One is to ignore the child. The other is to ask him to stay behind after class, an option to be taken in the knowledge, unfortunately, that this pupil would rather play games than learn to read, and that he considers his confinement to school ended when the bell rings at the end of the afternoon session.

That piece of rewriting quite efficiently comprehends the matter of the original text. What must emerge from a comparison of the two versions, however, is a feeling that this paraphrase presents the argument coolly, at a judicious distance. The writer proceeds dispassionately, as though avoiding any involvement with his topic, and the reader in turn is not invited to become involved. There is no direct pronominal address – *you* – as in the original, and there is a fastidious avoidance of the sort of vocabulary and phrasing that represents common talk in a cantankerous temper – 'a kid', 'loaded to the roof', 'packed', 'dumping', 'that poor ignorant jerk', 'damn well'. Even Hunter's text says HEY! LISTEN UP! Its questions imply, for the reader, angry directives and exclamations. It appears to eschew, impatiently, all notions of control and elegance in sentence structure. The third sentence, for example, almost bawls its way into breathlessness: 'And what do you do when those special reading classes are loaded to the roof, packed because there are kids who can't read in abundance, and you have to take only those who can't read the worst, dumping them on to a teacher who's already overloaded and who doesn't want to teach a remedial class to begin with?' (Hunh?) And yet this apparently headlong, headstrong harangue is not lacking in design. His seeming refusal to be self-possessed and sensible allows the writer to make his own stylistic rules with, for example, some striking turns of phrase: 'who can't read in abundance', 'who can't read the worst' (compare these 'hot' confections with the paraphrase's 'cold' rendering, 'with severe reading difficulties' and 'the poorest of poor readers'). It is grammatically incorrect, or at the very least an infringement of standard idiom, to say that someone 'can't read in abundance' or 'can't read the worst'. Standard idiom allows 'are extremely poor readers' or 'have the greatest difficulty in reading' or simply 'can't read very well', but does not recognise the adverbial collocation of 'in abundance' with 'read' ('can't read abundantly'? 'can't read in spades'? 'most exceedingly cannot read'?) or the adverbial use of an adjective in 'can't read the worst'. These expressions are grammatically 'wrong', yet rhetorically right, making their personal/emotional appeal with considerable force. What creates an acceptance for them, however, is the larger stylistic context designed by the author. They would appear as absurd strangers in the controlled sentences of dispassionate, 'functional' prose: 'In special reading classes there are inconveniently large numbers of pupils who *can't read in abundance*; teachers try only to refer children who *can't read the worst*, even then imposing a great burden on their reluctant colleagues.' That is a hybrid composition, in which the textual background does not match the lexical effect in the foreground. Unless the writer is deliberately planning some act of humorous dissonance, a jarringly incongruous choice of word, there should generally be be a sense of accord between the particular wording and the general textual design. That is one of the lessons this extract has to teach.

E

Incidental lessons in style and composition are taught by all non-fictional writings, if only we read attentively, cultivating a sense of what the writer is trying to do, knowing that we ourselves in due course will have our reports to write, our arguments to set out, our essays to compose, our polemics to script. From any literary journal or any good newspaper (in the British phrase, any *quality* paper) we can learn the techniques that frame the texts that form the styles appropriate to these various purposes. So-called 'creative' writing – meaning, usually, fiction – uses the same compositional techniques, but extends their range and adds other resources. We can hardly speak of a style 'appropriate' to the writing of a novel, for example. A novel is a complex of styles, sometimes incorporating, for fictional purposes, the imitation of styles 'appropriate' to non-fictional ends. Here is an example:

> Even the look of the house is vague to me. I laboriously transcribed into my diary a description of it that I found in a directory of Norfolk.
>
> 'Brandham Hall, the seat of the Winlove family, is an imposing early Georgian mansion pleasantly seated on a plot of rising ground and standing in a park of some five hundred acres. Of an architectural style too bare and unadorned for present tastes, it makes an impressive if over-plain effect when seen from the SW. The interior contains interesting family portraits by Gainsborough and Reynolds, also landscapes by Cuyp, Ruysdael, Hobbema, etc. and in the smoking-room a series of tavern scenes by Teniers the Younger (these are not shown).'
>
> (L. P. Hartley, *The Go-Between*)

This passage from a well-known English novel, a 'modern classic', describes the appearance of a country house, recollected after an interval of many years by a narrator who remembers having first seen it as a twelve-year-old boy. Here the novelist, we might think, had a choice of descriptive techniques: he could have let his narrator record impressions of the house in weary adult perspective, or he could have attempted to present it as seen freshly, through boyish eyes. In the event, he takes the task of description away from his narrator. To describe the house he chooses instead to imitate a functional style, the conventional procedure of the travel companion or topographical guide. This is the kind of thing he imitates:

> KEDLESTON HALL. The most splendid Georgian house of Derbyshire, in extensive grounds with a long undulating lake to the N, and to the S the slope upwards of a hill which tends to deprive the house of some of its effect on that side ... The paintings of ruins are by *Hamilton*, the grisaille panels between them by *Rebecca*.
>
> (N. Pevsner, *The Buildings of England, Derbyshire*)

The resemblances between this authentic sample of the guidebook method and the 'fake' description of Brandham Hall in L. P. Hartley's novel will be obvious. Hartley's mimesis is actually quite convincing; even though we know it to be an invention, we acknowledge its plausibility. What betrays it, if anything, is its tendency to over-elaboration, including a sly humour (those *tavern scenes* by Teniers the Younger which are *not shown*) hardly appropriate to the genre of guidebook writing. There is a muffled recollection here of Noel Coward's lyric, 'The Stately Homes of England', with its evocation of 'rows and rows and rows of/Gainsboroughs and Lawrences/And some sporting prints of Aunt Florence's/Some of which are rather rude'.

The description of Brandham Hall can be read as a parodic joke, devised for the benefit of those familiar with accounts of English country houses, their architecture, perspectives and furnishings; but there would be little point in it did it not serve purposes beyond humour and parody. The way in which the protagonist, Leo Colston, perceives the events of his own life and the shaping of his own personality is closely related to his perception, in imagination and fact, of the Hall. Certain crucial, damaging experiences are associated in his mind with the side of the building not mentioned in the guidebook account, the darker north side with its sheds and outhouses. His adult recollections of Brandham are deeply troubled, obscured by feelings of betrayal and lost innocence. Only in the closing sentences of the novel does Leo 'see' the house again, fairly, in a clear, conciliatory light. The present owner of the Hall has invited him to tea. He goes, with much uncertainty, but: '... hardly had I turned in at the lodge gates, wondering how I should say what I had come to say, when the south-west prospect of the

Hall, long hidden from my memory, sprang into view.' The ending of this fine book thus depends, for its effect of release and resolution, on a detail (the phrase 'when seen from the SW') occurring in the guidebook parody 250 pages earlier.

Hartley's mimicry is an example of what is sometimes called 'style borrowing', or 'register borrowing': the imitation of a functional style for imaginative purposes. It is not unusual for novelists to purloin registers in this way; among the styles they borrow are those of newspaper reports, legal proceedings, court circulars, tourist brochures, travel writing, technical accounts of machines or weapons. The purpose of the borrowing is commonly to make the narrative seem realistic, enhancing the factual plausibility of the fiction. But Hartley demonstrates a subtler use. His register-borrowing is related less to the factuality than to the symbolic implications of his narrative. It then becomes an important point of reference in the final cohesion of his text, that is, in establishing the sense that the whole piece hangs together and that ends are satisfactorily linked with beginnings. All well-written texts are cohesive, but there are degrees of immediacy in the pattern of connections. Most immediately, one sentence may embody a demonstrable connection with its predecessor. More loosely, the connections can show up as retrospective or prospective references within the course of a paragraph or a page. This is distant, or remote cohesion. The ultimately remote is the verbal linkage that spans a long text, such as a novel. In Hartley's narrative, the concluding linkage comes down to two words: the *south-west* of the final sentence recalls, in serenely spelt-out form, the laconic *SW* of the guidebook parody.

Here, then, are five texts, each with something in particular to teach about techniques of prose composition. Obviously, if we are looking for lessons from typical material, there will be texts beyond texts, the five extending to twenty-five and further to one hundred and five, and further yet into the exemplary distance. But the first five will serve for a representative account of what happens in some important varieties of prose composition. A typology might well begin with the proposed scope of the writing, from the author's point of view. These texts illustrate three major types: the objective, the affective, and the fictive – or, putting it concretely, what I do when I give an account, what I do when I am looking to have fun or raise hell, and what I do when I spin a yarn.

Passages **A** and **B** are samples of 'objective' writing, if by that we mean writing that assumes an impersonal descriptive stance in relating the acts and facts of what is known as the real world. That much the two pieces have in common; beyond that there are important differences. Passage **A** is journeyman prose, involving very simple and rather obvious techniques of reporting, competently laying out its facts, but with no insinuations of the figurative, no devices that allow the commingling of fact with comment. Passage **B** by comparison is 'crafted' prose, using a creative rhetoric working overtly and covertly to set out its exposition. It presents indubitable facts in a devious way, the way recommended by Emily Dickinson, who exhorts us to 'tell the truth but tell it slant/Success in circuit lies'. It *assumes* an 'impersonal descriptive stance', but the assumption will perhaps lead us to question the validity of describing this text as 'objective'. In the sense that it does not set out to call a spade simply and solely a spade but implies furthermore some reflections on agricultural implements, it is not 'objective'. Histories are seldom wholly 'objective'. Stark factual chronicles are boring; judgements creep in; interpretations are suggested. This text is nevertheless objective inasmuch as its topic is not something the author has invented and not a matter he takes personally.

Taking matters personally is the common characteristic of passages **C** and **D**. These are specimens of affective writing, meaning composition which takes as its principal aim the raising of *affects*, or emotions: anger, sorrow, delight, astonishment, laughter, the recognition of something felt. They are affective in different ways: **C** entertains, gently amusing the reader, **D** provocatively simulates the writer's despair and stimulates the reader's sympathetic anger. Passage **D** gets at the reader directly with its repeated pronoun of address – *you*. As soon as a *you* and an *I* enter our discourses, all pretence of 'objectivity' disappears – this is what *I* feel and what *I* think *you* should know, a matter between *ourselves*. Extract **C** is less direct in its personal appeal, and yet we recognise its intention as personal. There are no obvious pronominal clues to this; if there is in the text an important personal pronoun, it is not *I* or *you* or *we*, but rather *they*, *their*, in reference to *most people* – 'most people' being, by ultimate implication, *we*. Those rambling lists of commonplace events and household trivia represent the affective disorder of *our* lives, the exasperating intractability of things as we know them. (Once, in the high and palmy days of existentialism, Jennings mockingly propounded a philosophical theory with the motto *les choses sont contre nous* – a paradigmatic instance being the piece of toast that falls to the carpet butter-side down.)

Passage **E** is in a category of its own, and whatever lessons it has to teach about composition may be thought to lie outside the scope of whatever is to be taught in this book. The world of fiction is patently *other* than the 'real' world; it hardly needs saying, and yet it continually demands to be said. The novelist's 'objective' and 'affective' bear no *direct* relationship to the objects and affects of daily life on earth; a novel is not a history, though novelists may tease their readers with the illusion of historicity (as in *The History of Tom Jones*), and the feelings of fiction, whatever we may think, are not derived from common feelings about recurrent facts. Mr Micawber is not funny because of any place he has occupied in our worldly experience; he is funny because of the place created for him in the space of the novel, *David Copperfield*. His creator makes him humorous in relationship to David's openness and innocence, to Dora's vulnerability, to Aunt Betsy's quirkiness, to the Murdstones' malignancy, to Agnes' strength, to Uriah Heep's inveterate evil. We 'place' him in the novel, and find him funny there. We may sometimes think that we have met him in real life, but that is self-deception. What we meet is the fancied semblance of an illusion created by Dickens; Dickens, not 'life', got there first. It is sometimes difficult for us to acknowledge, and to persuade others, that characters and incidents are not 'based on' real-life characters and incidents, but are rather 'evolved from' the creative design of the writer. There is a common reluctance to let fiction be fictive.

The plane of the fictive, let us say, lies above, or aside from, the plane of the factual. The principal relationship between them is one of borrowing; fictions lift components out of fact – lift and adapt, lift and modify, the commonplaces of custom, social role, interaction, and so forth. Fictions lift functions – as we see in our passage from *The Go-Between*. In that respect we ordinary compositors can learn from the language and practice of fiction, because, in observing *how* the ordinary is modified to fit the fictional extraordinary, we can begin to learn what is essential to functional styles in themselves. Hartley's guidebook spoof, for example, at least makes us think a little about guidebooks, how their entries are written, what they necessarily include, how their information is presented, by means of what characteristic constructions.

But let us take examples, for the most part, from non-fictions such as those presented here in extracts from the writings of Professors Eysenck and Schama, from the humorous prose of Paul Jennings, from the angry polemic of Evan Hunter. There will be occasions in the common course of reading when we are struck by the quality of some such passage, and it is in such moments – the moment of saying to oneself, hey! not bad! – that we are most open to learning. Then there are questions to be asked about techniques of composition, questions ranging from the investigation of patterns of writing on a fairly large scale, down through hierarchies of construction, to the examination of sentence-types and structures, or the criteria for choosing and placing a word. Addressing these questions is the business of the chapters that now follow.

Three

About paragraphs

But what is a paragraph?

It is hardly possible to talk about techniques of composition without using this word over and over again; and yet it presents from the outset problems of definition. We know – or think we know – what *sentences* are. Grammarians describing the structure of the English language are agreed that there is such a thing as a sentence, a unit in a hierarchy of linguistic forms, constructed in accordance with a definable set of rules. Paragraphs have no such linguistic claims. Their formation depends on other criteria.

This, as it stands above, could be called a paragraph:

But what is a paragraph?

And similarly this, as it stands at the beginning of *Moby Dick*, is a paragraph:

Call me Ishmael.

Equally, this, as we find it in the Edinburgh University Calendar:

2.4. A candidate who satisfies the examiners in the Final Honours examination shall be awarded Honours in one of the three grades to be denominated respectively First Class, Second Class (Upper and Lower Divisions) and Third Class. The names of candidates shall be arranged for publication in alphabetical order according to the grades or subdivisions of grades.

And this, from a modern novel (A. S. Byatt's *Angels and Insects*) is just as surely a paragraph:

> Edgar Alabaster was dancing with his sister Eugenia. He was a big, muscular man, his blond hair crimping in windswept regular waves over his long head, his back stiff and straight. But his large feet moved quickly and intricately, tracing elegant skipping patterns beside Eugenia's pearly-grey slippers. They were not speaking to each other. Edgar looked over Eugenia's shoulder, faintly bored, surveying the ballroom. Eugenia's eyes were half closed. They whirled, they floated, they checked, they pirouetted.

Each of these, in its context on the printed page, as a piece of text standing complete in a defined space, answers to the notion we identify with the word *paragraph*. Already the notion begins to look odd – odd, shifty, yet inescapable. If 'Call me Ishmael is not a paragraph, what shall we say it is? Could there be a one-word paragraph – 'September', or 'Women', or 'Murder', the word sitting in its own space? That is not impossible. Beyond that device of layout, however, a typographical stratagem, it seems there is little that our extracts have in common. What holds each of them together, as text? What justifies their positioning? What signals do they diversely convey to a reader? Why did Melville choose thus to 'break' the text after his famous opening sentence, not continuing the narrative on the same line? Why did not the administrators of Edinburgh University make a separate section (numbering it 2.5) for their description of arrangements to publish successful candidates' names? And what prevented A. S. Byatt from shifting to a new line after 'pearly-grey slippers', or after 'not speaking to each other', or possibly after both, and then with a further break after 'half closed'? Thus:

> Edgar Alabaster was dancing with his sister Eugenia. He was a big, muscular man, his blond hair crimping in windswept, regular waves over his long head, his back stiff and straight. But his large feet moved quickly and intricately, tracing elegant skipping patterns beside Eugenia's pearly-grey slippers.
> They were not speaking to each other.
> Edgar looked over Eugenia's shoulder, faintly bored, surveying the ballroom. Eugenia's eyes were half closed.
> They whirled, they floated, they checked, they pirouetted.

Why not like that? For no reason at all, apart from the all-important subjective conviction that this re-arrangement of the text in some way 'means' something different from Ms Byatt's original. The author's − and subsequently the reader's − perception of paragraphing is formed through the imagination of a narrative context, a feeling for the rhythms and the relationships, the intimate or more distant perspectives, of a developing tale.

In other words, the concept of 'paragraph' (if there is indeed such a general, unifying concept, as distinct from an open-ended series of particular realisations) is aesthetic. Or stylistic. Or possibly, at its simplest, text-functional. The aesthetic of the paragraph is its appearance on the page (its 'visual impact'), and its conveyed suggestions of emphasis, rhythm and resonance as it is translated into an idea of speech and delivery heard in the mind of the reader. (Note, however, the assumption that author and reader must then share, at least in a general way, 'an idea of speech', some common notions of how to put things into words, a *rhetoric*; writing paragraphs for Martians or other exotics might require a different set of aesthetic principles.) The stylistics of the paragraph appear in its internal pattern of connections and transitions from sentence to sentence, and in its management of variations in sentence-length and sentence-type. The functional value of the paragraph is its role as the frame for a certain content, a phase in an argument, an account of a step in a procedure. The paragraphing in Edinburgh University's degree regulations is purely functional; in A. S. Byatt's text, the paragraph is an aesthetic/stylistic event.

There appears to be no finite set of choices regulating the formation of a paragraph. It is a subjective matter, and the options are open to the writer; always open and ever-changeable. We are aware, as we compose, that the paragraph is an arbitrary segment of the text, and this awareness takes two forms. One is retrospective. Having drafted a page or two, we look back over our work, find it, perhaps, too bulky to the eye, too extensive to hold easily in mind; and so we contrive one or two paragraph-breaks for the comfort of the prospective reader, seeking out those minor boundaries and semantic fissures that are to be found in any extended text. At some point the text will plausibly divide. The other kind of 'paragraph-awareness' is concurrent: a sense of the growing work as we develop it, arranging and grouping its points and emphases, realising the logical and psychological progress of discourse. One kind of paragraph, the retrospective sort, is *edited*; the other, 'concurrent' kind, seemingly more natural, more immediately responsive to the mind's self-communings, is, shall we say, *monitored*.

In monitoring the growth of a paragraph, writers habitually resort to certain rhetorical patterns which appear to be instinctive, or even innate, a matter of compositional competence; and in retrospective editing, they will often divide the text as an inherent patterning might seem to dictate. The psychology of the paragraph is analogous with the psychology of physical work-processes; at the workbench, or in the backyard, one devises ways of handling otherwise intractable material – taking it piece by piece, placing it here or there, making connections, distributing its mass, etc. Much of the labour is in the handling of the means to labour. So it is with the paragraph, the compositional shop. The simplest of procedural patterns is the Step – so called here because it takes the reader step by step through the presentation of a content. It emerges commonly in the making of instructional texts, in outlining simple arguments, and in some kinds of narrative. The step pattern distinguishes a 'linear' from a 'columnar' text. For example, the Instructions for Use printed on a packet of wound-dressings might read like this:

> Clean the wound
> Cut the dressing to the shape of the wound
> Moisten the dressing in a sterile saline solution
> Secure in place with a secondary dressing
> Change when maximum absorption is reached

Although the constituent sentences are set out separately, this will pass muster as a coherent text, the kind of text that ordinary people are reading and acting upon with each ordinary day that passes. For one thing, there is a common reference, explicit or implicit, to one topic, ie to dressings; further, the progression of sentences is implicitly marked by a repeated grammatical feature, the imperative ('clean' – 'cut' – 'moisten' – 'secure' – 'change') appearing at the head of each. But this text will not be perceived as a *paragraph* without some additional marks of continuity and linkage. It needs to to be set out as 'run on' prose, and the connections between sentences need to be more overtly indicated. Here is one possibility:

> First, clean the wound, then cut the dressing to shape. Next, moisten the dressing in a sterile saline solution, and then secure

it in position with a secondary dressing. From time to time change the dressing, when maximum absorption is reached.

That is a fairly crude instance of a 'step' pattern. The sequence of imperatives remains in place, but is further marked by expressions which emphasise steps in the procedural and temporal sequence: 'first', 'then', 'next', 'from time to time'. The same paragraph might be composed in a more fluent style, perhaps by introducing some participial constructions, e.g.:

> Having cleaned the wound, first cut the dressing to shape. Then, after moistening it in a sterile saline solution, secure it in position with secondary dressing. Subsequently, as and when maximum absorption is reached, the dressing may be changed.

But that still conforms to a step pattern. It is not noticeably more lucid or cogent than the preceding example, which in its turn is no more cogent than the 'columnar' text on which it is based. Instructions are as a rule best conveyed in column; but if a running text is called for, step markers usually have to be written into it somewhere: 'first', 'then', 'next', 'afterwards', 'subsequently', 'finally'.

Two recurrent features of the step pattern are the sequence markers noted above, and, as also noted, the repetition and regular positioning of some grammatical feature, such as the imperative, suggesting the textual continuity of a series of contextually associated items. Together, these characteristics go a long way towards designating the style of instructions, recipes and lists. Variations of step-patterning are observable, however, in other kinds of writing. It is usual for stage directions, for example, to conform to a step pattern:

> Round a centrally-placed coffee table there are three armchairs. To the left of the fireplace is an alcove with built-in bookshelves; to the right a table carrying a TV set. Against the wall facing the fireplace stands an upright piano.

In that example, the stepwise progression is emphasised by the regular location of a *place adverbial* ('round', 'to the left', 'to the right') at the head of each sentence. This sequence of adverbials does for the stage direction what the sequence of enumerations ('first', 'then', 'next') does for the instructional text. In that invented example, the step effect may perhaps seem too obviously contrived. Here, then, is a comparable instance of stage-directional prose, this time from an actual play, Ben Travers' farce *A Cuckoo in the Nest*:

> Parlour of the 'Stag and Hunt' Inn, Maiden Blotton. In the C. background a door giving direct access to the road through a porch. In the back wall and L. of this door, windows. The backcloth seen through these windows and also through the door when opened represents a country road. There is a door up R. with glass panel, also door up L. with glass panel entrances to bar. Just below the bar entrance there is a swing door, not a complete door, leaving an aperture at the top which is the entrance behind the counter. There is one other door down L. Above front door is a window with inscription set so as to be legible from without.

Thus a professional playwright imagines the setting of his play and describes it in detail, step by step, from position to position, in a tour of the scene, for the immediate benefit of the stage manager and his crew. The place adverbials show the way round: 'in the C. background', 'in the back wall and L. of this door', 'through these windows', 'through the door', 'just below the bar entrance', 'above front door', etc. This is strictly functional prose, clockwise composition (see p. 8) in the instructional register. A scene is 'set' in the strictest, most practical, workaday sense. But scene-setting also occurs in writings of a less *prescriptive*, more truly *descriptive* sort. How, for example, does George Eliot begin the narrative of *The Mill on the Floss*? Here is that wonderfully lyrical opening:

> A wide plain, where the broadening Floss hurries on between its green banks to the sea, and the loving tide, rushing to meet it, checks it passage with an impetuous embrace. On this mighty tide the black ships – laden with the fresh-scented fir-planks, with rounded sacks of oil-bearing seed, or with the dark glitter of coal – are borne along to the town of St. Ogg's, which shows its aged, fluted red roofs and the broad gables of its wharves between the low wooded hill and the river-brink, tinging the water with a soft purple hue under the transient glance of this February sun. Far away on each hand stretch the rich pastures, and the patches of dark earth, made ready for the seed of broad-

leaved green crops, or touched already with the tint of the tender bladed autumn-sown corn. There is a remnant still of the last year's golden clusters of beehive ricks rising at intervals beyond the hedgerows; and everywhere the hedgerows are studded with trees: the distant ships seem to be lifting their masts and stretching their red-brown sails close among the branches of the spreading ash. Just by the red-roofed town the tributary Ripple flows with a lively current into the Floss. How lovely the little river is, with its dark, changing wavelets! It seems to me like a living companion while I wander along the bank and listen to its low placid voice as the voice of one who is deaf and loving. I remember those large dipping willows. I remember the stone bridge.

This is a long opening paragraph, but it has its 'semantic fissures' (to use an expression previously suggested, see p. 41). From a description in broad perspective of the flood-plain of the Floss, with St. Ogg's at its centre, it proceeds, through the phrase *Far away on each hand*, to a delineation of features in the middle ground; then comes into nearer focus with *Just by the red-roofed town*; and finally closes on to the narrator, as beholder, standing near 'the stone bridge' and looking at *those* 'large dipping willows'. This is not at all like a stage direction, and yet it shares one feature of descriptive staging, the use of the place adverbials that progressively set the scene, until the perspective narrows down to the observing eye, when the demonstrative 'those', with its implication of things near at hand, displaces the adverbial expressions that tell of things seen at a distance. The paragraph in fact takes three long steps (broad view – middle view – close view), to its conclusion, and the steps are duly marked. There is even some internal marking of steps within steps – perspectives within perspectives; for instance, in the central section of this text, between 'Far away on each hand' and 'the branches of the spreading ash', we note 'at intervals beyond the hedgerows', 'everywhere', 'among the branches of the spreading ash' – turns of expression that read like an artist's annotations for a sketch or a painting. George Eliot's prose in this passage may indeed remind us modern readers of diverse yet complementary ways of looking at a scene: the playwright's careful directions; the painter's sketch-notes; most of all, perhaps, something that the author herself could not have known or guessed at, a filmic technique of 'tracking' and 'panning'. This artistic use of a step pattern is subtle and complex, but the steps are there to be traced, when the text is closely examined.

When narrative depicts action and its consequences (who did what? with what result? what happened next?) the steps are somewhat differently marked. The indices of sequence become redundant. No competent author of a hopefully hair-raising tale would write, for instance: 'First she picked up the gun. Next, she shot him. After that she ran from the room, screaming.' No, no. 'The gun was in her hand. She was shooting him. She was running from the room, screaming'. Perhaps like that. But here is a better example, for purposes of illustration. It comes from the first chapter of Raymond Chandler's *Farewell My Lovely*, and depicts the scene in a bar when an overweening bouncer tries to evict the mountainously unmoveable Moose Malloy:

> The bouncer tried to knee him in the groin. The big man turned him in the air and slid his gaudy shoes apart on the scaly linoleum that covered the floor. He bent the bouncer backwards and shifted his right hand to the bouncer's belt. The belt broke like a piece of butcher's string. The big man put his enormous hand flat against the bouncer's spine and heaved. He threw him clear across the room, spinning and staggering and flailing with his arms. Three men jumped out of the way. The bouncer went over with a table and smacked into the baseboard with a crash that must have been heard in Denver. His legs twitched. Then he lay still.

Here is only one overt marker of a sequence, the *then* of the final sentence. None of the preceding sentences carries any kind of introductory, step-marking phrase. Nevertheless, implications of 'then' – 'next' – 'after that' run through the paragraph. The sense of sequencing, or perhaps of *listing*, is effectively conveyed by a certain regularity of sentence structure. Each sentence, apart from the last, begins with a nominal or pronominal subject: respectively, 'the bouncer'. 'the big man', 'he', 'the belt', 'the big man', 'he', 'three men', 'the bouncer', 'his legs'. Of nine sentences, four begin with phrases designating the actors in the drama (two each for 'the bouncer' and 'the big man') and three with pronominal or demonstrative reference to the actors ('he' = the big man (twice); 'his legs' = the bouncer's). There is, in short, a catalogue of actions or brief events, mainly concerning the principal actors, and presented item by item, in a sort of descriptive inventory. This, though quite unlike the opening of *The Mill on the Floss*, and much more unlike a stage direction or a piece of instructional prose, is nevertheless an example of step-patterning.

The Step is a rhetorical principle underlying, as we see, diverse realisations. It is possible to discern four types, one instructional ('first do x, then y, and afterwards z'), one the propounding of an argument ('in the first place', 'furthermore', 'lastly'), a descriptive type ('here was this, next to it that, beyond, the other') and a narrative type ('something happened, then something else, and after that a further event'). This makes for a rather large family of texts, with two main branches, the general, practical usage of the instructional/expositional types, and the literary usage of the descriptive/narrative types. There are, no doubt, specimens of text not easily assigned to this 'branch' or that: some stage directions, for instance, fulfil their instructional role but also have literary claims on an audience that, having seen a play, will go on to read it. A classic example of this must be the introductory direction to Harold Pinter's *The Caretaker*:

> A room. A window in the back wall, the bottom half covered by a sack. An iron bed along the left wall. Above it a small cupboard, paint buckets, boxes containing nuts, screws, etc. More boxes, vases, by the side of the bed. A door, up right. To the right of the window, a mound: a kitchen sink, a step ladder, a coal bucket, a lawn mower, a shopping trolley, boxes, sideboard drawers. Under this mound an iron bed. In front of it a gas stove. On the gas stove a statue of Buddha. Down right, a fireplace. Around it a couple of suitcases, a rolled carpet, a blow-lamp, a wooden chair on its side, boxes, a number of ornaments, a clothes horse, a few short planks of wood, a small electric fire and a very old electric toaster. Below this a pile of old newspapers. Under ASTON's bed by the left wall, is an electrolux, which is not seen till used. A bucket hangs from the ceiling.

This is a stage direction – no doubt a conscientious stage manager would try to get hold of the items listed here, and arrange them in accordance with the playwright's wishes; and then again it is not a stage direction in the practical sense, it is a parody, a humorous mockery of the orderly proceeding that stage directions imply, with their customary circling and portioning of the 'set'. This 'direction' is defiantly indirect; the place adverbials take the eye here there and all over the place. Moreover, its wording tells of more things than are likely to meet a stage manager's eye, or that an audience really needs to see: for instance, those 'boxes containing nuts, screws, etc'. But this is not so much the specification for a stage set as the audience must see it; rather it is a specification for chaos as the author imagines it. It is a literary act, a piece of writing that begins clockwise (see p. 8) respecting the functional proprieties, but then turns convention about, in a creative counter-movement. Here the step-pattern is evoked, only to be mischievously disrupted.

More confined typologically is the pattern of the Stack, deriving ultimately from the figure of *anaphora* in classical rhetoric. The essence of a stack pattern is that a proposition, or 'topic sentence' is followed by a sequence of supporting assertions: a case is made by statements in evidence, or an argument is elaborated by amplifying comments. Advertising copywriters have frequent recourse to stack patterns, laying out the sales pitch in breakdown form:

> **WHIZZO** is the washing powder that fits your bill
> It works faster to make things whiter
> It takes away grease and ugly stains
> It is kind to your fabrics
> It is economical – a little goes a long way

Kind on your clothes and your pocket. **WHIZZO**. Today's wash

One might say, in imitation of the adman's style, that The Stack is the Pattern that makes Points – a series of points commonly rounded off by a summary formulation or a reassertion of the topic sentence. In expository prose, the argument or commentary is presented in continuous text, the successive points appearing to yield progressively, each one to its successor:

> There is something amiss with the morality of a saying like 'Honesty is the best policy'. The wrongness lies with equating virtue with profit. Any tolerably observant person must see that the equation is false. There are countless occurrences in life when doing what we believe to be right does not bring us material rewards. Indeed, we may sometimes suffer for it. To offer sound policy as an incitement to good morals is therefore

in itself dishonest. Honesty, if it requires a motive, must be valued for reasons other than politic.

In that moralising example – a piece of text devised to illustrate the stack pattern in use – the topic sentence is 'There must be something wrong with the morality of a saying like "Honesty is the best policy", and the summary of the stacked-up argument is "Honesty must be valued for reasons other than politic"'. In such instances it must often appear that the topic sentence and the summary are termini which writers establish in their own minds before they begin to work out points in argument. The working is displayed in the intervening sentences which form the stack. Each of these sentences extends the ground laid by its predecessor, but at the same time each sentence is an offshoot of the original proposition. This process of reversion, through developing stages, is a distinctive mark of the device.

It is in the formation of the stacked commentary, in the means used to order and relate the constituent items, that the interest of the pattern lies. Here, for example, the argument is made to cohere *lexically*; echoes and correspondences in the vocabulary are made to do the work of holding the text together. Thus, the phrase *something amiss* in the topic sentence is echoed by *wrongness* in the sentence that follows; the word *equating* in the second sentence is further echoed by *equation* in the third; and the words *policy, incitement,* and *good morals* in the penultimate sentence have semantic equivalents in the *politic, motive,* and *honesty* of the summary.

Stack patterns turn up quite often in newspaper editorials, when the writer temporarily quits exposition in favour of oration. Here, in a brief passage from a broadsheet editorial (in the *Guardian* of 23 February 1995) the journalist-orator does his declamatory stuff:

> Spain since Franco has done the easy things brilliantly. It has luxuriated and blossomed in freedom. It has embraced the European community as the bulwark of its new estate. It is genuinely vibrant. But, below the surface, many of the old industries and the old ways and the old nationalist tensions still lurk.

This is easily analysed: the topic, 'Spain since Franco has done the easy things brilliantly'; the conclusion, 'But, below the surface, many of the old . . . tensions still lurk'; and between, the stack, the anaphoric sequence defined by the repetition of the pronoun *it*. That is a typical ground plan for a great many examples of journalistic wiseacreage. Here is a more ambitious example from the same newspaper:

> Yesterday's Anglo-Irish framework document is a quintessential text for and of our times. It proposes rather than imposes. It has something for everyone, but no one gets everything. It is neither republican ramp nor sell-out to unionism. It recognises the importance of the nation state while acknowledging that this is no longer an age in which purely national solutions are deliverable. It respects sovereignty while ensuring that minorities and individuals are protected within it. It is a multi-layered, multi-dimensional, pluralist trade-off, or rather the groundwork of such a deal. Indeed it is not even a final statement of the two governments' intentions, as John Major was frequently at pains to point out yesterday. It is exactly what it says it is: a framework for an agreement, not a final, take-it-or-leave it solution.

To see how the statement of the conclusion brings us back to the proposal of the topic, we have only to put the two together. With no intervening stack: 'Yesterday's Anglo-Irish framework document is a quintessential text for and of our times. It is exactly what it says it is: a framework for an agreement, not a final, take-it-or-leave it solution.' Between these termini comes a long series of supporting assertions marked by the anaphoric *it*. A stylistic feature of the sentences in this series is the tendency to increase in length. There is some fluctuation, but a reader sensitive to the general rhythm of the paragraph must sense the contrast between the five words of 'it proposes rather than imposes' and the 24 of 'Indeed it is not even a final statement of the two governments' intentions, as John Major was frequently at pains to point out yesterday.' The stack *broadens*, as it were, on the way down from the topic to the conclusion.

Just as the step patterns of functional prose may be adapted to literary use, at times to subversive effect, so in fiction we may find examples of stacking that defy the implication of an orderly, regulated process from a topic to a conclusion. A stack-shape – call it that – is evident in this paragraph, the opening of a chapter in Michael Ondaatje's novel *In the Skin of a Lion*:

In 1938, when Patrick Lewis was released from prison, people were crowding together in large dark buildings across North America to see Garbo as Anna Karenina. Everyone tried to play the Hammond Organ. 'Red Squads' intercepted mail, tear-gassed political meetings. By now over 10,000 foreign-born workers had been deported out of the country. Everyone sang 'Just One of Those Things'. The longest bridge in the world was being built over the lower Zambezi and the great waterworks at the east end of Toronto neared completion.

Although this piece of narrative may seem to avoid the conventional stacking procedure of topic–stack–conclusion, that shape is, as it were, latently present. The 'topic' is 'In 1938, when Patrick Lewis was released from prison', and the 'conclusion' follows in due course with 'the great waterworks at the east end of Toronto neared completion.' This relationship between the top and tail of the paragraph may not be apparent to anyone reading the passage out of context; the reader of Mr Ondaatje's novel, however, will be aware of Patrick Lewis's history, and his quarrel with 'the great waterworks at the east end of Toronto'. The first and last words of this paragraph thus represent a strand of narrative; the stack of intervening sentences presents an impressionistic sketch of a moment in the history of the twentieth century – Garbo, Hammond Organs, a popular song, the 'Red Squads', deportations, etc. As a structure, the paragraph fulfils two concurrent purposes. It 'reconnects' the reader with a character from earlier chapters, and it pictures the world into which the character is emerging, having been locked away in the obscurity of prison.

The Stack and the Step are compositional patterns with a certain predictive value. That is, it is possible from the outset to decide how a proposed content might best be treated. We can anticipate, at least for a little while, the course of composition. The academic in his study goes into an automatic step-routine: 'In this paper I want to consider . . . First, I shall . . . In the second place, the discussion . . . Then and only then . . . etc.' The political speech-writer stacks up his points and punch-lines: 'The wibbly, the public must realise, not the wobbly, is the message for today . . . Wibblies are what the people want . . . Wibblies are economically sound . . . Wibblies are the foundation of health and happiness . . . Let us pay heed to the wibbly and leave wobbling to others . . . etc.'

Step or Stack become routine choices in some registers; they are, in effect, maps of possibility, routes to a predetermined goal.

These stereotypical patterns relieve the writer of one of the major burdens of composition: the bewilderment, sometimes bordering on paralysis, of not knowing quite how to proceed, or where the material is leading. The argument has to be thought through *currente calamo*, assembled on the run, paid out link by link. There are episodes in writing when one is looking to establish a connection with the preceding sentence and trying to anticipate a transition to the next sentence ahead. One feels one's way through a compositional labyrinth. The following passage imitates this process of verbal maze-threading:

> Britain cannot easily extricate herself from events in Northern Ireland. She must feel the burden of history, a history shadowed and tainted by tragic mistakes. Those mistakes, and the responsibility for their consequences, are not to be written wholly and solely to the account of a generation that included the likes of Lord Birkenhead and Lord Edward Carson. The debit is older and more complex, a tally dating back to the days of King William, and those famous apprentice boys of Londonderry, and then farther, ever farther into the past.

This is a sketch, thrown off in the style of an editorial or commentary article in a broadsheet newspaper. Sentences are successively linked by devices of vocabulary or grammar:

Sentences
1–2   events . . . history
2–3   mistakes . . . those mistakes
3–4   the account . . . the debit (+ tally)
4–5   Birkenhead/Carson . . . King William/apprentice boys

The lexical connections in that passage are made by repeating words from one sentence to the next (*mistakes*), or by synonymic variations (*events/history, account/debit/tally*), or by characterising allusions to persons and events (*Birkenhead/Carson, King William/ apprentice boys*). The one syntactic link in this short example is the demonstrative *those*, which has an 'anaphoric', or backward-pointing function, in one case to something specifically within the text ('*those* mistakes') and in the other to an extra-textual item, a feature of the cultural context ('*those* famous apprentice boys'), with which it is assumed that the reader will be familiar. The range of grammatical connectives is much greater than this example might suggest, but the topic can be put aside for the moment. The 'chains' of expository prose are usually constructed from lexical items supported by deictic ('pointer') forms from the grammatical repertoire. The method can be further illustrated by a passage from Nigel Barley's *The Innocent Anthropologist*. Dr Barley lived for two years among a people called the Dowayos, in the Cameroons. One of the many questions he had to ask, as an anthropologist, was why, among the Dowayos, blacksmiths appeared to be marked out as a ritually separate segment of tribal society. Here he is, pondering some of the possibilities:

> I found that blacksmiths were supposed to speak with a particular accent, different from the other Dowayos; their sexual isolation might be stressed by beliefs about incest or homosexuality. The last I found a particularly awkward area. My opportunity to broach the subject came on the occasion of the castration of a bull whose testes were being eaten by parasitic worms. I was interested to note that, had several cattle been due for castration, this would have been performed in the circumcision grove where boys are cut, another example of the identification of cattle and men. As all the cattle were driven in so that the diseased one could be caught, two yearlings tried to mount each other. I pointed this out, hoping that similar practices would be imputed to some group, with luck, blacksmiths. The further I went in my questioning, the more awkward and embarrassing it became. The truth seems to be that homosexual practices are largely unknown in West Africa except where white men have spread the word. Dowayos were incredulous that such things were possible. Such behaviour in animals was always interpreted as 'They are fighting over women'.

Essentially, the argument runs between a hesitant hypothesis ('their sexual isolation might be stressed by beliefs about incest or homosexuality') and a reluctant conclusion ('the truth seems to be that homosexual practices are largely unknown in West Africa except where white men have spread the word'). The progression between these points runs through a series of linkages perhaps not quite so obvious as those illustrated in the previous extract. Here, the first link, after the initial, 'hypothetical' sentence, is *The last,* referring back to *homosexuality*. Then, an *awkward area* ('area' in the sense of 'topic of enquiry', 'theme') finds its subsequent connection in *the subject*. Next in the chain, the word *castration* supplies the point of reference, in the sentence that follows, for the demonstrative *this* ('this would have been performed'). That sentence ends with *cattle and men*, and the next begins *as all the cattle*; repetition of a word makes an immediate lexical bridge across sentences. Another *this* ('I pointed this out') then makes anaphoric reference to 'two yearlings tried to mount each other'. The last link in the chain is a connection, perceived in the narrative context rather than made explicit in the text, between *I pointed this out* and *my questioning*. All this exemplifies the effort of a writer to work his way through a theme, to write 'closely', to stay in touch with the exposition as it is laid out on the page, not allowing gaps of explanation and understanding to occur between one sentence and the next.

Jumps in the expository argument or narrative are allowed for by a companion pattern, the Balance. Balances are made by 'but' and 'however' and 'though' and 'if' and 'nevertheless'. A particular symptom of the balance is 'on the one hand . . . on the other hand', that judicious turn of phrase so dear to the hearts of broadsheet newspaper editors. As a paragraph-informing device, the Balance takes several shapes. In some instances, the paragraph text is emphatically divided by an emphatic BUT; so that the paragraph presents argument and counter-argument in two balancing blocks. Another pattern propounds thesis – antithesis – synthesis: 'if *A* is the case' . . . 'against which *B*' . . . 'from which we conclude *C*'. Yet a third type explores the argument in stages, each stage presenting its own balance, as in this (invented) example:

> For some writers, the best time to work is in the early morning. For others, night is the consecrated time. The early birds rise fresh to their task in a reilluminated world, and claim to feel, and do, the better for it. The night owls seek the composure and tranquillity, the creative quietude that only darkness can bring. Do your writing while the rest are having breakfast, thinks one party, and so escape irritating phone calls and unwelcome enquiries; have the world to yourself. The others think, no, do your writing while the world sleeps, and be sure you have a whole universe to yourself. Perhaps these preferences are a

matter of temperament. Possibly they are a question of physiology. For my own part, I choose to *compose* at night, but *correct* in the morning, often cancelling more than half of what I have written. Darkness generates; daylight regulates.

There, the sentences run in pairs: 'For some ... For others'; 'The early birds' ... 'The night owls'; 'Do your writing while the rest are having breakfast' ... 'Do your writing while the world sleeps'; 'a matter of temperament' ... 'a question of physiology'. Even in the concluding sentences, offering some kind of arbitration between *this way* and *that way*, the balancing act goes on, with 'to *compose* at night, but *correct* in the morning'. And so to the balancing-out of the last balance: 'Darkness generates; daylight regulates.'

When paragraphs are obviously constructed round a single pattern to the exclusion of any other, this is usually a product of the *editorial* process, rather than of progressive *monitoring* (see p. 42 above). The writer makes conscious decisions about the rhetoric of his text. The psychology of writing, however, rarely allows for neat-and-tidy structures. Short paragraphs may cleave conveniently to a particular design, but the long paragraphing of a writer responding to compositional instincts generally presents a mixed patterning, a shifting from one procedural method to another, as the exploration of a theme appears to dictate. Here is a randomly-chosen instance, a passage from Bronislaw Malinowski's *A Scientific Theory of Culture*. It is a paragraph on the subject of fire-making, arguing that for this primitive craft to have practically possible there must have existed a theory, in the form of a set of concepts and principles that could be said to amount to a *science* of fire-making:

> One of the simplest and most fundamental primitive crafts is that of fire-making. In this, over and above the manual ability of the craftsman, we find a definite scientific theory embodied in each performance, and in the tribal tradition thereof. Such a tradition had to define in a general, that is, abstract manner, the material and form of the two types of wood used. The tradition also had to define the principles of performance, the type of muscular movement, its speed, the capture of the spark, and the nourishment of the flame. The tradition was kept alive not in books nor yet in explicit physical theories. But it implied two

pedagogical and theoretical elements. First and foremost, it was embodied in the manual skills of each generation, which, by example and precept, were handed over to the new growing members. Secondly, whether primitive symbolism was accomplished by verbal statement, by significant gesture, or by substantial performance, such as instructions where to find and how to store the materials and produce the forms, such symbolism must have been at work, even as I myself have seen it at work in my field research. That this is so we have to infer, because the final performance, that is, the production of fire, would never be possible unless general distinctions as to material, activity, and coordination were kept within the conditions necessary and sufficient for a successful pragmatic performance.

The first three sentences of that paragraph make a chain, the links of which are *fire-making . . . in this*; *tribal tradition . . . such a tradition*. The fourth sentence appears at first to extend the chain, but actually marks a brief transfer to a different pattern: the sentences beginning 'The tradition also had to define' and 'The tradition was kept alive' are 'stacked'. Then follows a major balance with 'But it implied, etc'. ('The tradition was not expressed in a theory BUT it implied theoretical elements – as follows'). What immediately follows is clearly marked as a step-pattern: 'First and foremost . . . ', 'Secondly . . . etc.' The sentence beginning 'Secondly' is, however, a very long one, and at its conclusion we return to the chain-structure: 'such symbolism must have been at work' is the explicit reference of *this* at the beginning of the final sentence, 'That this is so we have to infer'. Some of Malinowski's sentences are long, and to study properly how the patterns shift one might have to look closely at the changes of stance – so to speak – that occur *within* these long sentences. But even a cursory examination of sentence-linkages will suggest the image of a writer exploring his own mind even as he investigates his theme: brooding on promptings to connect, to exemplify, to contrast, to list.

The compositional skill of getting from one sentence to another is, like fire-making, 'one of the simplest and most fundamental crafts'. Like fire-making, it is a pragmatic accomplishment, observable in traditional practice, not made explicit in any body of theory, and yet implying theoretical elements. It might indeed be said that inability to grasp (not necessarily *formulate*) what the theoretical options are is the cause of many an onset of that dreaded affliction called 'writer's block'. Having some understanding of how compositional patterns are used and formed is one way of helping to remove a block. A companion remedy is to cultivate a consciousness of those resources that help a writer to bridge the gaps between sentences.

Four

Charley's tale, or the gaps between sentences

Unconstrained, with nothing particular in mind, no ulterior motive, no prompting from immediate experience, directed only by a random fantasy, I think of a sentence, a sentence I am fairly sure that no one has heard or read before. Nothing could be easier. I commit my sentence to paper. It is a declarative sentence, and it reads: 'Charley quit the accounts job towards the end of July.' I have, as the saying goes, 'dreamed up' this statement, quite freely. Thus prompted, I attempt to add other sentences, and now the constraints begin, the containing and steering of my fantasy. From this point on, it gets harder. I start to give shape to a narrative, and in doing so find that each sentence I add is in some way dictated, at least as to content, by its predecessor. My sentences are insisting, it seems, on their cumulative status as a text. While I ponder this evolution, I set out my sentences in list-fashion, the better to consider what each of them adds to the textual shape:

1. Charley quit the accounts job towards the end of July.
2. There was some difficulty in finding a replacement.
3. The applicants were well-qualified men in their mid-forties.
4. Charley's was not a highly paid post.

On the whole, I think that these four sentences make an intelligible opening to a possible tale of Charley, but then I have to ask myself, is it fully intelligible only to me, its originator? Are there not gaps, so to speak, between those sentences, gaps that, if filled, might slant the narrative in different ways, even confer upon its totality a different *sense*? I can leave the reader to fill the gaps, of course, but

I may not want to do that. In the interests of making things as clear as possible, to keep the unseen critic at bay, I decide to do a little gap-filling:

> Charley quit the accounts job towards the end of July. There was some difficulty in finding a replacement, however. For one thing, the applicants were well-qualified men in their mid-forties. For another, Charley's was not a highly paid post.

Now I have devised some linking expressions, to direct the reading and stay one step ahead of the reader. I write *however* to anticipate the phantom conjecture – 'Well, there would be no problem, surely, in filling a post in accounts?' Then I put in *for one thing* and *for another*, marking two good, and connected, reasons, for that *however*. I have shaped my text, and I have not left my readers much room for creative guesswork. Indeed, I have not left a very 'creative' text. This rudimentary method of constructing links produces a reading that resembles an academic exposition or a piece of boilerplate prose rather than a potentially interesting narrative. (On academic exposition, see p. 20 above.)

I then try to guide the tale along slightly different lines, using the same set of sentences but filling in the gaps in another way:

> Charley quit the accounts job towards the end of July. At that time of year there was some difficulty in finding a replacement. Inevitably, the applicants were well-qualified men in their mid-forties. Charley's was not such a highly paid job.

My linkers now are *At that time of year, Inevitably,* and, in the final sentence, *such*. The linkages are not so tight, in just-so expository fashion; they allow the reader to speculate, to participate in the invention, supply a narrative context. Why should there be difficulty in replacing an employee at the end of July? No real-world reason at all; but the adverbial *at that time of year* connects the sentences, and in doing so directs the fantasy. In this imagined world, the reader is allowed to suppose, July is not a good time for the job market. The linking phrase is thus not only a textual connector, but also a perceptual directive. Similarly, the making of an imaginative connection is the whole point of *inevitably*; this 'commentary disjunct' presupposes, again, a willingness to imagine a world in which certain things are 'inevitable', whatever may be the facts and probabilities of the 'real' world. This combination of textual marking and contextual perception continues with the demonstrative *such* in the last sentence. Textually, it points towards the preceding 'well-qualified men in their mid-forties'; perceptually, it invites the reader to suppose that such men would, of course, be looking for a highly paid post. Altogether, this is a much more open, speculative structure than the formulaic pattern of the preceding example. And it encourages the reader to ask further questions. For example, is Charley a man or a woman? (The spelling of the name could indicate either.) If Charley were a woman – or rather, were 'read as a woman' – it would explain quite a lot in this second version of the text, notably by giving a particular orientation to *inevitably*. Charley's parsimonious employers, the participant reader might then conclude, were hoping to replace her with another (underpaid, underqualified) woman, but *inevitably* the applicants were *men*, and highly-salaried men at that, who would turn up their noses at this low-grade post. (Is that elaborate reading really possible? The text is becoming leaky; some ideology is seeping in at those open seams.)

I try a third version, and now I am fully aware of the reader over my shoulder, he who sneers and pulls wry faces at every juncture. See how I appeal to him:

> Charley quit the accounts job towards the end of July. Unfortunately, there was some difficulty in finding a replacement. True, the applicants were well-qualified men in their mid-forties, but Charley's, alas, was not a highly paid post.

The appellant words are *unfortunately, true,* and *alas,* each of them conceding to the reader the right to question, to interpose, to deplore, to enjoy the participant emotions of the kibitzer. (This is an easy game to play. Try it: 'Adolf Hitler made a great impression on everyone. Unfortunately, he also made a lot of people cry. True, he had an unhappy youth, but that, alas, is no excuse for enslaving half of Europe.' This syllogistic way of going on is what the rhetoricians call an *enthymeme*.)

A feature of my third version is that the last two sentences of the original paradigm are now *conjoined*, so that they become one sentence, with the two declarative clauses internally linked by the conjunction *but*. Indeed, the entire narrative might have been compressed, by means of such internal linkages, into one sentence:

> When Charley quit the accounts job towards the end of July there was some difficulty in finding a replacement, because the applicants were well-qualified men in their mid-forties and Charley's was not a highly paid post.

When, *because* and *and* do all the linking that exposition requires, and the possibility of readerly intervention is, once more, greatly reduced. But that sentence, considered as a narrative 'core', might be expanded again, into a fuller narrative text:

> It was towards the end of July that Charley quit her job with accounts. Her going raised an unforeseen problem. The firm had some difficulty in appointing a replacement, largely because the people who applied were men − men in their mid-forties, moreover − whose qualifications presupposed a salary much higher than Charley's humble wage.

Now, however, our exercise has gone beyond sentence-connection − the management of gaps between sentences − and is entering on questions of sentence-type and sentence-structure, the control of the text in its variable patterns of clause order and word order. This must be matter reserved for a later chapter; our immediate problem is to consider the matter of *connection* in general, and in particular to describe the processes of transition between sentences.

CONNECTORS, THE BUSY AUTHOR'S FRIENDS

Connectors are indeed the busy author's friends, or, one might say, the author's busy friends, because they bustle about a great deal, fastening this to that or hooking those to the others, and there is really no building a text without them. Now pause: read that sentence again, and account for the presence of its third word, *indeed*. Why this? What on earth is this 'indeed' indeeding? Indeed, it is acknowledging the possible oddity, for the reader, of the preceding piece of text, the sub-heading of this part of our chapter, and it makes the promise of an expansion or explanation, which follows after 'because'. It is, in fact, a connector (as, indeed, is 'in fact'). Other kinds of connector occur in the unwinding of the rest of that long sentence: *and*, *or*, *because*, make it possible to keep the thread of the sentence running, to go on paying out the text without a break.

Conjunctions

The words 'and', 'or', and 'because' belong to the grammatical class of *conjunctions*. Conjunctions are so called because they conjoin words, or phrases, or clauses within the larger pattern of the sentence:

> The lion and the unicorn were staying at the inn.
> (The nouns 'lion' and 'unicorn' are linked by the conjunction *and*)

> Last night's cabbage or the day before's meat loaf was the option at lunch.
> (The conjunction *or* links the phrases 'last night's cabbage' and 'the day before's meat loaf')

> The unicorn chose the cabbage because he was a vegetarian.
> (The conjunction *because* connects the clauses 'the unicorn chose the cabbage' and 'he was a vegetarian')

Closer examination of the sentences making up that little fantasy may reveal the fact that the kind of conjoining done by *and* and *or* differs somewhat from the type of linkage represented by *because*. It is the difference between *coordinating* and *subordinating*. Coordinating conjunctions (*and*, *but*, *or*) link items of strictly parallel grammatical status: brother word joins hands with brother, sister links arms with sister phrase. Subordinating conjunctions, by contrast, express the dependency of one construction on another, the dependency of the child looking to the parent. Putting it less fancifully, the coordinating conjunction simply joins A and B without indicating anything in the way of priority or precondition or causality; whereas subordinating conjunctions (among others *because, therefore, although, yet, while, since, as, when, where*) furnish reasons, conditions, provisions, concessions, or attach some indication of time (e.g. the *when* of 'I was sleeping when he came') or place (e.g. the *where* of 'He told us where he found it').

This distinction between coordinating and subordinating, a

grammatical commonplace, is of some importance as a possible determinant and symptom of literary style. How did Ernest Hemingway tell his tales of simple, elemental action? Here is a brief, characteristic extract from his last novel, *The Old Man and the Sea*:

> The skiff was still shaking with the destruction the other shark was doing to the fish and the old man let the sheet go so that the skiff would swing broadside and bring the shark out from under. When he saw the shark he leaned over the side and punched at him. He hit only meat and the hide was set hard and he barely got the knife in. The blow hurt not only his hands but his shoulder too. But the shark came up fast with his head out and the old man hit him squarely in the centre of his flat-topped head as his nose came out of the water and lay against the fish. The old man withdrew the blade and punched the shark exactly in the same spot again. He still hung to the fish with his jaws locked and the old man stabbed him in his left eye. The shark still hung there.

That passage is not without its subordinating junctures ('*so that* the skiff would swing', '*when* he saw the shark', '*as* his nose came out of the water'). The scene is set in due form and order; but the impression this scene overwhelmingly makes is that of dramatic coordination. Count the coordinators: *and* occurs nine times in eight sentences (twice in a single sentence, 'He hit only meat and the hide was set hard and he barely got the knife in'). *But* occurs no more than twice; those two occurrences are, however, narrative neighbours ('The blow hurt not only his hands but his shoulder too', 'But the shark came up fast' – implying the almost simultaneous happening that leaves the old man no time to think about his bodily pain: he strikes – hands hurt, shoulder hurts, up comes the shark). One other word dominates, or at least *frames*, the drama: the adverb *still* ('The skiff was still shaking', 'He still hung to the fish', 'The shark still hung there'). Just so: whatever the action, the position is *still* the same, unbudgingly constant, a picture of a man desperately trying to bring effects out of causes but, stranded all the time on the effects of an effect – and ... and – and ... and ... and ... but ... and ... and.

Contrast this drama with a very short extract in a completely different style – almost a functional, 'clockwise' style (for 'clock-wise' see Chapter 1, p. 8). At the end of his novel, *A Passage to India*, E. M. Forster embarks on the necessary process of tying up the strands of the plot. The narrative ends despondently. There has been a religious festival, its splendour ruined by rain and floods. A Rajah has died. It is the melancholy recession of Forster's tale of cultures in contact and conflict. We are left to understand that the 'passage to India', the voyage of discovery, is coming to an end. The book's closing section then begins with these sentences:

> Friends again, yet aware that they would meet no more, Aziz and Fielding went for their last ride in the Mau jungles. The floods had abated and the Rajah was officially dead, so the Guest House party were departing next morning, as decorum required. What with the mourning and the festival, the visit was a failure.

Thus Forster effects a rapid transition into his final pages. There is one coordinator in those three sentences ('The floods had abated and the Rajah was officially dead', which might just as easily have read 'the Rajah was officially dead and the floods had abated'); apart from that, the significant linkages are all subordinating expressions – '*yet* aware that they would meet no more', '*so* the Guest House party were departing', '*as* decorum required', '*What with* the mourning and the festival'. The subordinators make for a compact textual structure; more than that, they supply a dimension, a kind of explanatory depth. This is the dimension of the conceded circumstance, of 'although', which is the purport of *yet*. It is the dimension of the drawn conclusion, of 'therefore', which is the sense of *so*. It is the dimension of the explanatory comment, represented by *as*. And it is the dimension of addition and elaboration, of 'among other things', which is the drift of *what with*. These paraphrases – 'though' for 'yet', 'therefore' for 'so', etc., suggest that there might be other ways of writing this short passage. And indeed other ways are available; subordination has quite plentiful resources.

Conjuncts

Among those resources are the expressions described as *conjuncts*. Conjuncts operate like conjunctions, with which, as a type of connector, they overlap. Like conjunctions, conjuncts may serve to link the components of a sentence, but they can be made to do more than that. A conjunct takes up where a conjunction leaves off; conjuncts can jump the gaps between sentences:

> Though Becker played well, he lost the match.
> Becker lost the match. He played well, though.

In the first of those examples, *though* is a subordinating conjunction, introducing the clause 'Becker played well'. (Note that *although* might also have been used, with the same function and implying the same meaning.) In the second example, *though* is a conjunct. It skips across otherwise discrete sentences ('Becker lost the match. He played well'), and – rather unusually for a conjunct – its placing is restricted to the sentence-end position.

Sentence-linking conjuncts most commonly introduce the construction, but they can often be placed in mid-sentence, and may also occur as a species of colloquial throwaway at sentence-end. Something depends on the specific instance. So with the word *nevertheless* in these examples:

> The smart money was on his younger opponent. Nevertheless, the German veteran made a hard match of it.

> The smart money was on his younger opponent. The German veteran nevertheless made a hard match of it.

> The smart money was on his younger opponent. The German veteran made a hard match of it, nevertheless.

The positioning of *nevertheless* is acceptable in all three instances, though it might be argued, as a matter of stylistic perception, that shifting the word involves some shifting of emphasis, a different intonation, a different focusing of the message. Some conjuncts sit more easily at the beginning or end of the sentence than in the medial position. Again, something depends on the specific item and the context. *All in all* as a conjunct is well suited to the introductory position:

> It rained every day, some of the delegates had valuables stolen from their rooms, and during the grand gala dinner a fire

swept through the hotel. All in all, this conference was a failure.

That could be written with the conjunct in the final position:

> It rained every day, some of the delegates had valuables stolen from their rooms, and during the grand gala dinner a fire swept through the hotel. This conference was a failure, all in all.

The placing of the connector, in such examples, is a matter of stylistic fine-tuning. One can imagine a writer brooding over it, switching phrases back and forth, asking himself temporarily unanswerable questions − 'what effect am I trying to bring off here?' − 'the angry emphasis? the defeated sigh?' − 'what is the narrative point of view?' − 'what positioning of the link-word will provide the best point of connection to other parts of my text?' − and so on. Such questions demand a great deal of meditation, a stewing-over that can go on until the script goes to the printer and reaches the proof stage (after which alterations tend to be frowned on). It is even possible that the labouring author could be seduced for a minute or two by the possibility of placing the conjunct medially, before or after *was*:

> It rained every day, some of the delegates had valuables stolen from their rooms, and during the grand gala dinner a fire swept through the hotel. This conference all in all was a failure.

That could be civilised a little by setting the conjunct parenthetically, between commas:

> This conference, all in all, was a failure.

The other possibility is to enter *all in all* after *was*, again marking the phrase with those parenthetical commas:

> This conference was, all in all, a failure.

Such readings, by fragmenting the sentence, suggest a rhythmic break and a consequent 'accenting' of the word immediately preceding the conjunct − in this instance *conference*, or *was*. It is thus demonstrably possible for a conjunct like *all in all* to be purposefully assigned to the medial position, but it is nevertheless an awkward, problematic choice.

Commonly occurring conjuncts are *however* and *nevertheless, moreover, furthermore, what's more, in addition, in fact, in brief, in sum, indeed, all the same, in other words, by the way, as a result, by contrast, on the other hand, meanwhile.* That is a mere fistful. One of the best ways to collect further examples would be to read with close, critical attention the editorial articles of some broadsheet newspapers; and after that, to study the relevant sections in a good reference grammar (for example Quirk *et al.*1985; Greenbaum and Quirk 1990).

Disjuncts

The reference grammar should also tell the enquiring student something about *disjuncts*. A disjunct is a word or phrase (sometimes quite a short word, sometimes quite a long phrase) 'disjoined' from the surrounding text, readily detachable from it, but serving to make some kind of comment on it:

She arrived later that evening. My goodness, I was relieved.

She arrived later that evening. Unexpectedly, there had been traffic jams on every major road.

My goodness and *unexpectedly* work as disjuncts in these examples – they do not conjoin sentence-units, and could be removed without centrally affecting the sense of the text – but they operate in slightly different ways. The comment, *my goodness*, is purely personal, a reflection of the speaker/writer's feelings or point of view, not a matter for 'objective' testimony. The comment *unexpectedly* does not represent the writer's state of mind – or if it does, it is only because the writer is one among many who did not expect the roads to be congested with traffic; what it represents is a matter of verifiable public consensus, and in that function it can be regarded as 'objective'. On the one hand, there is a kind of interjection or exclamation; on the other, an adverbial expression modifying the content of the sentence to which it is attached. The two kinds of commentary-item can be distinguished as *style disjuncts* and *content disjuncts*. Look at some further examples:

Some style disjuncts:

Oh: Nobody got on very well with Captain Bligh. Oh, he ran his ship efficiently enough.

Well: It is said that old men forget. Well, some of us can remember as clearly as some others, whoever they may be.

Frankly: The forecasters offered us the pleasing prospect of more warm weather to come. Frankly, I was getting tired of sweating all day.

To be honest: I was not surprised when Buggins was arrested for fraud, assault, arson, drunken driving and indecent exposure. To be honest, I always thought there was something odd about the man.

True: To be in the peak of physical condition is something I am learning to appreciate. True, I have diabetes and asthma and a nasty bed sore, but I am the right age for these things.

Sadly: My choice for the steeplechase, *Wideawake*, was leading by five lengths with a furlong to go. Sadly, the jockey nodded off at the last hurdle.

Face it: The Internet beckons many, but its allure is not for all. Face it, some of us have enough to do with the alphabet.

Between ourselves: *The Times* reviewer called Simpkins' book ignorant, illiterate, and destined for a short life in the 'remaindered' box. Between ourselves, I thought that an undeservedly favourable notice.

If I might venture to say so: You say you cannot sleep at night. If I might venture to say so, you could help yourself by staying awake during the day.

And so with many others, including *honestly, truthfully, as far as I am concerned, for my part, to put it briefly, strictly speaking, as a staunch supporter of the Kansas Chiefs*, etc.

Some content disjuncts:

Naturally: Henry was offered a Professorship in All Things Oxonian. Naturally, this involved living in Oxford.

Regrettably: They proposed a meeting of interested parties. Regrettably, some of the most important people were unable to attend.

Apparently: There was some uncertainty as to which side had won the battle. Apparently the British lost more battleships than the Germans, who lost more cruisers than the British.

Without a [shadow of a] doubt: The precipitation statistics for the Iberian peninsula leave no room for vague conjecture. Without a doubt, the rain falls mainly in the plain.

All things being equal: I am now making arrangements to travel towards the end of the month. All things being equal, we should be in Sweden by the 23rd.

Not entirely to our surprise: Jake was entrusted with the task of supervising the lottery. Not entirely to our surprise, his numbers came first out of the draw.

And so with others, among them *curiously, understandably, funnily enough, wisely, predictably, given these circumstances, taking one thing with another, everything else considered*.

The repertoire of disjuncts includes expressions that cautiously qualify 'content' statements, and thereby qualify, or protect, the writer's personal stance. Some scholars refer to such words or phrases as 'hedges'. *Admittedly* and *arguably* are common hedges; so are phrases like *in principle, generally speaking, as a rule, in most cases*. Some form of hedging comment is often used to connect pairs of sentences in which the first is a quite powerful statement, calling for a qualifying follow-up:

Such a warlike response was unjustifiable in the eyes of many. Admittedly, there had been great provocation.

To molest a child is the gravest of crimes. It is arguably worse than murder.

There is very little violence at football matches. Generally speaking, the fans are well behaved.

We are all free and equal before the law. That is, in principle, correct.

In those examples the second, 'hedging' sentence picks up the loose end of a possible challenge or query. ('What, no violence on the terraces?' – 'Generally speaking, no'; 'Are we really equal before the law?' – 'In principle, yes').

Adjuncts

There are some kinds of adverbial adjunct (meaning a phrase which specifies or amplifies the scope of the meaning denoted by a verb) that commonly serve to bridge gaps between sentences. The most usual types of sentence-linking adjunct are expressions of space and time, though other semantic categories (e.g. 'frequency', 'manner', 'contingency') may occur. Typical space adjuncts denote position, direction, or distance:

> Inexpensive restaurants were few and far between. I found a good one *in Marchmont Street*. (Note how the connection might be differently focused by presenting the adjunct at the beginning of the sentence: 'In Marchmont Street I found a good one'.)

> The town ended abruptly at the railroad station. *To the West* lay nothing but parched earth and cactus.

> The stillness of the morning was abruptly broken. *From far away, from the other side of the valley*, came the buzz and shriek of a chain-saw.

Time adjuncts denote periods or points in time:

> *For decades after the Restoration*, wigs were commonly worn. *Towards the end of the eighteenth century*, the fashion changed.

> We sat and waited for the doctor to come. *At 4.15 precisely* he appeared at the garden gate.

As noted above, other types of adjunct, common in internal sentence structure, may serve as agents of transition between sentences when the writer wishes to break the text into fairly short units. Thus:

> Bloggs was unimpressed. *With a scornful gesture* he dismissed my whole argument. [Manner adjunct. Compare this with the possibility of incorporating the adjunct in a single sentence: 'Bloggs, unimpressed, dismissed my whole argument with a scornful gesture.']

The computer may not recognise the file name you entered. *In that case* you must think again, and try again. [Contingency adjunct. Possible construction: 'The computer may not recognise the file name you have entered, in which case you must think again and try again.']

The next stage of construction requires care. *With a sharp knife and a lot of patience* the components may be cut out of strong board. [Instrumental adjunct.]

When adjuncts are thus used, to connect sentence units, they behave in many respects like conjuncts and disjuncts. The general principle is, that you may by all means keep your text simple by reducing the length and increasing the number of sentence units; but if the text so reduced and simplified leaves awkward jumps in meaning, or is likely to leave the reader in doubt as to the continuity of reference, then you must find and exploit appropriate mechanisms of connection. Connectors, we repeat, are the busy author's friends.

CONTINUITIES; OR, KEEPING THE TEXT IN MOTION

An important function of any kind of connector is of course to explain a linkage, or fill in a semantic gap; at the same time, these devices of connection keep the text in motion, sustaining a kind of rolling impetus from sentence to sentence. Our descriptions of paragraph patterning (in the preceding chapter) may have served to illustrate this. Here we add some further notes on the strategies of continuity, together with some of the phrases – a more or less automatic repertoire – that implement them.

Such 'strategies' can be described in general as (a) 'ticking off the points, or saying *first, second and finally*', (b) 'amplifying, or saying *for instance and furthermore*', (c) 'contradicting, or saying *on the other hand*', and (d) 'hooking up, or saying *this, that, the above and the following*'. Let us, for convenience' sake, label these 'strategies' respectively **enumerative**, **extensional**, **interruptive**, and **cohesive**. In each case there are words and phrases to which a writer has habitual recourse. Sometimes the range of choice is restricted because the stylistic task is relatively simple, not calling for any profusion of expressions; and sometimes, despite a greater availability of linking devices, the choice tends to be qualified by the 'register' (the writing about *what* and *for whom* and *in what tone of voice*) in which the text is cast.

There are, for example, comparatively few *enumerative* terms. We have *first(ly)*, *second(ly)*, *third(ly)*, etc., all the way through to *finally*, or *lastly*; and these basic indices of order and progression can be varied by periphrases, e.g. *first and foremost, to begin with, for a start, for starters, in the first place, ... second place, ... third place, ... next, ... in conclusion, to sum up, in short, last but not least*. These are stylistic variants, and it may be obvious that some are appropriate to purposes and contexts not served by others (for example, would anybody write *for starters* in sober academic exposition?); it will also appear that any one of these expressions may keep company more or less successfully with any other, given, however, the constraints of rhythm, register and word-form (so that a sequence beginning 'first' will go on to 'second', not 'second*ly*', and 'to begin with' tends to predict 'all in all', or 'taking one thing with another', rather than 'in conclusion', because 'to begin with' is rather more colloquial, and 'in conclusion' rather more literary).

The **extensional** repertoire is larger, so much so that it can be divided into stylistic sub-categories casually overlapping certain grammatical classes, particularly the conjuncts and disjuncts, some of which have been discussed above. A recurrent call on the extensional repertoire is for words and phrases that introduce an example or an explanatory comment: *for example, for instance, to take (quote, cite) a typical example (instance, case), a case in point, by way of illustration (elucidation, explanation), that is to say, that is*.

Other expressions under this general head are 'additioning' and 'specifying'; they expand a point, or indicate the particular scope of a given instance. *In addition* obviously belongs here; as do *moreover, furthermore, equally, similarly, in the same way, by the same token, also, besides, too, not only ... but also, in particular, particularly, chiefly, especially, mostly, mainly, even*. These 'additioning' words or phrases can often look a lot like cautiously cultivated 'hedges' – for example in the following (parodied) style of boilerplate prose:

Though the rain in Spain is conventionally said to fall mainly in the plain, the mountainous areas, especially the Pyrenees, can be similarly affected by heavy rainfall. Moreover, the seaboard provinces of the North, particularly Galicia, are moderately rainy, chiefly because of their exposure to the Atlantic westerlies. Even Andalucia is not quite bone-dry; rain falls, furthermore, in Seville.

Not much of substance is left in that passage if one eliminates 'mainly', 'especially', 'similarly', 'moreover', 'particularly', 'moderately', 'chiefly', 'even', and 'furthermore'. The piece is not a passage about the weather in Spain; it is, if anything, a passage about the possibility of talking about the Spanish weather.

Another sub-class of expressions in the 'additioning' repertoire marks results, or inferences drawn from a foregoing process of exposition. Here we find *consequently, in consequence (of which), as a result (of which), in view of which, in that case, in which case, so, so that, thus, therefore, then.* Among these, *so* is commonly the preferred item in the spoken language; the others come into their own mainly in writing of a quite formal kind (e.g. in philosophical or forensic discourse). The development of the inferential argument may then lead to attempts at 'reformulation', in which a preceding expression is re-phrased, or, in the search for better definition, a temporary expression is invented. This is the province of *or rather, in other words, alternatively,* and *differently put*; and of *so to speak, as it were,* and *if you will,* when the writer invents a term or assigns his own meaning to a familiar word. (But the commonest way of doing this in informal registers is to set the word in quotation marks: one 'allocates' a meaning typographically.) Beyond reformulation lie processes of disjunction and transition, when the writer indicates a revised point of view or denotes the passage to a further phase in the argument. Typical disjuncts are *admittedly, evidently, clearly, of course, indeed,* and *in fact*; moments of transition are marked by *now, as for, turning to, with regard to, as far as [. . .] is concerned.*

The various types of connective in the extensional repertoire suggest collectively the resources on which a writer progressively draws in developing a line of argument. Examples are followed by additional points, inferences are drawn, some expressions are corrected, a general stance is modified, the text goes forward to its next stage. That stage, however, may be **interruptive**, a breaking into the flow of the exposition, or even a reversal of its tendency.

The commonest interruptive is *but*, directly contradicting what has gone before; other powerful contradictions are expressed by *on the other hand, against that, on the contrary*, and *instead*. ('The new regulations were purportedly designed to help the poor and underprivileged. Instead, they brought great benefits to the rich') These contradictive phrases oppose absolutely or exclude a foregoing proposition. Other phrases have a contrastive purport, countervailing without excluding completely the argument of the immediately preceding text. Some conjuncts and disjuncts figure regularly here: *however, nevertheless, notwithstanding, yet, still, all the same, for all that, by contrast*. A somewhat milder form of turnabout makes a concession rather than a contrast or a direct contradiction. The concessives mitigate the severity of comment, forestall criticism, or imply awareness that something has been omitted or too easily dismissed. They are in effect 'hedges': *admittedly, naturally, of course, to be sure, [it is] true, certainly, assuredly*. The interruptive repertoire thus represents, for the writer's benefit, the possibility of showing the changes of one's mind. Brute contradiction can be modified by a more reflective contrast; and contrast itself may be mollified by conceding errors or omissions. 'But this is wrong', the writer declares; and then – 'However, that is not altogether right'; and so – 'Naturally, I may be at fault.'

The **cohesive** repertoire provides what is by far the most usual way of getting from sentence to sentence. The perception of linkages in a text is controlled either *exophorically*, when the reader's attention is systematically directed to a context, a 'world' (of narrative, report, etc.) to which the writing makes explicit and implicit reference, or *endophorically*, when connective clues are placed in the text itself, with the aim of making the actual writing a 'world', or self-explanatory domain. A brief illustration may help to explain what is essentially a difference of perspective:

A. Rationing continued here at home. These were hard times.
B. Rationing went on for two more years. That time seemed harder than ever for our people.

In A, the demonstrative *these* is exophoric; it points to something outside the text, and the connection between the two sentences can only be established if the reader assumes that there *is* an extratextual link, a connection dictated by inference. In B, another demonstrative, *that*, is endophoric; its primary reference is to something within the text, to the *two more years* of the first sentence. This pair of sentences is self-sufficing; the reader is not obliged to interpret them by scanning a potential context of situation.

Such text–internal references may be *anaphoric* (backward-pointing, the more usual function) or *cataphoric* (downward-pointing). Some of the grammatical indices instructing the reader to 'see above' or 'see below' will serve either purpose: for example, *this* and *here*:

A. The message was that the hostages had been killed. This turned out to be false. [anaphoric: 'this' refers back to 'the message']
B. The message came through at 4.30. This is what it said. [cataphoric: 'this' refers to what follows]
C. Despite the loss of life, it was decided to continue the attacks. Here was military stupidity at its worst. [anaphoric; 'here' takes into scope the main clause of the preceding sentence]
D. Some instances have been quoted and discussed in full. Here are a few additional examples. [cataphoric: 'here', like 'this' in B, presents a following text]

This, *that*, *these*, and *those* are recurrent anaphora; and also *here*, *such* and *so*. ('They said I had been paid twice over. Such was not the case'; 'I had submitted false accounts and solicited bribes, they said. But who would believe such lies?'; 'Napoleon's remaining option was to retreat. He did so with great reluctance'; 'The recession is over and the economy is on the mend. Or so we are led to believe.') Occasionally an anaphoric phrase is used – e.g. *the foregoing*, *the above* – when the backward reference implies stretches of text longer than a word, a phrase, a clause, or even a whole sentence. A paragraph-long argument may be included in the scope of 'the above' or 'the foregoing'.

Some cataphoric expressions overlap with the anaphora; e.g. *here* (see above) and the demonstratives *this* and *these*. *Thus* can signify 'as above' (inferring or concluding) or 'as below' (presenting):

A. By air, a ticket for a journey of 200 miles, lasting no more than 40 minutes, costs £35. The rail fare for the same distance, taking anything up to five hours, is £30. Thus air travel is in a real sense cheaper. [anaphoric *thus*, meaning 'given the preceding facts']

B. On the hills round the city there were geese, who raised shrill alarms at the approach of intruders. Thus Rome was saved. [anaphoric *thus*, meaning 'in that way', 'by such a circumstance']

C. The world may not be wholly round. It is, however, commonly represented thus. [once more, anaphoric *thus*, meaning 'in that way']

D. The argument is complex, but the main issues may be tabulated thus: [cataphoric *thus*, meaning 'in the following way'; it is usual for the word to be followed by a mark of punctuation such as the colon, the dash, or the colon-and-dash]

The cataphora may be expanded into phrase-form, e.g. as *the following, in the following way, as follows*; often, in academic exposition, the adverb *below* (as in 'the details listed below') does yeoman service. *Below,* like *above,* can imply more than a sentence, and sometimes quite a long reach of argument. They are expressions available not only for close (sentence-to-sentence) cohesion but also for the open span of an extended text. The demonstrator's 'above' and 'below' may refer ten pages back or two chapters down.

So-called *pro-forms* are the ever-present agents of close cohesion, pinning sentence to sentence as the text is constructed. Their grammatical name reveals their semantic function, as verbal 'stand-ins' for some preceding piece of text, often a noun (proper or common), but possibly a phrase or clause:

A. Harry yawned. Harry was bored and tired. [the proper noun is repeated]

B. Harry yawned. He was bored and tired. [the personal pronoun 'he' is used as a pro-form, standing in for 'Harry'.

C. Something long, green and shivery came across the lawn. It looked a lot like a snake. ['it' is the pro-form for 'something long, green and shivery']

D. Cecilia came waddling across the lawn. It was not an elegant movement. ['it' is the pro-form for the verb 'waddling'; but also a kind of anticipatory pro-form for the noun 'movement']

E. Jeremy tried hard to dress roguishly. It did not suit him. ['it' stands as pro-form for the verb and adverb group 'to dress roguishly'; or possibly for the whole clause, 'tried hard to dress roguishly'; pro-forms sometimes cause ambiguities]

As the examples may suggest, the pro-forms are often personal pronouns, whether in their subjective ('he'), objective ('him') or possessive ('his') forms. They also include pronouns and demonstrative adjectives like *one, all, some, any, many, each, none,* and *[the] same.* Since possessive pronouns and demonstrative adjectives pertain to nouns, double linkages, by grammatical item (the pro-form) plus dictionary item (the noun, in repetition or by way of a synonym) are common:

A. Not everyone was content to sit and wait. Some passengers got down from the coach. [*some* refers to *not everyone*; but *passengers* is included in the linkage]
B. Ella complained that her steak was overdone. Mine had been cremated. [*mine* is the simple pro-form link with *steak*]
C. Ella complained that her steak was overdone. My chicken was underprivileged. [the link is, first, the pronoun plus noun link, *her steak, my chicken*; then, at a different − here playful − level of linkage, the lexical counterpoise of *overdone* and *underprivileged*]

The last example points to another mode of sentence-connection, as yet untouched upon in this chapter. It is a method of cohesion by *lexis*, that is, by the vocabulary that invades and sustains a text, whether by authorial choice or because the subject demands it as appropriate to a technical domain. This is a matter of such large scope that discussion of it is best postponed to a later chapter.

CONNECTIONS AND REGISTERS

There are, then, various ways of clinching the structure of a text and bridging the gaps between sentences. No one text or sentence-sequence will display them all; furthermore, every text or sample of text will appear to be framed in accordance with one or two 'connective themes', repetitions of particular devices. The expository prose of essays, academic papers and editorials relies a good deal on grammatical connectives, because the scholar or the editor is committed to the principle of textual cohesion, a careful, unremitting demonstration of how the writing hangs together. Here is an opening paragraph, taken at random, from a *Guardian* editorial. The subject is the 'peace process' in Northern Ireland, the editorial stance one of demurral at the apparent lack of vigorous political action:

> Anniversaries are for taking stock. From today, however, the test of the Northern Ireland peace process cannot be about what was done in the past but must be about what is to be done in the future. It is already clear that next week will be crucial in answering this question, with the British-Irish summit announced for Chequers on Wednesday and the Ulster Unionist leadership election two days later. These are vital events which will together determine whether the process is to regain the momentum which it badly needs.
>
> (*Guardian*, 1 September 1995)

What is in this editor's mind? The thought, surely, that time has passed, is passing, and should be used before more passes away. The principal 'connective theme', accordingly, is the time-adjunct. The first word of the piece, *anniversaries*, sets up the theme which is subsequently realised in a sentence-spanning sequence of adverbials: *from today, in the past, in the future, already, next week, on Wednesday, two days later.* A lesser theme is the anaphoric linkage in *this question* (but what is the question? – no doubt 'what is to be done in the future') and *these [vital] events* (but what events? – evidently 'the British-Irish summit' and 'the Ulster Unionist leadership election'). A still smaller link, but a very important one, is the conjunct *however* in the second sentence. Anniversaries are for taking stock, the opening sentence declares – that is, for looking back and summing up; *however* – the topic is promptly turned around with that interruption – the present need is for looking forward and making plans. Probably none of these marks of connectedness thrusts itself upon the reader's attention; each is involved in the texture – so to speak – of the unfolding message.

Compare that steady pursuit of connectedness with the restless movement of a few sentences from a book which, in style, falls somewhere between free reportage and fiction. The book is Andrew O'Hagan's *Missing*, a disquisition on missing persons and the disruption of a sense of community in modern Britain:

> Gloucester was very quiet that day, and it rained. Four weeks had passed since the press first arrived in their black cabs, ready to win. They had moved around easily – professionally – with all the help that comes from gentle banter and loud chequebooks. The journalists had made the most of this one, and the local police were still hopping up and down. But the cabs were gone now, and the local folk were left to contemplate the threat of a normal day.

This narrative presentation may seem at first glance to be 'hopping up and down' like the policemen. But the sense of an apparent disconnection vanishes almost immediately, as we realise that the connective principle is *exophoric*: *that day* and *this one* refer to a context, a story, with which we are not as yet fully acquainted, but which we assume will be explained by and by. The sense of an exophoric connection, a linkage with the story behind the telling, readily extends to *the press*, *the journalists*, *their black cabs*, *the local police*, *the local folk*. It all exists 'out there', behind and beyond the text. Grammatical connectives within the text are few – for example the anaphoric *they* at the beginning of the third sentence; other endophoric connections are made through the vocabulary, e.g. through the synonymy of *press* and *journalists*, through the repetition of *cabs*, through the rhetorical echo of *local police* and *local folk*. This piece of scene-setting is not particularly remarkable for any display of sentence-connection; a more striking feature, no doubt, is its management of narrative tense, in the fluctuations between the past ('it rained'), the past continuous ('were hopping up and down') and the past perfective ('had passed', 'had moved around', 'had made'). The sense of time – of scenic time, as it were – is conveyed through these verb-forms rather than through any adjunct.

O'Hagan's writing presents factual matter in fictional style. Here, for comparison, is a short piece of pure fiction, the beginning of Virginia Woolf's story *Lappin and Lapinova*:

> They were married. The wedding march pealed out. The pigeons fluttered. Small boys in Eton jackets threw rice; a fox

terrier sauntered across the path; and Ernest Thorburn led his bride to the car through that small inquisitive crowd of complete strangers which always collects in London to enjoy other people's happiness or unhappiness. Certainly he looked handsome and she looked shy. More rice was thrown, and the car moved off.

This is not untypical of Virginia Woolf's narrative style, in which she habitually records a discrete consciousness of various and simultaneous events, some immediately relevant to the action of her story ('Ernest Thorburn led his bride to the car'), others quite casually occurrent ('a fox terrier sauntered across the path') The method is wholly exophoric, the aim being not to construct a text but to adumbrate a scene; 'that small inquisitive crowd of complete strangers', for example, is a crowd the reader is asked to imagine ('you know, that sort of crowd'), not to identify in textual reference ('that particular word, the one I mentioned above'). There is an absence of commonplace textual linkage, the linkage of exposition. Even *certainly* does not read quite like a normal disjunct whereby a writer, anticipating some objection, makes a self-protective move. (As, for example in 'You may find this argument impossibly hard to follow. Certainly it is intricate.') Woolf's *certainly* reads more like a reply to some hidden conversational partner. ('Was he handsome? Oh, certainly.') Indeed, throughout this short paragraph there persists a feeling of the offstage questioner asking for details of the scene, and of the writer, not wholly free to arrange things at her own will, supplying answers. Here, as in so many instances, fiction becomes a dialogue between writer and reader, in ways that are not always apparent, or perhaps not always available, to the newspaper editor or even to the documentary reporter.

But then, are 'apparent' and 'available' quite the right words – the one implying the possibility of choice, the other suggesting a kind of concession? Does the writer *choose*, or are certain things *chosen for* the writer, chosen by virtue of the very nature of the proposed text, so that in effect *the text chooses*? Let that question now recall Charley's Tale, and the way it is told. Supposing that a writer were quoting Charley's case in a newspaper article entitled 'Changing Jobs in a Man's World'; would the composition of that article, its pattern of linkages, sentence by sentence and paragraph by paragraph, differ much from that of a magazine story, written by the same author at about the same time, called 'Promoted to Love'? The supposition has to be – though of course it remains to be tested by anyone interested in the experiment – that there would be more than a few compositional differences, but mainly that 'Promoted to Love' would rely on connections of *story* rather than linkages of *text*. (There might well be some laborious attempts at filling in the background, supplying an explanatory context of situation: 'She had so enjoyed working in the accounts department, but then Jeremy had come along and all thoughts of an office career had been driven, wonderfully, excitingly, out of her head.') The composition of 'Changing Jobs in a Man's World', on the other hand, would supposedly demand rather more attention to the endophoric scheme, the pattern of explicit connections in the text. Of course there would be other differences. In each instance there would be a typical vocabulary, or an *expectation* of a vocabulary conventional to the topic. We expect things like 'economic status' in 'Changing Jobs in a Man's World', and things like 'blissful stirrings' in 'Promoted to Love' – though expectation might be confounded, by skill or mischief. And there might be significant variations, as between the two pieces, of sentence type and structure; but to study that possibility we have to assume that we now know how to cross the gaps between sentences, and hence must begin to explore the routes that lead through the sentences themselves.

Five

Sentences: penning and parsing

Grammarians tell us that sentences contain clauses, that clauses contain phrases, that phrases contain words, and that words, if we wish to pursue the matter so far, contain morphemes. Each of these elements can be classified and analysed, the relationship of one unit to another can be identified, the function of each in the developing pattern of the text can be stated, the constraints upon order, placing and combination can be determined. Sentences are there to be dismantled, or *parsed*, an activity somewhat removed, however, from what writers do as they struggle to put things together, mumbling and brooding and scribbling and experimentally turning phrases this way and that until at last a sentence or a sequence of sentences can be *penned*, or provisionally committed to writing. Penning is a dark, vague, instinctive synthesis; for the writer, the analytic process of parsing might only come in useful at an editorial or revisory stage of writing, or when things begin to go wrong, or possibly when a point of composition has to be demonstrated for the sake of objective criticism. 'Might only' is perhaps an unfairly belittling reservation. The 'only' includes quite a lot; it is certainly helpful to have some clearly articulated knowledge of what you are doing, and of the resources that are available to you as you write. There are writers, too, who sometimes write badly because they evidently cannot parse, or at least lack the objective sense of construction that parsing implies. A little book–grammar never comes amiss. Nevertheless, it is fair to say that writers in general parse, if they parse at all, to learn about what they have penned, and seldom if ever study parsing in order to prepare for penning.

THE SENTENCE AS ART (OR THE LADIES ARE NOT FOR PARSING)

Go, for example, to your favourite novelist; consider her works – the gender is probably feminine – and wisely discover what she has to teach about sentences. As an act of creation, a sentence is an intricate, ingenious, endlessly variable thing, adapted to rules and conditions of *discourse*, which go beyond the limits of the sentence itself. Nowhere is this more evident than in the high art of fiction, which provides innumerable examples of simple and complex sentences, presenting an impression of simplicity or complexity not so much in relationship to their internal construction as in their relevance to an overriding principle of discursiveness. We have seen (p. 79 above) how Virginia Woolf begins her story *Lappin and Lapinova*:

> They were married.

Add to that the opening sentence of A. L. Barker's *The Gooseboy*:

> Bysshe could be seen, not so old nor so young, walking in his garden, a dusty lusty place of greed and rapine.

Then add a longer piece of text, the two opening sentences of P. D. James' *Original Sin*:

> For a temporary shorthand-typist to be present at the discovery of a corpse on the first day of a new assignment, if not unique, is sufficiently rare to prevent its being regarded as an occupational hazard. Certainly Mandy Price, aged nineteen years two months, and the acknowledged star of Mrs Crealey's Nonesuch Secretarial Agency, set out on the morning of Tuesday 14 September for her interview at the Peverell Press with no more apprehension than she usually felt at the start of a new job, an apprehension which was never acute and was rooted less in any anxiety whether she would satisfy the expectations of the prospective employer than in whether the employer would satisfy hers.

There are two sentences only in that last passage; the first 37 words long, the second a slow-unwinding, laboriously lucid 80 words; and this is at the beginning of a popular narrative, truly a dragon-tailed construction coiled in the very mouth of the story-teller's cave.

Each of the three examples cited above is in its own way a remarkable instance of cunning in the framing of a narrative sentence, short or long. Virginia Woolf's is the shortest, a construction so simple as to be almost beneath a parser's notice. Discursively, however, it is more complex than it might at first appear, because it makes the narrative begin, not inappropriately, on a note of ambiguity. *They were married* could be tantamount to 'they *got* married', that is, 'they went through the wedding ceremony'. Then again, it might (and almost certainly *does*) intend, as its primary sense, 'the ceremony had just finished', or 'that fact was accomplished, and the marriage could begin'. (It could also suggest 'this was the state of this particular couple before our story begins' – but the ensuing text promptly excludes that possibility.) This tiny flicker of ambivalence in an opening sentence which Virginia Woolf could have rewritten, had she so chosen, in order to establish a single, uncompromised sense, is a preliminary signal, a kind of anticipatory vibration, in a narrative which is disturbingly equivocal throughout and which ends on a similarly 'compromised' sentence: *So that was the end of that marriage.* (To know why the meaning of the last sentence is 'compromised' you will have to read the story.)

Now this is a matter of creative instinct, owing little or nothing to grammatical analysis. It is hardly reasonable to suppose that Virginia Woolf, conceiving her tale and beginning to get it onto paper, could have told herself, 'Now I shall construct a little sentence, the predicate of which could be parsed either as the past tense, passive voice, of a transitive verb *to marry* (meaning "they were married by a priest") or as the past tense of the verb *to be* complemented by a participial adjective *married* (with the sense of 'they were a married couple').' Nor will we imagine A. L. Barker as she embarks on the first, deliciously surreal paragraph of her novel (read it – her style sparks with irony and wit), murmuring 'So here we go with a main clause in the passive voice, governing a dependent participial construction – but hey, now, between the main clause and the participle clause why don't I wedge one of those adjectival phrases that you might expect to follow imme- diately after a main clause subject – you know the sort of thing, "Makepeace, brown as a berry, walked over the fields", or "Waldo, pale and intense, could be found in his library" – something in that style, except that *my* phrase, coming off-handedly, so to speak, eccentrically placed in a by-the-way position, just after the verb, will come in with a teasing effect, casually not answering the question the reader has had no time to ask. Crafty. Work the grammar and keep 'em reading, that's the ticket, my dear.' And work the grammar she does, with considerable success, all the way through the book; but she quite certainly does so at a level of choice and organisation deeper than that of conscious analysis.

As for P. D. James, whose way with her opening sentence would be almost inconceivably bold were it not for the nearly calamitous audacity of her way with a second sentence, are we to think of her as judiciously reflecting, 'Now, I propose to begin my detective story with a pre-posed subordinate clause, running to 22 words in length and functioning as the grammatical subject of the sentence – nothing simple, oh no, a real *belter* of a subject, something like "For a temporary shorthand-typist to be present at the discovery of a corpse on the first day of a new assignment".' Would she approach her creative business in quite that way? Hardly. And she would probably not think of her second sentence as a sequence of apposed phrases and recursively dependent clauses – in effect, a grammatical game of dominoes. If we dare speculate on the workings of the author's creative instinct in this instance, two points suggest themselves. One is, that at the beginning of her story Ms James is concerned to plant, or rehearse, or propound, in as brief a space as possible, as much information as possible. The two opening sentences, taken together, tell the reader a great deal (try ticking off the items) about the what and where and who of the impending narrative, rather as the introductory shots in some television serials give the viewer a forewarning or preliminary scan of the action. The second point is that, almost through sentence-structure alone, James succeeds here in establishing a 'dry', ironically objective narrative tone. Her first sentence, *For a temporary shorthand-typist to be present at the discovery of a corpse on the first day of her assignment, if not unique, is sufficiently rare to prevent its being regarded as an occupational hazard,* is a construction in the same ironic *genus,* so oblique, so unrelentingly arch, as that other more famous opener, the chief exemplar of a stylistic type, *It is a truth universally acknowledged, that a single man in possession of a good fortune, must be in want of a wife.*

(Jane Austen may, of course, have smiled with anticipatory relish at the prospect of beginning her novel with the playful extraposition of a clausal subject, but somehow one doubts whether she would have thought of it in those terms.)

These ladies are not for parsing. Their sentences can be parsed, of course; but the point is that they, and any other writer at work, must assess a sentence by its *feel*, rather than by its frame. They must ask, in dark creative puzzlement, 'is this *right*?', 'does this *fit*?', 'will this *work* at this point in my discourse?'. And so it is, even for the rest of us who have no pretensions to being literary artists but who wish nonetheless to present a subject and engage a readership. We, too, must learn – 'hands on' – about penning; and afterwards we can confirm our discoveries and insights in the light of a little parsing.

PENNING FOR BEGINNERS: FIVE NOTIONS TO BEAR MORE OR LESS IN MIND

The particular terms do not matter, but there are some five ideas-in-general to keep accessibly in mind as composition proceeds. Call these notions **content**, **weight**, **pattern**, **position**, and **stance**. In practice, each is involved in one or more of the others, but if one is to be given primacy, it must be **content**. This implies a view of the sentence as a process of information-giving, controlled by the writer, who is under compulsion to tell his reader some things but is also at liberty to withhold or postpone the telling of others. What sentences have to tell is compactly summed up in the designations of Rudyard Kipling's 'six honest serving men', whose 'names are *What* and *Why* and *When* and *How* and *Where* and *Who*'. That catalogue may need a little expansion, to include, for example, *With what result?*, *For whose benefit?*, and *Being or doing or suffering what?*, but as a mnemonic it will serve well enough to account for and direct a great many acts of penning.

In so-called 'simple' sentences (see below, p. 99) there is an evident match, a procedural symmetry between promptings of penning and the divisions of parsing. Thus the sentence 'My father kept his insurance policies in an old tin box' can be parsed in terms of *Subject* ('who?' – 'my father'), *Verb* ('doing what?' – 'kept'), *Direct*

Object ('what?' – 'his insurance policies'), *Adverbial Adjunct* ('where?' – 'in an old tin box'). That analysis, however, denotes the simple rationale of the sentence without purporting to represent the dynamic drive of more ambitious or protracted structures, born out of the writer's endless self-questioning – 'What am I going to write about?' 'Now?' and 'Next?' and 'After that?' and 'What, then, goes in to this determinable stage, this particular piece of the topic I have conceived?'.

Note further that the primary questions of penning ('who?', 'what?', 'where?' etc.) would be much the same if the sentence were subsequently to read, 'My father, a prudent man with a dread of fire, had been keeping a motley collection of insurance documents, some more important than others, in a battered old tin box given to him by his grandmother'. In that case, however, the parsing would be more elaborate, with more dividing and sub-dividing of the text, and the contrast of 'synthesis' and 'analysis' in penning and parsing would thus become more apparent. Penning synthesises – 'a prudent man with a dread of fire' is incorporated piecemeal into the synthesis of *Who?*, in the sense that the writer conceives of a whole idea that must somehow be got, in its wholeness, onto the page; whereas parsing analyses – 'a prudent man with a dread of fire' is taken as a separable piece of text, a 'complex noun phrase' said to be 'in apposition' to 'my father', its complexity further divisible into underlying constituents, eg. 'a prudent man' and 'with a dread of fire'.

That example will serve to illustrate the next consideration of penning, that of *weight*. (Which might also be called *length*; but *weight* is sometimes a more useful figure). Feel the increasing weight of the following sentences:

A. My father kept his insurance documents in a tin box.

B. My father kept a large collection of insurance documents in a battered old tin box.

C. My houseproud father, a prudent man with a great dread of fire, kept a motley collection of insurance documents in a battered old tin box given to him by his grandmother.

D. My happily houseproud father, a prudent man with a great dread of fire, had been keeping for years a motley collection of insurance documents, in a battered old tin box given to him by his grandmother on the occasion of his eighteenth birthday, at which time it was no doubt more ornamental and not so brutally 'distressed' (to use the antique dealers' word).

These examples raise the practical question, 'how much can you put in at a time?', which involves the query 'how heavily dare you burden the reader?' and 'how will your own concentration bear up under the load?' – for you must sustain a recollection of what you are writing even as you are producing it. As more and more information is incorporated into the mass, so the sentence grows weightier, and the weight – in these instances – tilts increasingly towards the end of the construction.

Sentence D above presents an example of heavy end-weighting. It is common – one might risk saying 'normal' – for the weight of a written English sentence to fall towards the end in this way. (We have already seen a notable example in one of the sentences by P. D. James, quoted on p. 83). This is how writers, prompted by the common order of syntactic elements in English, generally like to distribute the weight of a sentence, though at times they may opt to lay the weight at the 'front', i.e. the beginning of the construction, thus:

> In a battered old tin box given to him by his grandmother on the occasion of his eighteenth birthday, at which time it was no doubt more ornamental and not so brutally 'distressed' (to use the antique dealers' word), my happily houseproud father, a prudent man with a great dread of fire, had been keeping for years a motley collection of insurance documents.

For such an inversion of the weight there might be stylistic reasons, touched upon below under the headings of **pattern** and **position** and relevant to the wider context of discourse.

A heavily weighted sentence may threaten to run out of the author's supervisory control, and it is here that a little parsing, or some activity akin to parsing, can be helpful. Punctuation is a form of practical parsing; if the sentence cannot be broken down convincingly with the aid of those old punctuational soldiers the comma, the semi-colon, the dash and the bracket, then the writer must accept that the sentence needs to be lightened, and may then attempt a re-writing in the form of several 'lighter', shorter sentences. Like this, perhaps:

> My father was happily houseproud. A prudent man with a great

dread of fire, he had been keeping for years a motley collection of insurance documents. He kept them in a battered old tin box given to him by his grandmother on the occasion of his eighteenth birthday. At that time the box was no doubt more ornamental and not so brutally 'distressed' (to use the antique dealers' word).

That is one solution among others. It uses the same words as the original sentence, but as a text it is not quite the same. It handles the original content in a way that suggests differences of emphasis, of cohesiveness, of rhythm and pace, even of *stance*, the author's attitude, to texts as they are told and to readers as they are imagined. Adjusting the weight of sentences nearly always brings with it the adjustment of other properties in the writing.

One of these properties is that of **pattern**, which parsing can help us to understand objectively, in set terms. In penning, however, the feel for a pattern is instinctive, or sometimes a matter of trial and error. Here are some simple sentence–patterns, arranged in contrasting sets:

A(1) My father kept his documents in an old tin box.
  (2) In an old tin box my father kept his insurance documents.
B(1) He kept his personal letters in his bureau.
  (2) His personal letters he kept in his bureau.
C(1) My father was a prudent man.
  (2) A prudent man, my father was.
  (3) He was a prudent man, my father.
D(1) A kind old lady gave my father that tin box.
  (2) My father was given that tin box by a kind old lady.
  (3) That tin box was given (to) my father by a kind old lady.
E(1) No one could call him improvident.
  (2) Improvident no one could call him.
  (3) Him no one could call improvident.

Of these examples, some will appear 'normal', while others may seem more contrived, or acceptable only in the context of some particular purpose (e.g. the purpose of focusing meaningfully on the sentence-initial *him* of 'him no one could call improvident').

These ostensibly deviant patterns are known by grammarians as 'marked' forms. We need samples of discourse, longer stretches of text, to see how they work stylistically:

A. My father kept his insurance documents in an old tin box. Some of them dated back to 1923. There was a policy for his bicycle. Another covered the possible theft of his *wireless*. The house, of course, was insured against every species of calamity, including subsidence resulting from the activities of burrowing animals. A prudent man, my father.

B. Ephraim once laid out six months' savings on a holiday trip to Spain. People called him improvident. Amos took flying lessons. This also was deemed improvidence, of a more spectacular kind. Bernard was something else. Bernard never went anywhere, never did anything, and hoarded up all his money against a lifetime of rainy days. Him no one could call improvident.

In those samples of text, the marked pattern comes in with the effect of colloquy, of spoken commentary rather than written observation. Putting at the beginning of the sentence ('preposing', 'fronting') some word or phrase that we would normally expect to come later in the order is a recurrent feature of emphatic 'presentation' in speech. ('Cold again, the weather', 'Clean out of the park he hit it', 'Stupid I call them', etc.) By contrast, in the following patterns the locus of attention, or 'focus', and with it, potentially, the weight, is shifted towards the end of the sentence:

A. There will come a time for rejoicing.
    (Compare: 'A time for rejoicing will come.')
B. It was in London that they first met.
    (Compare: 'They first met in London.')
C. It was unfortunate that you failed to qualify.
    (Compare: 'That you failed to qualify was unfortunate' – which in this case would be the 'marked', or less usual form.)

These are samples of variable sentence patterns, answering in general to the writer's preoccupying questions, 'what is going on?' and 'where do I put the emphasis?', and 'how is the reader's attention to be guided?' The same questions are asked when the simple constructions are linked into complex, so-called multi-clause sentences. (On these, see below, p. 107.) The following examples illustrate a recurrent and familiar problem, that of adjusting the order of clauses in a complex sentence, in order to find the pattern that best reveals a writer's intention (revealing it to himself, it may be, as much as to his reader):

A Although he was not formally qualified, Jim decided to apply for the job, because he badly needed the money.

B. Because he badly needed the money Jim decided to apply for the job, although he was not formally qualified.

C. Jim decided to apply for the job because he badly needed the money, although he was not formally qualified.

D. Jim decided to apply for the job although he was not formally qualified, because he badly needed the money.

E. Because he badly needed the money, although he was not formally qualified, Jim decided to apply for the job.

These examples present the familiar process of juggling with notions in a compositional pattern. Here are three such notions, the *who does what*?, the *why not*? and the *why*?, represented by the clauses 'Jim decided to apply for the job', 'although he was not formally qualified', and 'because he badly needed the money'.

It might seem at first that the order of representation is of no consequence, all that matters being that the sentence should strike the author as fitting the rhythm of the text, of 'sounding right' or 'reading well'. There are other considerations, however. There is the question of how efficiently the sentence will slot into a developing sequence of constructions, taking up the transition from its predecessor and passing on a connection to its successor; there is the question of what differences of posture – formal? colloquial? ironic? humorous? – these variants of order might convey; there is even the question of whether the ordering of the elements affects the actual *meaning* of the sentence. Several strands of meaning are entwined here: 'Jim applied because he needed the money'; 'Jim applied although he was not qualified'; 'Jim needed the money although he was not qualified'. These 'strands' cannot be presented simultaneously, but have to be unwound in a linear process; then how do changes in alignment serve to convey the prominence of one inherent meaning over another?

That same question may be asked with reference to the **position** of the proposed sentence in the proposed text. There are sentences that open a narrative, sentences that conclude a paragraph or clinch a point, sentences that stride along in fluent mid–argument, sentences for pausing and changing direction; and there are no rules or recommendations to supply recipes for the right kind of sentence in any of these positions. *Weight* is an important connection: the positional choice is commonly between 'light/short' and 'heavy/long' units. Fiction writers not infrequently opt for the short sentence at the beginning of a story: 'They were married', 'Miss Sideley was her name and teaching was her game', 'The girl lay naked on the bed with a knife through her heart', 'Lily the caretaker's daughter was literally run off her feet.' In such sentences (the examples are all taken from actual works of fiction), *who*? is the question that motivates the pattern, so that grammatically they are all 'subject-led', with a pronoun, a common noun or a proper noun. This is how apprentice hands in the composition class instinctively prefer to begin a story. They have the feeling that brevity means business. They may choose to write, for example, 'Kolkhov sneezed', rather than 'On the 26th of April, at precisely 4 p.m., in the Ostrogoth Park whose leafy alleys and arbours offer a cool resort for the citizens of Gonzoburg in the warmest days of their overwhelmingly humid summer, Vladimir Kolkhov, a refugee housepainter, down on his luck and with no immediate prospect of gainful employment, did something that was to affect almost disastrously the life and health of every man, woman and child in the Duchy of Monomania. He sneezed.' Their instinct is possibly sound, to begin light and put on weight gradually; it is perfectly possible, nevertheless, to start a narrative, or indeed an argument or a report, with quite heavy constructions. P. D. James does it in her novel *Original Sin*, quoted on p. 84 above. Her first sentence there is already quite heavy, but its weight apparently franchises (so to speak) an even heavier second sentence; after 'longish', the reader is genially persuaded to accept 'longer still'.

Writer and reader alike are caught up into the rhythms of a well-made text, where lighter, shorter sentences are positioned to relieve the burden of longer, heavier units, or to create a cadence – as, for instance, when a short sentence concludes an otherwise weighty paragraph. The pacing of a narrative, through the adroit positioning of a relatively short sentence, is beautifully illustrated by the opening paragraph of James Joyce's fine story, *The Dead*:

Lily, the caretaker's daughter, was literally run off her feet. Hardly had she brought one gentleman into the little pantry behind the office on the ground floor and helped him off with his overcoat, than the wheezy hall-door bell clanged again and she had to scamper along the bare hallway to let in another guest. It was well for her she had not to attend to the ladies also. But Miss Kate and Miss Julia had thought of that and had converted the bathroom upstairs into a ladies' dressing room. Miss Kate and Miss Julia were there, gossiping and laughing and fussing, walking after each other to the head of the stairs, peering down over the banisters and calling down to Lily to ask her who had come.

The first sentence in that passage is the shortest; the longest and weightiest is the second, and after that the last sentence. It is the third sentence, 14 words in length, coming after the 45 words of the second, that crucially and gracefully shapes the style of the whole paragraph. Here we pause a little, the pace drops for a moment, as the author comments gravely on Lily's situation. Some idea of the workmanlike quality of the writing, the skill of weighting and positioning, might be gathered from an experimental merging of the third and fourth sentences: 'It was well for her she had not to attend to the ladies also, but Miss Kate and Miss Julia had thought of that and had converted the bathroom upstairs into a ladies' dressing room.' That merger (resulting in a sequence of sentences with a word-count of 10–45–35–38) sadly levels the narrative rhythm. It *feels* wrong. Joyce, resisting any levelling impulse, makes two sentences out of one (incidentally defying the schoolroom embargo on sentences beginning with *but*).

In studying more closely the patterning of these Joycean sentences, it is important not to overlook the placing of certain words, for example *hardly* and *also*. Try altering the word-order a little. Instead of 'Hardly had she brought, etc.' write 'She had hardly brought'. Instead of 'she had not to attend to the ladies also', write 'she had not also to attend to the ladies'. For various reasons these adjustments will produce a text that instinct deems wrong – wrong in accentuation, wrong in connectedness, and above all wrong in **stance**. *Stance* is the sidelong squint of the text, the writer craftily looking at his subject while keeping a clever eye on his audience. Most commonly it appears through choices, and juxta-positions of choices, in vocabulary, idiom, metaphor, everything known to linguists as *lexis* (see our next chapter). But the patterning and placing of a sentence can also express a stance. As between 'It was well for her she had not to attend to the ladies also' and a possible 'She had not to attend to the ladies too, luckily for her', there is a considerable difference in stance. We can hardly miss an impression of demure formality, almost of courtliness, in Joyce's prose, an impression which certainly accords with the setting and events of his story ('a great affair, the Misses Morkan's annual dance'), and is appropriate to his role as the omniscient, slightly distant, but not unsympathetic narrator.

How many ways are there of beginning the story of *The Dead* – apart from Joyce's, which of course we must accept and honour as the best possible way? The question can only be answered by making attempts at rewriting, of which the following is one:

> The caretaker's daughter was called Lily, and she was having a busy time of it. There she was – taking each gentleman into the little pantry behind the ground floor office, helping him off with his coat – when clang!, the hall-door bell would be ringing again in that wheezy way it had, and off she would go, scampering through the hall to let the newcomer in. She could count herself lucky that she didn't have to take care of the ladies too, but Miss Kate and Miss Julia had thought of that and converted the upstairs bathroom into a place where the women could leave their coats and powder their noses. They were up there waiting, Miss Kate and Miss Julia. They gossiped and laughed and fussed a bit, and now and then they would follow each other to the head of the stair, peer over the banisters, and call to ask Lily who had come.

Many of the differences between that and the original text are lexical – for instance, 'a busy time of it' and 'a place where the women could leave their coats and powder their noses'. These variants certainly affect the stance of the revised text, suggesting a much less formal, almost *chatty* approach to the narrative. In a subtler way, the constituent sentences, by virtue of their distinctive grammar, contribute to this sense of lowered formality. One example is 'They were up there waiting, Miss Kate and Miss Julia', which revises the original's 'Miss Kate and Miss Julia were there.' The 'postponed theme' (compare 'They're a good team, Liverpool', 'He's a crafty beggar, Harry', 'He was a prudent man, my father') suggests, rather than written description, the language of colloquial commentary. Another example: in Joyce's text, the second sentence is long, and linear: 'Hardly had she brought one gentleman into the little pantry behind the office on the ground floor and helped him off with his overcoat, than the wheezy hall-door bell clanged again and she had to scamper along the bare hallway to let in another guest.' This is called 'linear' because of the way in which the text is marshalled: the sentence is a sequence of coordinated and dependent constructions which the reader must patiently follow as the writer has laid them out, one by one. In the rewritten text the structural line is broken (the dashes and the exclamation mark are a symptom of this), and the content of the sentence is managed as though the writer had the ambition of presenting everything *simultaneously* rather than *sequentially*. Again, the spoken language is evoked: speech often tends to be 'presentational', ignoring the linear conventions associated with written texts.

Content, weight, pattern, position and *stance* are our convenient terms (no magic in terminology – make your own, if you please) for a complex of notions pertaining to the business, now brooding now bustling, of penning a text. Some of these are more easily related than others to the formal business of parsing. There is not much that a parser might have to say about *position*. There is no general analysis of this; it all depends on the particulars of a specific context. Someone may be able to convince a writer that a sentence is badly placed, but no one can teach the craft of placing. Experience does it, after a long time, and by God's grace, and never perfectly.

Stance is a similarly unteachable matter, a topic uneasily handled in manuals of rhetoric, but with no real place in the grammar books. There are no numbered paragraphs on 'ironic sentences' or 'funny sentences' or 'rather cool sentences' to go along with the sections on simple and complex and compound-complex sentences. But *pattern* has a descriptive base in grammar, as do *weight* and *content*, and that is useful for the writer who would like to achieve some understanding, above all, of the structural *resources* of composition. To know explicitly what is available, what alternative choices there are, what operations on the text may be performed, and under what constraints, is the reward of a parsing that involves, intelligently, the exercise of creative perceptions.

SOME POINTS ABOUT PARSING

By 'parsing', let us then understand 'everything grammarians do when they classify the forms of words and phrases, and describe word-relationships and word-order in a language'. That 'everything' is a very large domain indeed, and writers who aspire to a grammarian's comprehensive knowledge of it not only take on a ponderous task, but might also be in danger of raising a great obstacle between themselves and the prospect of fluent, uninhibited writing. Write first and do the parsing afterwards, must be the general rule; and the parsing will then be confined to matters affecting the evolution and clarity of the text. Such parsing, a writer's current awareness of procedures, may not be particularly detailed or 'delicate'. It should include, however, a knowledge of how sentences are constructed, of how their components are defined and ordered, of the cohesion, or hooking-up, of elements within and across sentences, and of the means used to script an emphasis or bring some part of a message into prominence. It is in these matters particularly that parsing helps to define and give cognitive voucher to the instinctive procedures of penning.

SENTENCES AND DISCOURSE FUNCTIONS

A writer probably needs to feel that the forms of sentences are boundless, and that there are no limitations on creative possibility. Any way I want it, let me write it. Write it in my own way you can in all confidence bet your boots I will, understand? In my own way. Sure. Without that heady illusion of liberty, often a puzzlement as much as a privilege, there might be little inducement to embark on the adventure of writing. But obviously we are not utterly free to go as we please, and there are, after all, certain constraints to be accepted, and certain prescriptions as to the form English sentences can take.

To begin with, sentences can be typified in accordance with their discursive function – that is, what they are intended to do, or what response they are presumed to elicit, if we prudently think of the text as a form of interaction between writer and reader. Some make statements; some ask questions; some apparently issue commands. These discourse types are known respectively as *declarative*, *interrogative*, and *imperative*, and they are realised in characteristic constructions:

A. Jack went out and bought the papers today. [declarative]
B. Did Jack go out and buy the papers today? [interrogative]
    Who went out and bought the papers today? [interrogative]
C. Go out and buy the papers, Jack. [imperative]
    Don't forget to buy the papers today, will you, Jack? [imperative]

Most of the examples presented for discussion and analysis in these pages will be of the declarative type, and will assume full predication, that is, they will not be sentences of the truncated sort, so-called 'minor sentences' like *sure*, or *not now*, or *on Friday, maybe*. This assumes that writing is mostly a matter of making statements, though in fact that assumption is more convenient than accurate. Lively writing is forever asking questions – asking questions of itself, asking questions of its readers; and not infrequently it issues directives and recommendations, as though the reader could jump to it then and there. Even a textbook like the present work, a book setting out to lay down the instructional law, must occasionally appeal to its readers with a 'Why is this?', or urge a participatory response upon them with 'Consider the following' or 'Let us turn to another matter'.

The writing of instructions and demonstrations conventionally demands frequent use of the non-declarative forms, but in the composition of other, less conventional kinds of text an author may still want to consider the creative potential of a question or a directive. Here are three versions of a sentence imagined as occurring in the course of a biographical narrative:

A. For no reason that any of her numerous friends and advisers could see, this supremely talented woman, an artist at the height of her career, decided to take her own life.
B. Who among her numerous friends and advisers could say why this supremely talented woman, an artist at the height of her career, should decide to take her own life?
C. Let her numerous friends and advisers suggest, if they can, why this supremely talented woman, an artist at the height of her career, should decide to take her own life.

The substance of the sentence, its 'message', is the same in all three instances, but there are potential differences of stance, and also of *positioning*; just why the sentence is so framed will depend on just where it comes in the text, and just how the author wishes to enhance or diminish the sense of rhetorical appeal to a reader.

Interrogative sentences are handy for relieving the predicament of a text apparently in danger of getting lost in its own verbosity. Every teacher knows the stratagem: ask a question and make the class sit up. (Furthermore: ask a question and clear your own head.) Interrogatives are also useful, at times, in managing what can otherwise be wearily wordy transitions. Some illustrations:

A1. Despite the labours and the obvious sincerity of the negotiators, the dispute broke out again within three months as a direct result of the Government's failure to meet its declared commitment to provide the requisite funds.

A2. Despite the labours and the obvious sincerity of the negotiators, the dispute broke out again within three months. Why did that happen? Primarily because of the Government's failure . . . etc.

B1. Scripting a piece for a lecture or a broadcast involves a conscious attention to the relationship between speaking and writing, and thence to a variety of features, the most important among which may be briefly listed here.

B2. Scripting a piece for a lecture or broadcast means paying attention to differences between speaking and writing. What are the most important features? The following is a brief list . . . etc.

Examples A2 and B2 are 'lighter', less wordy, than A1 and B1; they present an obvious difference of stance, in that they appeal more directly to an assumed reader; and the interrogative sentences give particular definition to the moment of turning from propositions to explanations or examples. These forms are thus rhetorically useful, but they should be employed sparingly. It is all too easy to fall into the mannerism of asking the reader empty questions, merely to circumvent the problem of managing a possibly cumbersome transition in the text.

In spoken language we often imply one discourse function in the grammatical guise of another; a query masquerades as a declarative sentence, or an imperative implies a statement. 'Masquerades' like the following are frequently noted:

A. Declarative form implies question: 'He's coming, then' (= 'Is he coming?')

B. Declarative form implies command: 'Supper's on the table' (= 'Come and get it')

C. Interrogative implies statement: 'Whatever gave you that idea?' (= 'That's not so')

D. Interrogative implies command: 'Have the papers come?' (= 'Go and fetch them')

E. Imperative implies statement: 'Believe what you please' (= 'I don't care what you believe')

Such instances represent an oblique style of discourse, common in speech, usually as an expression of the interpersonal stance; a sense of ironic or sardonic distancing is never far from these usages. They do not transpose easily into writing, however; authors generally have to find other ways of scripting their ironies and directives.

Simple sentences

The writer's basic implement is the simple sentence, and some are very simple indeed. Many resemble this:

Kolkhov/sneezed **SV**

There, the proper noun 'Kolkhov' represents the syntactic element called the *subject*, **S**, of the sentence, and the verb, **V**, 'sneezed' constitutes its *predicate*. Verbs 'predicate' – have something to say about something – in relationship to the subject. We denote this basic declarative structure **SV**. The predicate can be augmented by other elements that in some way extend, or *complement* the meaning of the verb, for example the adverbial, **A**, of 'Kolkhov/sneezed/ furiously' (symbolised **SVA**), or the direct object, **Od**, of 'Kolkhov/took/a pinch of snuff'. In English, elements like **O** normally follow the **SV** stem-structure, for which reason ours is called an **SVO** language.

'Kolkhov', 'sneezed', 'took', 'a pinch of snuff' are words and phrases that are said to *realise* the abstractions of 'subject', 'verb', 'adverbial' and 'object'. There are one or two other relationships in the pattern of the sentence, e.g.:

The Russian housepainter/was/furious. **SVCs**

[There, the word 'furious' says something, not about the verb, but about the subject, 'the Russian housepainter'. Its role is accordingly identified as *subject complement*, symbolised **Cs**. The **Cs** can also be a noun or noun phrase, e.g. 'The Russian housepainter/was/an angry man']

His landlady/made/him/an indigestible pie. **SVOiOd**
['An indigestible pie' is the direct object, **Od**, of 'make', but there is a secondary, or *indirect* object, **Oi**, represented by 'him']

His colleagues/made/him/unhappy **SVOdCo**
[This is the standard SVO pattern, with one additional element – realised by the word 'unhappy', which adds to, or 'complements' the meaning of the **Od**. The name of this element is the *object complement*, and it is symbolised **Co**. The **Co** can also be a noun or noun phrase, e.g. 'His colleagues/made/him/ chairman']

To summarise the basic sentence patterns:

SV: The roof/collapsed
SVA: His best suit/hung/in the wardrobe.
SVO: The thieves/stole/all the medical supplies.
SVCs: The policemen/were/visibly annoyed.
SVOiOd: Shakespeare/left/his wife/an old bed.
SVOdCo: Large dogs/make/children/nervous.

Add to these one further pattern, **SVOdA**, in cases where an adverbial is an obligatory adjunct to the verb, e.g.:

   SVOdA: The movers/put/the tallboy/in the kitchen.

The verb 'put' in that example necessitates **A**, the place-adverbial; without **A**, 'the movers put the tallboy' does not make sufficient sense.

Compositional scope of simple sentences

These patterns admit of some useful manipulations in composition. The **SV**+ order of elements is not altogether rigid; 'fronting', or moving an element up into a position before **S** is a possibility to be exploited more or less freely with **A**, particularly when there is more than one kind of adverbial in the sentence:

> The old professor/lectured/every Friday/in the small seminar room. **SVAA**

That example can be rewritten thus:

> Every Friday/the old professor/lectured/in the small seminar room. **ASVA** [AtimeSVAplace]

Or thus:

> In the small seminar room/the old professor/lectured/every Friday. **ASVA** [AplaceSVAtime]

Or thus:

> Every Friday/in the small seminar room/the old professor/ lectured. **AtimeAplaceSV**

Or even thus:

> In the small seminar room/every Friday/the old professor/ lectured. **AplaceAtimeSV**

The choice among these alternative constructions is governed in particular by the writer's sense of *position*. Shifting the **A**s about can redistribute the weight (and thereby affect the rhythm) of the sentence. Putting the **SV** stem at the end opens the sentence to the possibility of further extension: 'Every Friday in the small seminar room the old professor lectured before a limited but appreciative audience' (**AASVA** = Aplace AtimeSVA-circumstance). But perhaps the most important consequence of moving the position of elements in this way is that some part of the sentence is 'highlighted', or brought into special prominence.

Other elements may be highlighted by fronting, not so readily as **A**, but often with stark rhetorical effect. The following examples show respectively subject complement, direct object, indirect object, and object complement in position as the first element in the sentence:

A. A prudent man my father was **CSV**
   A proud and happy man was Harry **CVS**

B. Three attempts he made in all **OdSVA**
   Four pages of notes I gave those idiots **OdSVOi**
C. Her children she left nothing **OiSVOd**
D. His country's saviour they called him **CoSVOd**

Such inversions of the customary order of sentence-elements may intuitively suggest the heated medium of speech rather than the cooler process of writing. They can nevertheless be put to use in scripted discourse, along with other methods of implying focus and emphasis.

Highlighters

These 'other methods' involve constructions so formed as to imply a discursive slant towards, for example, the emphasis of 'I tell you this is so' or the acknowledgement of 'I grant that such is the case'. Principal among these highlighters are the *existential sentence*, the *extraposition*, and the *cleft sentence*. It may be necessary at this point to rehearse the details of their formation – they are, indeed, almost formulaic structures –after which we can consider their place in the creative pattern of writing.

Existential sentences

Existential sentences are constructions that, in the rapper's phrase, 'tell it like it is'. The existential sentence to end all existential sentences reads 'There is a God'; but here are some less austere samples:

> There were three sailors of Bristol city
> There can be no excuse for neglecting one's
> duty
> There occurred a most sinister event

The characteristic form is THERE + BE + COMPLEMENT. (On *complement* see above, p. 100). *Be* is the usual verb, though some others are occasionally used, e.g. 'occur', 'appear', 'come', 'befall', all implying 'exist' or 'come into existence'. This invites a good deal of commentary, but let us defer for the moment a consideration of the usefulness of the existential sentence and its scope as an alternative to 'normal' declarative structures (compare, for the moment, 'There occurred a most sinister event' with 'A most sinister event occurred').

Extrapositions

Extrapositions are sentences that leave the important message until the end. 'It is a truth universally acknowledged, that a single man in possession of a good fortune, must be in want of a wife', is a classic extraposition. Here are some less distinguished inventions:

A. It was a pity that she was ill
B. It appeared that the train was late
C. It became clear that he had not learned his part
D. It seems nothing can be done
E. It doesn't matter who did it
F. It is important what you say
G. It is a mystery where she left the keys
H. It was an honour to know her
I. It was nice talking to you

The formula for this commonly recurrent structure – as common in speech as in writing – is as follows:

1. IT as the sentence's 'anticipatory subject', or 'dummy subject', or 'slot filler'. The pronoun simply marks the grammatical subject-position.
2. The VERB, commonly *be*, though others are possible, eg. *appear, become, seem, matter.*
3. The SUBJECT COMPLEMENT (i.e. 'pity', 'clear', 'important', 'a mystery', 'an honour', 'nice' in examples A, C, E, F, G, H, I above)
4. A NOUN CLAUSE (beginning 'that'/'what'/'where'/ 'who', etc.) or a NON-FINITE clause (with an infinitive or a present participle, e.g. 'to know her' and 'talking to you' in H and I above. This clause is the 'postponed' subject of the sentence, the part of the construction for which the 'dummy' or 'anticipatory' IT is the forward-pointing marker.

Such a breakdown shows how the sentence is programmed, a

computational metaphor which is not out of place; it might indeed be said that such sentences have a keyed input, rather like a word-processor's macro. Once again, there are things to be said about the stylistic importance of these structures; and let us once again defer comment while we consider another highlight form, the cleft sentence.

Cleft sentences

Cleft sentences couple two clauses in tandem. 'It was I who chopped down the tree' is a mythic instance (it was George Washington, the story goes) of a cleft sentence. That kind of cleavage, or tandem-riding, is further represented in the following examples:

It was Rossini who wrote *The Thieving Magpie*
It was in Oxford that Jack met his wife
It was poor old Joe they made president
It was a blue waistcoat she bought him

All of those instances could be be written as simple declarative sentences, with various patterns, thus:

Rossini wrote *The Thieving Magpie* **SVO**
Jack met his wife in Oxford **SVA**
They made poor old Joe president **SVOdCo**
She bought him a blue waistcoat **SVOiOd**

From the simple sentence is derived the cleft form, which presents an emphatic, 'focused' response to questions like 'Who?', 'Whom?', 'What?' and 'Where?': 'Who wrote *The Thieving Magpie*?', 'Where did Jack meet his wife?', 'Whom did they make president?', 'What did she buy him?'. The emphasis may also be corrective: *A* 'Wagner wrote *The Thieving Magpie*' − *B* 'Wagner did not write *The Thieving Magpie*. Wagner wrote *The Flying Dutchman*. It was Rossini who wrote *The Thieving Magpie*.'; *A* 'Didn't he meet his wife in Paris?' − *B* 'No, it was in Oxford he met her.'

The cleft construction has (as the name must imply) two parts. One is the 'focusing' phrase, 'It was Rossini', 'It was in Oxford', etc., which highlights the who-what-where of the sentence, and the other is the 'background' phrase which explains the relevant circumstances ('he met his wife somewhere', 'she bought him something') that call for the explanatory or corrective highlighting.

Stylistic potential of highlighters

In writing, these highlight constructions are a useful resource in several ways. They allow the writer to allocate the particular emphasis and scope of a sentence, to control and distribute the 'weight' of a construction; and they are stylistically involved in matters of 'position' and 'stance' (see above, p. 86), affecting the continuity of the text and projecting a sense of relationship with the overseeing reader. Some of these properties may be appear from the following variations on a compositional theme:

A. The room was still more than half empty. By 7.30 all the invited dignitaries had arrived. I began to realise then that Bodger had sold very few tickets.

B. There were still a lot of empty seats in the room. It became apparent by 7.30 that all the invited dignitaries had arrived, and it was only then that I began to realise how few tickets Bodger had actually sold.

C. There were still a lot of empty seats in a room that could easily have accommodated the audience of a small orchestral concert. It became achingly obvious by 7.30 that all the invited dignitaries whose attendance we might reasonably anticipate had now arrived. Then and only then was it that I finally began to realise how few tickets the miserably incompetent Bodger had succeeded in actually selling, as opposed to giving away.

Obviously, B and C are a good deal 'heavier' than A; not necessarily more efficient as narrative, for A gets through its basic business well enough, but heavier in the elaboration of the constituent sentences, observable in B, running towards extremes in C. There are no highlighters in Text A. Texts B and C, on the other hand, are constructed round a sequence of three highlighters: an existential construction ('There were still a lot of empty seats in the room'), an extraposition ('It became apparent . . . that all the invited dignitaries had arrived') and a cleft sentence ('It was then that I began to realise . . .'). Text C exploits, with a relish perhaps only permissible in comic narrative, the inherent possibilities of highlighter syntax. Since the tendency of all highlighters is to postpone the content-bearing phrase, elaborate end-weighting becomes possible. 'There were three sailors' can be teased out and stretched into 'There were three fairly drunken and totally bewildered sailors'; 'It is a known fact that he is a thief' will expand quite easily into 'It is a known fact that he is the sort of man whose hand strays with fatal persistence towards the cash register'; and 'It was in Peoria that I met my first wife' permits the elaboration of 'It was in Peoria that I met the woman whose astonishing dexterity at the pool table first persuaded me to make a proposal of marriage'. Furthermore, 'It was in Peoria' will allow a touch of rhetorical inversion – 'In Peoria it was' – and one highlighter may embody another, as in the following example, which embeds an existential construction in a cleft sentence: 'In Peoria it was that I met the woman whose sagacious conduct of a hand of contract bridge first persuaded me that there is more than one definition of the word nubile.'

One can have a lot of compositional fun with highlighters, but they are not wholly designed to convey the comic stance that may be apparent in the above examples. They certainly have designs on the reader, but the purpose is more often than not one of explanation, of half-excuse, of elaborating, sometimes in a rather stilted way, the implicit appeal of 'Let me explain', 'You ought to know', 'You may wonder why I am telling you this', 'I must emphasise', or even – in narratives – 'to begin at the beginning'. As a general rule (with numerous exceptions in particular) there is a potential correspondence or equivalence between 'normal' and 'highlighted' constructions. The existential 'There was a tall dark man waiting by the door' supposes the alternative of 'A tall dark man was waiting by the door', or even 'Waiting by the door was a tall dark man'. It is commonly possible for the postponed clause in an extraposition, e.g. 'It was obvious that he would be found guilty', to be brought forward into the subject position: 'That he would be found guilty was obvious.' Cleft sentences present a focusing, or accentuating, that can be effected by other means:

A. It was Thomas Jefferson who wrote about liberty and kept slaves.

B. Thomas Jefferson, as all the world knows, wrote about liberty and kept slaves.

In that example, as in many others, the 'straight' alternative to the cleft sentence has to include some interjection or parenthesis that will fulfil the necessary focusing effect. (Compare 'It was Harry who forgot to bring the beer' with 'Harry, wouldn't you know it, forgot to bring the beer'; or 'It was in respectable Eastbourne that my wallet was stolen' with 'In Eastbourne, of all places, my wallet was stolen.'.) The suggestion that every form has an equivalent, a stylistic transformation, will hold good only till the first awkward instance comes along; nevertheless, it is worth a writer's while to take mental note of the many cases in which simple declarative sentences, existential sentences, extrapositions and cleft sentences form a complex of interchangeable resources.

MULTI-CLAUSE SENTENCES

Simple sentences contain only one *clause.* 'The boy kissed the girl' (**SVO**) is a clause. 'The boy who had behaved so badly kissed the girl' is a sentence with the overall pattern **SVO**, but it is no longer a simple sentence. It contains more than one clause, i.e. 'The boy kissed the girl' and 'who [= "he"] had behaved so badly' (**SVA**). In that example, one clause is contained within the other; it is 'incorporated' or 'embedded'. In the sentence 'The boy had behaved badly, but he kissed the girl' (**SVA + SVO**) two clauses are linked (by the conjunction *but*), not incorporated. In 'The boy had behaved badly, although he kissed the girl', the relationship of the two clauses is slightly different. This is not a linkage of equals. One of these statements – 'although he kissed the girl' – is *dependent on,* or *subordinate to,* the other, the dependency/subordination being expressed by the conjunction *although.*

All these examples are instances of *multi-clause* sentences (or 'multiple sentences' as they are sometimes called). The type illustrated by 'The boy behaved badly, but he kissed the girl' is called a *compound sentence.* Children habitually construct these in their narratives: 'The princess was disobedient and the king was angry and he banished her from the kingdom and the wolf nearly ate her but the handsome prince saved her.' Adults write in this way only when they are being designedly artful or artless. 'The boy who had behaved so badly kissed the girl' and 'The boy had behaved badly, although he kissed the girl' are examples of *complex sentences,* which involve the embedding or subordination of one or more of the constituent clauses. All writing that is not stultifyingly simplified has frequent recourse to the complex sentence, and often to sentences that combine the complex and the compound. Authors have sometimes rather notable preferences: where for good examples of compound sentences in stylistic action one might turn hopefully to Ernest Hemingway, for complexity or compound/complexity a promising source could be Henry James or Joseph Conrad.

The subordinate clauses in the above examples all have so-called *finite* verbs, meaning verbs that can be inflected for tense ('kiss' – 'kissed'), person ('I kiss' – 'he kisses') and number (singular, 'he kisses', plural 'they kiss'). Some dependent clauses, however, are constructed on the *non-finite* forms of the 'marked' infinitive (e.g. the *to*-infinitive of 'to kiss') and the participles, present ('kissing') and past ('kissed'). In some of the following examples the non-finite clause is embedded, as subject or object of the parent clause; in others it is a linear dependent of the main clause:

A. Kissing the girl/was/enormous fun.
B. To kiss her/was/both a pleasure and an honour.
C. Someone/suggested/starting up the boiler.
D. It/should have been/the work of a moment/to start up the boiler.
E. Everyone/tried/to start up the boiler.
F. Starting up the boiler/was/harder than anyone could have imagined.
G. Kissed under the mistletoe, the girls went away to fix their make-up.
H. Starting up the boiler, Jake began his morning's work.
I. Jake went crazy starting up the boiler.
J. Miss Kate and Miss Julia were there, gossiping and laughing and fussing, walking after each other to the head of the stairs, peering down over the banisters and calling down to Lily to ask her who had come.

Examples A–F show the use of the non-finite clause as the subject or object of the sentence. In D, an extraposition, the clausal subject, 'to start up the boiler', is postponed. (The alternative construction being 'To start up the boiler should have been the work of a moment'.) In G–J, the dependency is 'linear': there is a separable main clause ('the girls went away . . .', 'Jake began . . .') to which the subordinate clause is added as a kind of comment ('kissed under the mistletoe', 'starting up the boiler'). Example I is elliptical – something is left out, the 'something' being a subordinating *when* or *while*, or even *through* ('Jake went crazy through starting up the boiler so often'). Example J, finally, shows a sequence of participle clauses in literary prose, in the opening paragraph, quoted earlier, of Joyce's *The Dead*. (Joyce's use of non-finite clauses may be compared with the re-writing of the paragraph, on p. 94, where the sentence about Miss Kate and Miss Julia is based on finite verbs.)

Another kind of non-finite clause is *verbless*, and as a rule functions adjectivally, as modifier to the word or phrase that realises the subject of the sentence: 'Fearful of an explosion, Jake tried to start the boiler'; 'He threw the switch, his face a mask of sheer terror'; 'Bysshe could be seen, not so old nor so young, walking in his garden'. In their modifying relationship to clause subjects, these verbless adjectival clauses are sometimes comparable to certain adjuncts (see p. 70 above) which relate to a following verb: compare 'Relentlessly persistent, the rain in Spain falls mainly in the plain' (verbless adjectival clause, modifying 'rain') and 'With relentless persistence, the rain in Spain falls mainly in the plain' (content disjunct, qualifying 'falls'). This is a minor instance of the kind of choice, among diverse syntactic possibilities, that a writer is called upon to make, sentence by sentence, all the way through the text. A little study of clauses in complex sentences (for instance in Greenbaum and Quirk 1990, or most conveniently in Greenbaum 1991) will reveal a pattern of intermeshing resources in composition, and in developing an objective awareness of what is possible may even serve as a stimulus in those unfortunately rather frequent moments when there appears to be no way forward and no way round. When in doubt, parse a little; it may not solve your problem, and it is no substitute for the instinctive certainties of penning, but it helps at least to clear the head.

Six

Plausible words in possible places

'The right words in the right places' is an old definition of style; but every writer knows just how hard it is to attain that degree of elegant precision. Genius can do it: the rest of us are apprenticed to compromise. For us, the process of writing brings frequent intervals of bafflement and near-despair when almost any word will have to do, whether the place is right or not. There are times, indeed, when composition is completely halted, blocked by the mind's inability to find the right word, or its refusal to accept the word that is not quite right enough. This is what holds the modern author transfixed, staring at the computer screen, at the cursor that blinks and blinks in one immutable position.

Here are some familiar versions of blockage in the writer's search for words:

1. No word suggests itself – not even an echo, not the poorest possibility of a word. The writer contemplates the apparently unsayable. This desperate situation is usually a compound of the puzzlements listed in 2–4 below.
2. A word fills the gap, but feebly; e.g. 'thing', 'fact', 'good', 'make', 'do', 'tell', 'say', and other normally efficient common-places of the common tongue, when the immediate context of writing demands something more powerful and specific. (But we are not to confuse 'powerful' with 'showy' or 'imposing'.)
3. The word that first comes to mind is strong enough, but inexact, the off-centre choice among a set of possibles (on 'sets' see below, p. 124): e.g. 'conversational' where the context

properly requires 'colloquial'. The inexact choice very often blocks the recall of the better word – much as a wrong guess at an imperfectly-remembered name will stubbornly impede accurate recollection.

4. The word at first chosen is an awkward repetition of a word in the immediate or recent context. This is the problem of 'lexical variation'. You cannot allow yourself to write, for example, 'Lexical variation is a problematical problem'. You must find an alternative for 'problematical', or you must change the word 'problem' itself – perhaps to 'question', or 'issue', though in doing so you accept the compromise of the inexact word. A 'question' is not exactly a 'problem'; but if you have already used 'problem', and 'topic' will not fit, then 'question' may have to do – for the time being.

All but the most competent writers – or in some cases, perhaps, the most cheerfully insensitive or brutally boilerplated – will recognise these difficulties of finding, pointing and revising words crucial to the tenor and harmony of the text, words that vividly or precisely or at least adequately fill gaps. (A typical 'gap' occurred in the composition of that last sentence: 'these difficulties of finding, ————— and revising'. The problem – question, task, matter – was to find a word with the suffix *ing*, compactly expressing the notion of 'pointedly conferring the desired sense'. *Pointing* was the invention prompted by a mental rehearsal of 'pointed', 'pointedly' which followed initial thoughts of 'exactly' and 'explicitly').

There are solutions to these difficulties (questions, problems, puzzlements, perplexities, predicaments); routines of enquiry to which writers have more or less unconscious resort. Such routines take the form of **scans**, **prompts** and **escapes**. The terms are invented for the nonce; here are some preliminary notes for further reference:

1. A **scan** is a quite systematic review, systematic even at a half-conscious level, of the lexical resources of the language as the author knows them, or 'possesses' them, and as they apply to a particular instance. The search, mentioned above, that led to the choice of the word 'pointing', is an example of a scan. (It also exemplifies a prompt – see below.) The most usual object of a scan is a set of synonyms, or hyperonyms, or hyponyms, or antonyms, or meronyms (on all of which, see further); however,

part of the process of scanning for a word may be a review of grammatical constructions, briefly exemplified in 4 below.

2. A **prompt** is a phonetic or visual cue. Some words are finally chosen because they 'sound right' or even 'look right' in the context; and the sounding or looking right often has to do with the impetus given by an earlier word. Alliteration is a common form of phonetic prompting; one might, for example, be prompted to the choice of '*k*indly' after a preceding '*c*ourteous'. Word-forms suggest visual as well as phonetic prompts; for example the *ing* suffix of 'find*ing* and revis*ing*', at once a sound in the head and a shape on the page, makes a prompt so powerful as to dictate the necessity of a comparable form for the intervening third term, 'point*ing*'.

3. An **escape** is a re-framing of the text, in the hope that changes of order, position and emphasis may ease the way to choosing a word. This is essentially the re-casting of a clause or a sentence, though altering one construction may further necessitate the alteration of others around it. Possible re-framings might be:

(i) the change from active voice to passive voice, allowing the writer to escape the fumbling with a not–quite–exact noun, as in 'The authorities (people in charge? officials? governors?) announced a change of policy', which becomes 'A change of policy was announced'.

(ii) switching from transitive to intransitive constructions and vice versa, as in 'The defence … ? … an objection', SVO transitive, becoming 'The defence objected', SV intransitive (assuming that one has searched in vain for the transitive verb 'lodged'), or 'Prosecuting counsel spoke', SV intransitive, becoming at first 'Prosecuting counsel made a speech', SVO transitive, then developing into 'Prosecuting counsel addressed the court', SVO transitive – a typical escape-and-discovery move.

(iii) making changes of focus and highlighting (see previous chapter) in an attempt to 'empower' the banal or fairly weak expression, or to open the perception of an alternative choice. 'He felt so sad' might in the right context transform more emphatically into 'So sad did he feel'; 'They behaved inexcusably' can be re-cast in the existential form, 'There was no excuse for their behaviour', possibly leading to 'There was no justification for their behaviour'. In examples like the latter, it often seems that a word − e.g. 'justification' − is hidden from mental view until a change of construction allows the seeker to begin a scan, in this case a scan that reviews the synonyms of 'excuse'.

These are some of the difficulties that challenge writers looking for words, and some of the resolutions open to them. Note, only 'some'; for nearly every sentence we write involves questions within questions and answers growing diversely out of answers. It is a subtle, fugitive process; and to understand something of this diversity we need to look a little more closely at the structure of the lexicon.

LEXICAL ITEMS

'Lexicon' is a technical term, signifying what non-technical usage calls 'vocabulary', or simply 'words and phrases'. Words such as 'house', 'elegant', 'calibrate', 'punctually', and phrases like 'spick and span', 'at loggerheads', 'by and large', 'Tom, Dick and Harry', are *lexical items*, as opposed to grammatical items like 'the', 'a', 'and', 'by', 'though', which are words without content or extra-textual reference, used to organise the syntax of sentences. These 'grammar words', furthermore, are members of so-called closed classes. *The* and *a*, for example, are the only two members of a grammatical class of *articles*. There are no others; whereas *house* belongs to an open class, capable of indefinite extension, via 'dwelling', 'mansion', 'cottage', 'villa', 'bungalow', 'semi', and so on, into the next century and the inventions of future generations of architects and estate agents.

It is important for writers to realise that new lexical items can be invented, whether on existing models of word-formation or in the free fantasy of imagining sounds and syllables. I can invent a noun meaning 'the cutting off of an ear' ('ototomy' − 'Vincent at this time underwent a do-it-yourself ototomy'); I can invent an adjective meaning 'embarrassingly dog-like in manner' ('waggly' − 'The manager arrived, all fawning and waggly'); a verb meaning 'to sneeze explosively and messily' ('shumblate' − 'We did not invite Jennifer to sit at table, in case she might get a tickle in her nose and shumblate all over the cucumber sandwiches'); an adverb meaning 'with a deceptive air of insincerity' ('falsiveritably' –'She smiled falsiveritably, as though questioning her own honesty'); a phrase expressing the notion of moving crabwise ('lateral-oblique displacement' – 'This political party is being compelled to head busily for the future in a mode of lateral-oblique displacement'). I can indulge myself with any of these inventions, and put them into writing, with the proviso that they are defined or that their meaning is clear from the context. I am allowed to invent a lexicon; but I am not permitted to tamper with the closed classes of grammar, tempting though it might be to invent a third article or a completely new preposition.

IN THE HEAD AND ON THE PAGE; HOW DO WE HAVE WHAT THEY HOLD?

If we measure the lexicon by the number of items recorded in dictionaries, it appears that the holdings of the English language are huge, running to hundreds upon hundreds of thousands of words in use, words out of use, words it sometimes seems that no sensible human being can ever have used. But in what sense does this vast catalogue represent the facts of current usage in English?; and what part of it can any of us, as individuals, be said to 'have'?

Learners of foreign languages are familiar with the distinction between 'active' and 'passive' vocabularies, the one kind consisting of words in regular use, mainly in speech, the other comprising words not used but recognised, usually in the course of reading, or else by way of particular necessity. The learner of Spanish, for example, may expect to know and use the word for 'bus/train timetable' (*horario*) but not (unless he/she is diabetic), how to ask for 'blood glucose test strips' (*tiras reagentes para el analisis de glucosa en el sangre*). In time, as knowledge of the language increases, the learner's holdings in the vocabulary settle into what is 'given' – the everyday requirement, the automatic product – and what needs to be 'sought' – the particular demand for a special purpose.

Comparable distinctions between the 'given' and the 'sought' may be applied to the speaking and writing of the mother tongue. Descriptions of the English lexicon usually require, in some form, a contrast between a 'central' or 'core' vocabulary and diverse items accessible as non-central, peripheral varieties. (See, for example,

Carter 1987). This contrast implies, about the language as a whole and in its current state, the existence of a vocabulary so well-established, so central to common usage, as to be virtually indispensable; and beside it another realm of vocabulary, existing for purposes of stylistic variation and differentiation, or for technical description. The verb *speak*, for example, must certainly qualify as a part of the core vocabulary of English. Items like 'murmur', 'mumble', 'babble', on the other hand, are not core words, though they have something to do with speaking. They can be defined in relation to *speak*, i.e. 'speak almost inaudibly', 'speak indistinctly', 'speak rapidly', but *speak* itself cannot be defined in relation to any of them. It is the prior holding, as it were; at need we can manage without mumble, but we cannot dispense with speak.

The distinction of 'active' and 'passive', if applied to mother-tongue usage, generally overlaps with 'core' and 'peripheral', without being exactly the same thing. The core/peripheral distinction suggests a general representation of the language as it exists now, and as it is used now by a significantly large body of users. 'Active' and 'passive' refer to what individual users know. My 'active' may include items that for other people are 'passive' (e.g. 'hypoglycaemia', which yields the familiar 'a hypo', whence 'going hypo', which may one day be playfully elevated to the status of metaphor – 'As soon as I try to add up, my arithmetic goes hypo'). My passive vocabulary may contain more or fewer items than the next man's (poor soul, he may not have come across 'liposuction' or 'hypostasis', or even 'shim'). In short, I 'have' a vocabulary which I use, or recognise in use, and I 'have' it against the background 'holdings' of core and peripheral items in the general stock of usage at the present time.

VARIETY AND REGISTER

One way of recording the holdings of a vocabulary is to list them alphabetically, as in standard dictionaries, but that is not the mind's way of storing and retrieving lexical items. We have dictionaries in our heads, but inasmuch as we understand any method of storage, it appears that words become accessible to us through some principle of association, by sound, by form or by sense. The most powerful principle is that of contiguous notions or 'ideas', and that is the system upon which the kind of word-list called a *thesaurus* is constructed. Here is a sample of a thesaurus entry (from Roget 1982); it occurs under the headword **speak**, and the recurrent numbers followed by clue words in italic refer the reader to other, contingent or associated entries, thus establishing nodal points in an ever-elaborating network:

Vb. *speak*, mention, say; utter, articulate 577 *voice*; pronounce, declare 532 *affirm*; let out, blurt out, come clean 526 *divulge*; whisper, breathe 524 *hint*; confabulate, talk, put in a word 584 *converse*; emit, give utterance, deliver oneself of; break silence, open one's mouth *or* lips, find one's tongue; pipe up, speak up, raise one's voice; wag one's tongue, give tongue, rattle on, gossip, prattle, chatter 581 *be loquacious*; patter, jabber, gabble; sound off, speak one's mind, tell a thing or two, have one's say, talk one's fill, expatiate 570 *be diffuse*; trot out, reel off, recite, read, read aloud, read out, dictate, speak a language, speak with tongues; have a tongue in one's head, speak for oneself; talk with one's hands 547 *gesticulate*.

orate, make speeches, speechify, declaim, deliver a speech; hold forth, spout, be on one's legs; take the floor *or* the stand, rise to speak; preach, preachify, sermonize, harangue, lecture, address 534 *teach*; invoke, apostrophize 583 *speak to*; perorate, mouth, rant, rail, sound off, tub-thump; speak like an angel, spellbind, be eloquent, have the gift of the gab; talk to oneself, monologize 585 *soliloquize*; speak off the top of one's head, ad-lib 609 *improvise*.

One might think that with so much detailed guidance, indicating so many of the points and tributaries in a network of potential meanings, any writer at a loss for the word that speaks his meaning should be able to find it by diligently searching in Roget or a similar thesaurus. There is, however, a significant omission from Roget's scrupulous catalogue: the book can tell us about possible words, but it cannot tell us much about the contexts in which the words will be plausible. A foreigner consulting Roget would not be able to tell *how* the words are used, whether seriously or humorously or ironically, in what context, to whom addressed, and whether they normally occur in spoken usage, or more often in writings of the literary or technical kind.

Such questions concern the many varieties of text that are nested (NB not found in Roget with this sense – therefore requiring 'so to speak'!) within the general concept of writing. The term *register* is often used in reference to the various practices, for divers purposes, that characterise texts in the societal actions and relationships of every day. A sense of *register* can be gathered from the perusal of a single copy of a broadsheet newspaper, preferably one with a Sunday supplement. Read the sports pages, look over the finance columns, dip into the fashion section or the holiday guide, glance at the art reviews, at the notices of new issues of CDs and pop albums, at reports on the latest and shiniest automobile, at the advertisement pages, and even, if you are at last driven to it, to the editorials and feature articles. You may assume that on any page of the paper you are reading English; but you cannot escape the awareness of reading different *kinds* of English. The most obvious differences will be in lexical choice and variety. Now look through these passages, all taken from newspapers, illustrating varieties of lexical register:

A. Cape View Merlot 1994 is typically leathery, giving and aromatic. A wine of deep flavour and charm. It has an extremely attractive partner, also at Victoria Wine; this is the Cape View Cinsault/Shiraz 1994. This is rich and soft and it has a friendly gluggability along with a serious mien.

(*Guardian Weekend*, Food and drink section)

B. The Safari Make-up Gift Set is presented in an elegant burgundy and gold coffret bound in silken cord. Inside, you'll discover an exquisite 50ml Safari Eau de Parfum Spray, a Climate Response Sun Sheer Bronzing Powder in a sheer, natural Berry shade perfect for all skin tones. At just £30 any woman who delights in exploring life's adventures will find it irresistible.

(*Guardian Weekend*, advertisement)

C. Think of 1995 mod as a continuation of the minimal design which has been the main theme of Nineties fashion. The graphic colour contrasts and modern body-contouring fabrics make this season's look starker, more confident, sexier.

Stark, however, does not mean bleak. The mod uniform is friendly. The components, the boxy jacket with three-quarter length sleeves, the single-breasted masculine tailored coat, low-waisted trousers and knee-length straight skirts, turtlenecks or zip tops, are all interchangeable.

(Guardian Weekend, Fashion pages)

D. I definitely liked the convenience of the in-mast reefing system but I'm afraid that's about where it ended. The Bavaria 33 has a relatively high aspect-ratio mainsail anyway so when translated into a sail without a roach, for me the trade off in efficiency drive on the wind was just too much of a compromise. We found it difficult to stop leech flutter without several attempts at adjusting the leech line, and the top of the sail appears so narrow that it's difficult to see that it does anything at all.

(Practical Boat Owner)

E. Robins' goal was a simple affair as Hill's routine punt forward beat Barnsley's offside trap and, with the goalkeeper Watson stranded, Robins executed a simple lob.

Leicester could have gone two-up by the interval, particularly when Archdeacon swept the ball away from Joachim after Watson had parried from Robins.

(Observer, Sports review)

F. The lack of advance screenings for film critics suggests *Assassins* may be a dog. Warner Brothers' tactic of opening the film nationwide looks like an attempt to capitalise on Stallone's box-office clout. With luck, his name may ensure a few days of big takings before any hostile word of mouth spreads.

Assassins, directed by Richard Donner, the man behind *The Goonies*, *Maverick*, and *Lethal Weapon*, claims to be a sophisticated *noir*-style psychological thriller, yet has Stallone in the role of the contemplative killer. ('Contemplative' in this context, means he only gets to kill one bad guy in the whole film, not one every 15 seconds.)

(The Observer Preview, 'Fast Foreword')

G. L'Escargot for me is the true manifestation of Matisse's noble spirit. Apollonian, detached but soberly joyful, nature transformed seemingly effortlessly above the sordid world of the streets, it has none of the shrill theatricality of Bacon or the turgid worthiness of Auerbach and Freud. It soars. The painting is elemental but humble. It follows the structure of a snail's form but is a masterpiece of chromatic and achromatic harmony – black and white working as colour structure – together with the full spectrum of his chromatic range.

(Guardian 2, Arts page)

H. Lloyds bank's share price plunged 6 per cent yesterday – wiping £435 million off its value – as City brokers turned bears on news of worse-than-expected interim results.

Lloyds unveiled pre-tax profits of £498 million for the six months to the end of June, a 35 per cent improvement year on year, and provisions of £138 million against £209 million in June 1992. But, while forecasting at least £1 billion for the full year, the majority view was that the bank's performance was far from impressive in terms of recovery potential.

(Observer, Finance section)

I. Powered by twin Moogs, driving beats and noise squiggles, much of the set unreasonably echoed Kraftwerk. Shades of the Velvet Underground and Nico, too, in the churning riffs and French chanteuse Letitia Sadier's aloof European vocals. However hypnotic the music, the band's boffin-like demeanour bolstered the impression of a daze of futures past.

(Guardian 2, Review pages)

J. TechnoSphere originated when Jane Prophet proposed an art installation in which people would interact in real time with projected, three-dimensional creations. She soon encountered the gap between virtual hype and reality ... TechnoSphere is designed to overcome some of the limitations of hardware affordable by civilians, by being distributed over space and time. Separate processors can handle the evolution and rendering, the e-mail to sponsors, and the World-Wide Web interface. Currently the project is running on two Pentiums under Microsoft Windows.

(Guardian, 'OnLine' supplement]

To describe and analyse in depth the lexical varieties apparent even in a relatively small sample like this would be a protracted task. One might suggest, however, a few stylistic recurrences apparent in the texts briefly represented above. They all contain **names**, whether of products, places, or personalities. Some names merely denominate – a name is a name is only a name; others are stylistically important, a matter of calculated invention, especially in the language of advertising. (Call a pharmaceutical product *Magnivite*; or a piece of office equipment *Deskmaster*; or a plant fertiliser *Grofast*; or a heavy perfume *Seraglio*; or an after-shave for the unassumingly handsome man, *Jim*.) A second property of the lexicon in our sample passages is that much of it is **techno-talk**, the necessary jargon and nomenclature of particular trades – 'high aspect ratio', 'three-quarter length sleeves', 'chromatic range', 'offside trap', 'hardware', etc. Along with the techno-talk come words and collocations (standard phrases) expressing **genre-stance**, that is, the 'tone' or 'attitude' or 'affective key' conventionally associated with a recognised genre (wines are 'leathery', perfumes are 'exquisite', clothes are 'confident' and 'friendly', public figures have 'clout', goals are 'simple', share prices 'plunge'). Finally, there are some words and phrases that do not seem particularly appropriate to the chosen register, but put themselves distinctively forward; such words as 'dog' in passage F, or 'shrill' in G, or 'a daze of futures past' in I; let us call these **mavericks**. The maverick word expresses a stance somewhat different from 'genre-stance'; the maverick is commonly the mark of a writer intruding on the conventions of register, innovating, playing, seeking both to entertain the reader and please himself. (On this sense of *stance*, see the previous chapter, p. 93).

It may be of interest to see how the varieties of lexical/stylistic items defined above are distributed among our sample texts. Here is a cursory breakdown of items listed as **Names**, **TT** (techno-talk), **GS** (genre-stance) and **Mav** (mavericks):

A. (on wines)
Names: House names, of wines and vintner. No stylistic significance.
TT: In this passage, it is hard to separate TT from GS.
GS: 'leathery, giving and aromatic', 'deep flavour and charm', 'attractive partner', 'rich', 'soft', 'a friendly gluggability', 'a serious mien'.
Mav: None, unless 'gluggability'.

B. (on perfume)
Names: 'Safari Make-up Gift Set', 'Safari Eau de Parfum Spray', 'Climate Response Sun Sheer Bronzing Powder', 'natural Berry shade'. In this kind of advertisement copy, names count a good deal, for what they 'connote' rather than what they 'denote'. 'Romantic adventure', 'warm climate', 'bronzed', 'brown as a berry' are notions lurking among the names.

TT: 'skin tones', possibly. Otherwise there is no TT in this extract.
GS: 'elegant', 'silken', 'exquisite', 'natural', 'irresistible'. The piece is virtually all GS.
Mav: None.

C. (on fashion)

Names: None(!) – apart from 'Nineties' and, possibly, '1995 mod'.
TT: Lots – 'minimal design', 'graphic colour contrasts', 'body-contouring fabrics', '[this season's] look', 'three-quarter length sleeves', 'single-breasted tailored coat', 'low-waisted trousers', 'knee-length straight skirts', 'turtlenecks', 'zip tops'.
GS: Comparatively little, but note 'starker', 'confident', 'sexier', 'friendly'; also 'boxy'.
Mav: None, apparently.

Interim note: 'Wine' and 'Perfume' appear to be high on the GS vocabulary: 'Fashion' is more explicit on TT.

D. (on boating)

Names: Only the commercial name of the product.
TT: Profuse – 'in-mast reefing system', 'high aspect-ratio mainsail', 'roach', 'efficiency drive on the wind', 'leech flutter', 'leech line'. The text is in effect a thread on which these technical terms are strung.
GS: None to compare with winebabble and perfume prattle, but there is an element of 'stance' in the casual talk (the chapchat) that occurs at intervals during the technical recital – e.g. 'I definitely liked', 'anyway', 'just too much of a compromise', 'anything at all'.
Mav: None.

E. (on football)

Names: Not important – names of teams and players.
TT: The common football parlance of players and fans alike: 'punt', '[beat the] offside trap', 'lob', '[go] two-up', 'interval'.
GS: 'simple' ('a simple goal'), 'stranded', 'executed [a lob]', 'swept the ball away', 'parried'. The cliches of the football commentator: an easily-taken goal is 'simple', goalkeepers who

use their fists to punch the ball away 'parry', defensive clearances are 'swept' or 'swept up', moves are 'executed'. These terms are cliches of the genre, amounting, indeed, to a kind of TT; in which respect footballing jargon has something in common with wine jargon.

Mav: None

F. (on film)

Names: Names of films, of a studio, of persons.

TT: Sparse: 'screenings', 'box-office', 'takings', 'directed', 'role'.

GS: 'a sophisticated *noir*-style psychological thriller', 'clout'.

Mav: 'dog' (meaning 'flop', ie 'failure') and – remarkably – 'contemplative'. The writer himself is amused by his own choice of this word, as his bracketed gloss indicates.

G. (on art)

Names: Denotations – the name of the picture, name of the picture's creator, names of other artists. But note that these other names – Bacon, Auerbach, Freud – have resonances to which the reader is obviously expected to respond.

TT: 'chromatic and achromatic harmony', 'colour structure', 'full spectrum of his chromatic range'.

GS: In the adjectives: 'true manifestation', 'noble spirit', 'sordid world', 'shrill theatricality', 'turgid worthiness', 'elemental', 'humble'.

Mav: 'soars'. Also 'shrill' and 'turgid' (in connection with the nouns they modify). Also the striking collocation 'elemental but humble'.

H. (on finance)

Names: None, apart from 'Lloyds'.

TT: 'share price', 'bears', 'interim results', 'pre-tax profits', '35 per cent improvement year on year', 'provisions of . . . against . . .', 'performance', 'recovery potential'.

GS: Some words, about the 'movement', or 'behaviour' of shares, etc., conventional to this genre: 'plunged', 'wiping off', 'unveiled'.

Mav: Not to be expected in a financial report (unless the news is truly disastrous!).

I. (on pop music)

Names: The impression comes across that the namings are intended to resonate: 'Moogs', an adjunct to pop technology; 'Kraftwerk' and 'the Velvet Underground', names of bands the informed reader must know. (Compare a similar use of names in passage G.)

TT: 'driving beats', 'riffs', 'vocals', 'chanteuse'.

GS: As in passages A and E, some GS could be read as TT: '[noise] squiggles', 'churning [riffs]'; but also 'aloof', 'hypnotic'. The point of the GS words is evidently to convey the physical feeling, the presence, of the music as it squiggles and churns.

Mav: 'unreasonably echoed' (almost an oxymoron), possibly 'squiggles' (see above), 'boffin-like demeanour', 'daze of futures past'. In this, as in many reviews of pop music there is a striving after stylistic innovation, a pervading 'maverick' spirit, which is a characteristic of the genre.

J (on computer games)

Names: Apart from the personal name, Janet Prophet, note TechnoSphere, World-Wide Web, Pentium, Microsoft Windows. Among these, 'Sphere', 'Web', and 'Windows' have figurative implications that invest the names formed upon them.

TT: This outdoes all the preceding extracts as a sample of techno-talk: 'art installation', 'interact', 'real time', 'three-dimensional creations', 'virtual hype', 'hardware', 'processors', 'the evolution and rendering', 'e-mail', 'sponsors', 'interface', 'running'.

GS: Hardly discernible. In this kind of text, the technical terminology expresses the genre-stance.

Mav: None. This is a sphere which does not readily accommodate mavericks; the system rules, OK?

Some of these passages – most of them, in fact – are manifestly 'register bound', making frequent demands on the appropriate technical vocabulary or the conventional style of the topic, and leaving scant room for the maverick intervention, the personal style of a writer conversing with a reader. 'Conversing' may suggest speech ('confabulate, talk, put in a word', says Roget), and indeed an *idea of the spoken*, or an *aura of conversation*, as much as the direct transcription of speech, is profoundly involved in some registers. Humorous composition depends upon it; but addition-ally requires an ever-present *idea of the written*, an acute sense of the bookish, so that extremes of bookishness and chattiness may clash upon each other in jocular fashion. ('Last night' – says the stand-up comedian – 'last night – no, listen, you might learn something – last night I was taking a jar – what? – Guinness if it's any of your business – I was taking a jar round at the old Dog and Biscuit – nice pub – very clean – oh yes, very clean, no spitting allowed – expectoration prohibited – don't faint now, missus, save it till later – swoon ye not – where was I? – taking a jar, I was – yes I was – and confabulating – DO YOU MIND?? – confabulating with this voluptuous totty'.) Thus for the abrupt swings and side-steps of comedy; a more subtle blend of book-style and speech-style occurs in other registers. The vocabulary of newspaper editorials, for example (broadsheet papers), is worth studying in this connection.

SORTS OF SETS

How does the joker discern the relationship of 'confabulate' and 'talk'? He can look it up in Roget, of course; but the nearer possibility is that there is a sort of Roget-in-the-mind, and that when he thinks about words he thinks about them in clusters – what's another word for this? what's the opposite of this? what does this include? what does this 'go with'?, and so on. The linguist's name for such clusters is **sets**. One kind of set is a cluster of **synonyms**, which are traditionally defined as words of the same or similar meaning, with the traditional warning that no two words mean exactly the same thing. The entries in Roget are not so much lists of synonyms as lists of sets of synonyms, and the problem of using a thesaurus is consequently the problem of finding the right set, or of finding the set that will lead one to the right set. Another kind of set consists of **antonyms**, or opposites. A thesaurus will also list these, making *suffering*, for example, the companion-entry of *joy*. The problem with antonyms is establishing the particular synonym of which they are supposedly the 'opposite'. In some contexts the antonym of *love* is *hate*, when 'love' is in the set that includes 'like'; in others the required antonym may be *fear*, when 'love' belongs to the set of 'accept', 'assent'. ('There is no fear in love, but perfect love casteth out fear' – 1 John iv, 18.) In settling these matters,

Roget-in-the-mind is generally more helpful than Roget-the-book, which bemuses with an excess of instances.

Other sets are **hyponyms** and **meronyms**. Hyponymy is the principle of associating subordinate instances under a superordinate notion; 'emotion', for example, is a superordinate term, or *hyperonym*, implying the *hyponyms* 'love', 'hate', 'fear', 'admiration', 'pleasure', etc. Hyponyms may in their turn be hyperonyms to further hyponyms, 'pleasure', for example operating as hyperonym to the possible hyponyms of 'walking', 'swimming', 'music', 'cards', and so forth. For the writer, the hyperonym is a word that sums up, or abstracts, a notion-in-general, while hyponyms specify particular instances of a notion. It is not unusual for a set of hyponyms to require a covering hyperonym:

> *Wining, dining, cards, womanizing, gambling*, occupied most of Bertie's time. None of these **pleasures**, however, could match his genuine **delight** in *gardening*.

(There, the hyponyms are picked out in *italic*, the hyperonyms in **bold**.)

A **meronym** specifies a part of a (usually physical) whole; e.g. 'hands', 'pendulum', and 'chime' are meronyms of *clock*, 'rim', 'hub' and 'spoke' are meronyms of *wheel*, 'root', 'bole', and 'branch' are meronyms of *tree*, etc. In the mental thesaurus, this principle of meronymy may be extended to include what is felt to be 'contingent' – as the scratch is upon the itch – if not physically 'incorporated' – as the finger is with the hand; thus 'frost' and 'snow' have a meronymic relation to *winter*;'din' and 'confusion' are pseudo-meronyms of *battle*; 'store', 'counter', and 'check-out' are included meronymically in *shopping*. Most descriptions require some degree of meronymy, in the interests of being 'concrete', 'realistic', or 'convincing'. One does not write, for example: 'On Friday my wife went shopping, and despite some difficulties of access to goods, and unpleasant confrontations with other customers, she made all her purchases.' Rather, one writes 'On Friday my wife went shopping. The store was crowded, the food counters were almost unapproachable, and she got into a fight at the check-out. But she brought home the bacon, and the coffee, and the Stilton cheese, and whatever else she had set out to buy.' Meronymy, in short, is a way of *diversifying* a topic and giving a theme a familiar human face.

It is a necessary part of a writer's competence to be able to hold in mind, and have rapid access to, these patterns of association, these clusterings in the vocabulary. They are not wholly like the sets arrayed on the pages of the thesaurus. As we write, one word finds another; no word is found without bringing with it, as a kind of penumbra, the possibility of some other word or words; our mental 'sets' merge and intersect with each other as we review them, constantly opening up new possibilities, new configurations. The image of the kaleidoscope comes readily to mind: the coloured particles remain the same, but the pattern they create is changed as the viewer turns the mirrors. The writer stuck for a word, unable to find the revelatory pattern of associations, has to go on turning the mental mirror, or, to change the metaphor and use a term announced earlier, he must *scan* his resources, looking for light on the synonyms, antonyms, hyponyms, meronyms, already present in his own mind. Project number B17 on p. 217 is an attempt to illustrate how the writer may grasp, intuitively, the intersecting of one set with another.

There are other patterns of mental association. Sound and rhythm can play a determinant part in the selection (or rejection) of words. Alliteration and assonance are often predictive clues. Rhyme in prose is a different case. Rhyme will often lead to the discovery of a word, which will then be rejected *because* it rhymes. If I write about the facility of Juggins' *prose*, the awareness of a hovering rhyme may suggest *flows*; but I will not then tell the world how Juggins' prose flows, or even about the flow of Juggins' prose, for fear of ridicule. Better to write that Juggins' prose is fluent, or tell of the fluency of Juggins' prose. Scan the sets; then try shifting formal categories, between noun, adjective, verb, adverb.

Another associative power is that of **collocation**. A collocation is a recurrent, sometimes fixed, turn of phrase. 'Reap a reward', 'ride a bicycle', 'fair play', 'stormy passage', 'hit the nail on the head', 'open and shut case', are collocations. We would seldom be tempted to write or say, other than in fun, 'Harvest a reward', 'pilot a bicycle', 'righteous play', 'inclement passage', 'bang the tack on the top' or 'unlocked and bolted case'. We have as a rule a sedate respect for the terms of the cliché. At the same time, those terms can be oddly productive as prompts and mnemonics. *Reap* and *reward* for example, might invite a compound or collateral scanning with interesting consequences for the formation of a text:

She hoped that in time she might *reap* the *reward* of her patience. As yet, however, it seemed that there was little to be *gathered in*, no *bonus* or *bounty* for all those patient years of research. Her small pension was secure, but if this was to be her sole *repayment*, her only *recompense*, she had to feel that all her *labour*, all her hard hours of *field work*, had yielded a at best a stunted *harvest*.

That example conveys a principle of compositional **texture**, based on a feeling for conventional associations, which is also a feeling for cliché. (We are not to despise cliché: it is the common currency that supports our speculations in writing.) As a result of the scan on 'reap' and 'reward', the text is pervaded by a kind of lexical harmony; it observes what Renaissance rhetoricians would have called a *decorum*. It would be possible to write that same text in a quite indecorous way, relying on the power of the maverick word to shock or amuse:

She hoped that in time she might reap the reward of her patience. Increasingly, though, her chances of carrying off any of the promised booty looked rather thin. Where was the gravy, where was the well-merited greenstuff, the generous reimbursement in consideration of all those patient years of pigging it in sordid provincial libraries? She had her minuscule pension, of course, but if that was to be the whole kit and caboodle, the loot, the ultimate lolly, the swag of a lifetime, the last word from her steatopygous sponsors, she could only feel that she was not so much reaping as being reaped, or rather, ripped-off.

To ask which of those two texts is 'the better' would be pointless, inviting the counter-questions 'better for what purpose?', 'better in what context?', 'better for conveying what?'

They are not to be read as lessons in composition. What they should convey is a sense of texture. Think of the text as something analogous to a fabric or a wallpaper or a decorative hanging. Look at it, feel it – what impressions does it convey? Of being smooth? Fine-grained? Coarse? Heavy? Light? Warm? Cool? Restrained? Flashy? Patterned? Plain? Some of those feelings about the text as a sensual object can be traced to the penning of sentences, described in the previous chapter; but mostly they are the products of the writer's lexicon, employed as the painter employs his pigments, as the musician uses his harmonics and dissonances, as the architect combines the materials of building – for indeed, do not the critics commonly speak, in their brand of techno-talk, about a 'vocabulary' of painting, of music, of architecture? It might be useful to explore this theme a little further by looking at the way writers go about one of the component tasks of writing, that of *description* – description being a painting in words, an *étude* in words, an edifice in words; but this must be the topic of a new chapter.

Seven

Objects and varieties: description as active participation

WRITING TO PARTICIPATE: LITERARY DESCRIPTION

There is a new folk saying of sorts occasionally quoted by teachers and students of Composition studies: 'The writer writing is never alone.' The act of writing envisaged here is very intensively *involved* – as a well as somewhat counter-intuitive. It goes against one of our most common conventional notions about writers to say that they *do not* work in isolation from society. According to this aphorism, writing reaches beyond solitude. 'Writing' refers to something beyond the immediacy of inscription, beyond the material, substantial weight of the pen wrapped up in the fingers or the electronic hum of anticipation in the fingertips on the keyboard. 'Writing' is part of a gerundal phrase *and* an adjective, tensed to the present and pitched toward the active. The writer writing is wide awake, wholly aware of her audience, and wholly involved in her subject and purpose. To be a writer, then, is to participate wholly and actively in a community *while writing*. Even at midnight, scribbling forlornly by candlelight in his lonely room at the top of the house, the writer is not alone, not while writing, because his pursuit is an especially intensive activity that binds mind to body and self to society.

One of the most effective ways of involving yourself in your writing and of assuring the involvement of your readers, is to vividly describe the persons, places and things you present.

Generally speaking, we regard strong description as virtually a universal value of good writing. As a guide rather than a rule, the detailed description is better than the generalised standard statement. We prefer lively demonstrations to tired tellings; the nimble verb over the dull version of 'to be' or 'to have'; the concrete noun over the abstract nominalization; the sensory image over the bloodless abstraction; the striking new phrase rather than the boring cliché. These characteristics of text are seen as marks of energetic involvement. They tell readers that you are really writing – and writing really. They show you moving beyond the isolated self of the writer not-writing. You wrestled with words and meanings, and discovered something important in what you wanted to say *while you were trying to say it*. You engaged your reader as a writer writing.

It is true, of course, that some occasions for writing – and therefore some kinds of text – do not need to be colourfully engaging. And then again, on the other hand, some descriptive intentions seem to overpower all other purposes in order to make a portrait of a person or an event stand out by itself. As with everything else, it depends on purpose. There are forms of text that do not need to point beyond an immediate reality and therefore avoid or suppress description, while other kinds of writing create their own worlds of reference and therefore prompt fulsome, extravagant performances. Both extremes, shall we call them, close down upon the involved engagement of the writer writing and the reader. In the first case, a formattable purpose excludes any need for interpretation of expectations on the part of writer and readers relating to one another as interlocutors, so that the meaning of *a* message is clear and unequivocal. 'First pull up, then pull down': these few words, inscribed in red letters on the little pane of glass on the cover of the fire alarm box, were all the instructions a schoolchild of my generation needed to be able to sound the fire siren. Vivid description disappears from a text when perfect clarity is the absolute need. In the case of description-onto-itself, a picture or portrait rendered in words goes forth into the world on its own. Again, there is not much to be involved in; when writing tries to compete with the camera eye or the painter's brush, there is little for a reader to do in the way of response. A reader assumes a passive, receptive role. He looks at the picture, audits the lecture, accepts the revelation, beholds the scene, suspends disbelief, and admits into his consciousness this world the writer has made as the only world there is.

For the writer writing, the new-proverbial writer-as-participant, description takes a middle path towards effective communication. Lively descriptions of people, places and things endow your text with energy. They give you material for developing your subject, and most importantly, they involve the reader in your meaning. In this sense, description can be purely modal, which is to say that it can be attached to anything, as a means of helping that thing to become more of what it already is. If this sounds vaguely philosophical – or philosophically vague – remember that writing is a ponderous process! Skilful description can be thought of as a perfectible effect, a technically useful intuition into how you can help an idea or thing become more of what it wants or needs to be. You discover this intuition in and during the very act of trying to describe something in writing, and once you have found it, it becomes an intention to revise for; it folds in with various other purposes as a means of drawing the reader into the process of making meaning. The achievement of a vivid description is a practical effect, a general impression, a pertinent mood or an apt atmosphere – that helps you make your say. Description makes your writing memorable and appealing whether you are telling about, analysing, or arguing a subject. You can describe things, ideas, persons and events so that the reader can see, hear, smell, taste and feel more exactly what it is you have in mind to say.

THE PARTICIPATORY PARADOXES OF LITERARY OVER-DESCRIPTION

Description in literary storytelling presents a bit of a paradox. Literature (and this is one of the reasons we study it) is simultaneously the most and the least participatory kind of writing and reading. In one sense, there is nothing for a reader of a story to do beyond passively accepting a writer's verbal images of a world. It's a simple social contract: a writer of a story presents in vividly detailed sensory images a *scene*; a reader accepts this scene as a background setting for characters performing significant actions that make up the story's plot. All the activity seems to flow in one direction, from writer to reader, and yet the writer wants the reader to accept and believe in and 'see' this world. The reader has to help the writer make sensible reality out of the writer's proffered world, by bringing imagination to bear upon the stuff of description. In this sense the reader's imagination is as important as the writer's. Readers have to help writers create the worlds they share together, and to do this they must activate the imagination.

Let's consider for a moment some of the formal and thematic purposes of fictional description – the better to understand and practice the general arts of description ourselves – by looking at an instance of imaginative description in literature.

> At almost one o'clock I entered the lobby of the building where I worked and turned toward the escalators, carrying a black Penguin paperback and a small white CVS bag, its receipt stapled over the top. The escalators rose toward the mezzanine, where my office was. They were the free-standing kind: a pair of integral signs swooping upward between the two floors they served without struts or piers to bear any intermediate weight. On sunny days like this one, a temporary, steeper escalator of daylight, formed by intersections of the lobby's towering volumes of marble and glass, met the real escalators just above their middle point, spreading into a needly area of shine where it fell against their brushed-steel side-panels, and adding long glossy highlights to each of the black rubber handrails which wavered slightly as the handrails slid on their tracks, like the radians of black luster that ride the undulating outer edge of an LP.
>
> (*The Mezzanine* 3)

This is the first paragraph of a novel, so its main purpose is, as you might expect, the establishment of the scene of a story. This particular opening scene describes a place rather than an action; there is of course an event occurring here – although admittedly not a very dramatic event. A man enters a building at the end of his lunch hour. He is carrying several objects. He sees an escalator. This much is evident – simply enough – because the writer has foregrounded the activity of naming the things his gaze comes upon.

That's the first job of description: to observe closely and to *name* things. At first glance, perhaps, the writer, Nicholson Baker, seems to overdo it here. The space he describes is not densely crowded with the objects of his perception; nonetheless, he seems to be naming everything in sight. But look again: this is a skyscraper in New York City. Where are the many people one would see at the end of the noon hour in the lobby of an office building in Manhattan? That's the second job of description: to *select* the things you name. From out of the manifold flux of all the things there are, you name but a few. Every situation is unique in its particulars, as the philosopher likes to say. To the extent that the writer has to create *everything* in an imagined world, literary description is different from the naming and detailing used in more expository modes of writing. Not everything can be named, of course, so that things that are named in a story have to 'stand for' more – and it is up to us as readers to imagine the people that are surely there, whether the writer includes them in the scene or not. In storytelling, description is devoted in this manner to the establishment of a situation in its entirety, often called 'the world' of the story. Literary description is dedicated to the whole of a situation, much more so than the kind of descriptions you will use in expository description. Readers have to use their imaginations to fill in the gaps in the world of the story, and in that sense literature requires more participation than any other kind of writing. Description signals an imagined world that has to be seen as a whole; it's the same activity that goes into sensory images used in other modes of writing, but employed to a different degree.

Circumstantial (Over)Description, Step 1

What public building is most important in your life? Is there an entrance-way – to your workplace or school perhaps – with which you are over-familiar? Is there a set of doors somewhere that you go through, day after day, without ever really thinking about or noticing the details? Choose that place, either where you go to work or where most of your classes meet – or any place else you would like to spend some time in descriptively exploring. In your mind's eye, walk through the main entrance of that building.

As you come through that doorway – in your imagination – what room, hallway, corridor, lobby, or 'mezzanine' greets you? Whatever kind of space it is, start from the far left of your periphery vision, and pan slowly to the very centre of your gaze, then move on to the far right of the view. List the objects you see – every one of them. For now, do not think of anything else beyond getting down *everything*; try to list every possible detail by naming every single thing you see.

Analysing and practising close description is a way of demystifying the processes of creativity (the better to participate in these processes ourselves), because in essence, the naming and selecting of details is a matter of practical workmanship, not innate genius. In effect, the creativity of fiction writers consists in building a world, recognisably parallel to the social world(s) we live in, out of sensory images. Sensory images are both the tools and the material of the work, and crafted narrative action is what interests us as readers of stories. What people do and say in the imagined world of the story is what catches and keeps our interested imagination. The relationship of imagistic background scene, or setting, to the action of the characters, or plot, is called *dramatisation*. A writer tries to dramatise events in ways that keep a reader's attention. Thus there is this all-important connection to keep in mind between descriptive detail and narrative action: they must 'fit' one another.

Most of the action of Baker's created world occurs inside the mind and body of the main character. A reader's attention to this opening event of the book, this man entering a building and heading for the escalator, may be distracted by the build-up of details that serve, ostensibly, as the setting for this action. Traditionally or conventionally, we expect a vivid description of a fictional scene to serve as the background for a significant event, which is why it is sometimes regarded as a novelistic fault to 'overwrite' a scene in such a way that the details of the setting overpower the action, unless the theme requires, as in highly realistic or naturalistic settings, that the situation powerfully determines (or even 'over-determines') the action taking place within it.

Circumstantial (Over)Description, Step 2

There are so many observable details in any given situation that you can never actually use all of them in a description of any given single scene or event. To get the feeling of what this means – that you must select carefully observed details to match narrative action (and then theme, as we'll shortly explain) – here are some activities with which you can practise observation and 'over-describing'.

From memory, you have just made a list of things to be found at a place that is important to you. Now it is time to supplement your memory's reality with the objective reality of the place. This you can do by going to the actual place to 'see it anew' and to collect *everything* you find there.

At your next opportunity, go back in person to the location of your entrance-way. Take with you a pen and notebook or a micro-cassette recorder – or a powerbook computer if you have access to one. Pause for a moment before you actually go through the doorway.

There are two objectives in what you are being asked to do here. For the first one, you must put aside the list you have already made from memory. Do this creatively. Imagine yourself in the physical act of putting the list into a drawer and then closing the drawer. For the purposes of seeing things 'as they really are,' tell yourself that you can 'mentally file away' that list and everything on it. Perhaps you can assist your visual imagination with your word processor: move (point, click and drag) the file you have created for this list over to another subdirectory, and leave it there. However you want to do it, put that list off to the side somewhere, and as you put it away, make sure that you attach to it all of your everyday associations, good or bad memories, and habitual expectations of this familiar place. Close your eyes, right here and now, before going through the doorway to this building. Pretend that you are a child seeing this place for the very first time.

Now, as you go through the doorway, simply LIST everything you SEE: pictures on the wall, lifts, stairways, bulletin boards, people (porters, security guards, secretaries, etc.), *everything*. Do not use full sentences. You will want to use quickly jotted phrases or 'scratchings' of what these different things look like. This time, start with the dominant features of the scene. What strikes your eye as soon as you come through the door? Get down those first things first. Then, as you did before in your memory, move from the far left of your view to the far right, jotting down what you see. Be sure to add any and all new items, people, objects, nouns, *things*, to the list you made from memory.

Another aspect of the activity of describing that this exercise may demonstrate to you is how 'eye-minded' we normally are in our everyday perceptions. The sense of sight dominates practical patterns of description. However, even though literary and other kinds of description are primarily concerned with sight, this does not mean that we can neglect other sensory details in a descriptive account of a scene. You should record here any of the other sense impressions besides sight, and the best way to do this, of course, is by concentrating on each sense faculty one at a time. Listen carefully for a few minutes to the sound(s) of this place, and write down what you hear. How do voices and footsteps register here? Do they scuff or squeak like track shoes on a gym floor? Do they resound or reverberate church- or museum-like? Do carpets mute and muffle every footfall? Are there any interesting or unusual smells that you haven't noticed before? Is there anything visually textural? Do you want to reach out and touch any surface that you see? What would it feel like?

Another word for 'selection' is *focus*. In descriptive writing, the writer's *impression* of a situation governs focus. Objective aspects of a situation are public, in the simple sense that you and I can point to them and agree upon their names. An impression however, is subjective, and therefore not as public as objective naming, at least not initially, but neither is it wholly personal or private. An impression belongs less to the situation you and I share and more to the eyes that see and the mind that perceives. It belongs to you, in other words, and when you name things you select them for focus. When you name an object you give it central attention. You have chosen, centred, magnified it. You have singled it out as a figure of attention and set it against the ground of total perception.

It is what we might call the primary condition of effective description that details must be selected and shaped in order to serve an impression. This is why a descriptive focus is said to consist of subjective and objective properties blended together in equal parts. A writer selects details according to a point of view that belongs to him or her. The details themselves are, or at least should seem to be, recognisably objective: they belong to the situation and can be named, pointed to, selected. The point of view belongs to you, the writer writing.

Circumstantial (Over)Description, Step 3

To create or formulate an impression of your entrance-way, start by dramatising your own entrance into this building you have chosen to write about. Look at the lists of things you remembered and observed. The lists will probably be long and perhaps a bit unruly. The things, objects, and people you have noticed in your building should seem a bit unmanageable by now, and that is fine and good, for good writing, as we have implied by now, takes the long way around through multiple considerations of perspective. Strong description copes with copiousness.

It is time now to wade into this sea of things, as it were. Enter the scene. Make something happen. Give yourself something to do. Imagine yourself entering the building, and as you come through that door, do something.

Make certain that the action, whatever it may be, is 'in character.' Look again at the way Nicholson Baker has someone move through a doorway; now, imagine a motivation for yourself. Where are you coming from and where are you going to? Why? This is a fictional event, remember, which means that you have other interesting options. If you do not want yourself at centre stage, so to speak, cast a friend – or an enemy – in that role. He or she could even be a composite figure made up of your brother or your sister – or your brother *and* your sister – and your best friend. You have complete freedom here. This is fiction, and fictional happenings are fantasised. They never truly occur. They are always actions that have been made up or imagined. What does your character look like? Where is he or she coming from and going to? Why?

It can be a very non-obtrusive action, like Baker's character carrying a book and a bag and thinking about what he sees. (Actually, he is thinking more about *how* he sees, but more about that in a moment.) It can be even more inner-directed and intensely subjective than Baker's barely perceptible actions, or it can be swashbucklingly dramatic. You decide, merely keeping in mind that whatever you *do* here, it is going to affect your description of the scene, to which we will shortly return.

In order to convey an impression of a situation or scene – this only *seems* to go without saying – a writer must have a point of view. That point of view affects and is affected by the action of the writing, whether it be the actions of characters in a story or the movement of mind in an informative, analytic, or argumentative essay. And here in our discussion of description we meet an interesting point about the way that writing intersects with thinking. A point of view is not a given, nor is it entirely personal, and it is never merely relative. You do not inherit it and it cannot be assigned to you by a teacher. You don't stumble across it, and you cannot order it from a catalogue or download it from the Internet or pick one up at a shop. To have a point of view as a writer you are once again called up to actively participate – as a writer writing – in the creative and critical processes of making meaning with your readers. You must discover and create an impression, find and invent a point of view. You must turn and look at the way you think or feel about something. You must *write*, in other words, to find out about your feelings and thoughts. What's more, your impressions of this or that person, event, thought or situation are never 'mere opinions'. As a writer, you are called upon to investigate what goes on inside your mind and heart, and then you must furthermore interrogate these thoughts and feelings for their origins and implications. What do you think or feel? Why do you think or feel this way? How does your stance affect other people? 'Know thyself' is, as you know, the great humanist mandate. Self awareness is good, but critical self awareness is even better. You must find out about what, how and why you think and feel as you do.

This matter of investigating impressions through writing is a circular or recursive process. It has everything to do with the matter of description. A writer takes a perspective by forming an impression, and then that impression guides a further selection of details. Those details, then, are consistent with or 'fit' the action or plot of the story, as we have said. When we describe something, in storytelling or any kind of writing, we choose from among all the possible details of a particular situation, those details that best represent what we want to convey about that situation. We leave out the rest. The close observation that writers bring to situations always reveals a world of genuinely copious detail. Any time you pick one thing to name, you leave behind everything else.

Circumstantial (Over)Description, Step 4

Literary description is like any other kind of writing in that it is not too difficult to generate a lot of material. To have 'too much material' is a good thing in a writing process. Even though it may seem overwhelming at times to have a lot to work with, your writing will have more depth, complexity and interest because of all the many different perspectives on your subject you search out and think about.

At this point we will generate some new material for you to work with by trying a slightly different approach to formulating an impression of your entrance-way. To start, take a step back from the action you have just added to your scene. Put it aside for a moment and have another look at the lists of details you have generated. You should have two lists, one made from memory and another one from your visit to the actual place.

You may feel that you know, straight away and without thinking much about it, exactly how you feel about this doorway onto your workplace or your classroom building. Perhaps it means absolute drudgery, to have to haul yourself out of bed early in the morning and then get yourself to the same place every day – day in and day out – to do the same silly thing over and over and over again. Or perhaps this doorway opens onto the place you love best in the world. This is the office of the company you have worked so hard for so long to join, or the classroom for the course you care about, the church you love to visit, the gym you work out in, the cafeteria where you know you'll see your girl- or boyfriend.

Then again, perhaps you are not so perfectly certain of how you feel about this place. Even if you are sure about your feelings, there may be more to learn about them. You can use writing to explore and discover both the larger outlines and the finer shades of your impression. The most common kind of writing-to-discover, as you may know, is called 'freewriting'.

Several different kinds of freewriting have been developed for students of writing, some of which you may already know. The different methods share one common purpose: *flow*. Fluidity is *the* solution to The King of All Writing Problems: how to begin. Writers often tell of the various terrors they feel in front of an empty piece of paper or the blinking cursor on a blank screen. Freewriting is a way through this and similar kinds of writer's block. Freewriting urges you towards ideas that might not automatically come to mind. It gets you started. It solves the problem of beginning by effectively skipping the formal beginning – and pitching you immediately *in medias res*. It propels you beyond and around and through the 'censor' of your conscious thinking processes, that voice inside you that says you have to wait until you know everything there is to know about your subject before you are entitled to speak and start to write. The sometimes fierce continuity of freewriting is not unlike the feeling of 'flow' reported by long-distance runners: you want to experience a breathless rush of words and meanings – too many coming too quickly for you to 'get it all down'.

Because the writing produced in freewriting is meant for your eyes only, you need not worry about how it looks. In fact, messiness is a virtue in this kind of thinking-on-paper. You are churning up ideas, trying to stimulate thinking, fomenting new notions, not putting carefully considered conceptions into perfect shape. It is a kind of writing meant to liberate thought processes and excite associations, which is why the emphasis in freewriting is always on creative speed and imaginative fluidity rather than on logical sense or correct and proper form.

There is only one rule to freewriting: start to write and do not stop. At first it may seem hard to do, because it calls for an intense form of relaxation, a letting go of an immediate need to make perfect sense, a surrender of any inbred desire you may possess to get it right the first time/every time, as the saying goes. In freewriting you cannot worry about spelling, grammar or punctuation. There are various ways of tricking yourself into a continuous, carefree (or indeed careless), fast movement of pen or pencil across and down the page. You can set a time limit so that you don't have to worry about anything other than not-stopping. Start at one minute. Then try three, then six, then fifteen minutes. If it seems an odd thing to do at first – recklessly unchecked, yet timed – it quickly gets easier to 'go with the flow' after you try to do it a few times.

A wholly unstructured freewriting does not have a topic or title. You simply pick a subject and start writing. If you can't think of anything to say, you start to scratch little Xs or numbers or boxes or circles across the line of the page – anything so that your pen does not come off the very top of the piece of paper. Try writing your name, over and over again; anything will do. Very soon, you will find, inner speech reasserts itself and you are back on track.

And what you are back on track towards is some kind of idea about what kind of track you might like to be on. Freewriting may seem like a funny thing to do, and it is; in our busy, product- and goal-oriented everyday lives, this writing activity, meant only to get things started, can be as formless as it is useful. This is not its only paradox. Freewriting is the only kind of writing you will ever do that is 'good' insofar as it messy, 'incorrect', hard to read, uncontrolled. All of the qualities one would normally aim for in writing are *wrong*. The more this looks like 'bad' finished writing, the better it actually is – as freewriting.

Freewriting is never wholly unstructured. One form of freewriting is particularly good for generating several 'different sides' to every story. It's called 'looping', and is simple to do. After you have reviewed the lists of things you have found at your entrance-way, and then considered some aspects of the character and action that could take place there, try to come up with a title for your scene. Nicholson Baker used 'the mezzanine'; you can use a similar phrase or a sentence that seems to sum up the way you feel about this place. 'Here I am in a hurry again,' for instance, or 'Out out out!'. Think of a snapshot of you or your character coming through the door. What might you write beneath that photo to explain it? If this were a cartoon, what would its caption say?

Put that word, phrase or sentence at the top of a piece of paper. Place the point of your pen on the line beneath this title. Take a deep breath. Begin. The objective is to write very quickly, and once you have started you must not stop. Try to write like this, as fast and furiously as you can, for a full five minutes. If you run out of words or cannot think of what to say next, start to make squiggles or circles or wavy lines – whatever you need to do to keep the pen moving. This is a dissembling manoeuvre, a holding pattern. As you do this, glance up at the word or phrase at the top of the page. Keep your eye there. Keep moving the pen. Shortly, you will feel the next idea make its way to the surface of your attention. If you keep focused on the title of this freewriting, the word or words at the top of the page, you can trust that the flow of words and ideas will resume.

Another method for finding out more about your own thoughts and feelings with freewriting is to do it 'invisibly'. Originally this was done using the treated paper used to make copies on old-fashioned ditto machines. To write invisibly, you simply removed the protective slip from between the two pages and wrote on the back of the second page. You could not see what you were writing until you turned the page over. Nowadays invisible writing is more likely to be done on a computer screen. You simply turn the monitor down low, by adjusting the knobs governing the 'contrast' and 'bright' functions so that you cannot see the letters as you type them.

Once again – it probably needs to be said – the intention here is not to act mysteriously or to produce mumbo jumbo. The intention is merely to allow ideas to start out on their path of development towards public form. An idea needs a chance to grow before you check it for accuracy, truth, form, readability. All of these qualities are important, of course, but they come later. The skills, concepts and conventions that make written forms meaningful are very powerful, and can stop an idea from germinating. Invisible freewriting is merely one more device for thwarting the knee-jerk impulses of the perfectionist in you, for checking that part of your mind or personality that does not believe in language as the key to learning about self and world. All freewriting will ever do for you is help you find and start to develop ideas. It will tempt inspiration. It is an aid to thinking about your subject, no more no less, and the most important skill to be associated with it is not, finally, the long flow of words that you can generate. What is most important is what you do with those words (and not-quite-words) once you have them.

Looping can be particularly helpful for finding out about your impression of a situation precisely because the freewriting loop forces you to attend carefully to your own writing. And because that writing has been 'freed,' it can make for strange reading, at least at first. A looped freewriting forces you to *start* working with this weird soup of a text you have produced in one or three or five minute spurts. This is an important challenge because freewriting, if it is done correctly, looks disposable. It looks like a piece of paper you would wad up and throw away. It looks like something you would stop with, not start from. When you start freewriting in a loop however, you must begin to practice and develop the skill of reading your own sloppy scrawl. You must examine these strange, disorganized jottings *for what they are able to tell you about your thought processes.* You will learn to regard this messy business as a transcript of your own creative processes at work. Take seriously the idea that writing is an extension of thinking, and you will be able to examine and develop your rough thoughts into more finished kinds of writing.

Freewriting requires a kind of decoding that is not very much like reading a finished essay. The first skill peculiar to an analysis of freewriting is zen-like: you already know how to do it, but you may not be aware that you do. And as the zen master might be imagined saying: only you can read your own writing. Further, you are reading not to find out what is there in the text, but what is *not* there – or not quite there yet.

Meanings in freewriting are there to be discovered, and *not* there to be discovered. Meaning in freewritten expressive discourse does not rise out of the depths of the script. What you want from freewriting lies on the surface of the text. If you don't know how to 'see through' the content, to let go of a drive for 'inner' or deep meaning, you may have to practise this kind of analysis as a new art. Freewriting presents you with a sometimes-odd sense of your own doubled voices: here you are, it says, trying to tell yourself what you're interested in. 'Listen to me!' it commands, and 'me' is you, or 'the other me' of the always virtually postulated audience that we mentioned early in Chapter 1. This duplicity, this doubled perspective of inventive freewriting, requires that you learn to read the look of the page. More often than not, the signs of what will interest you are in the gaps and breaks, the doodles and stars and spaces, as much as in the semantic content of the words and phrases positively there on the page. In other kinds of writing these would be marks of incoherence, but not here. What is *not* here is probably more important that what is here. Now you are reading your own words as if they were written by someone else. Now you are your own first reader. A writer reading writing.

The loop is as good a place as any to try out this new intuitive skill of self-analysis in freewriting. Read over what you have written so far. What is it trying to say? What are you trying to talk to yourself about? Can you phrase it? Is there a bottom or a base, sometimes called a 'centre of gravity' to it? Skip a line at the bottom of your first freewriting entry, and put that centre of gravity into a full sentence. Skip a line again and place the tip of your pen on the page again. Look carefully at the sentence you have just written. Stare at it for a moment; it has become the title for the next freewriting session, which you are about to begin. Hold the pen steady. Take a deep breath. Go.

Looping is the continuation of the process. You freewrite, find the centre of gravity, then freewrite again using the centre of gravity as a topic. In the end, you have a collection of sentences that function less as links between freewritten passages than as discrete moments in a line of loosely associated thinking, all of which is now available to you in an image of itself on paper.

In fiction, writers construct descriptions with details guided by impressions that reinforce themes. The place Baker depicts in *The Mezzanine* is the lobby just below the mezzanine that gives his book its title. This is the lobby, here are the escalators: this much is public and objective. In realistic storytelling, we expect the details associated with a scene to add up, as we have said, to a recognisable background setting *and* a subjective impression. That setting captures or projects a theme. A theme in fiction is like a thesis in more expository kinds of writing. It can be thought of as an amplified and dramatised impression. We can expect the chosen details of a scene to assume symbolic significance as thematic 'correlatives' of the governing impression. Details match, embody or convey the author's intention to make a meaningful comment on this character in this situation, and the writer's observation or insights we characteristically call the theme, point, moral or message of the story.

As a reading from start to finish of Nicholson Baker's *The Mezzanine* would show, Baker's use of description happens to be consistent with a theme, a theme that happens to be useful for our purposes here. Informally summarised, this theme might be phrased thus: 'It is fun to describe closely the products of our manufactured world that we ordinarily take for granted.' Another version might be: 'The functional objects of our every-day lives are important not only for what they do for us but also for the way they look.' At the beginning of his novel, in service to this theme, Baker has selected certain details of the building's lobby, and ignored, avoided or rejected many other details.

A large amount of circumstantial detail that has been selected is dedicated to setting the stage behind and around the simple action of a man entering a building and carrying some objects. We might even say that the scenery tends to take over the action, purposefully overwhelms it, when the speaking 'I' dissolves here into the accumulating detail of the paragraph. Description in this passage concerns itself to a very high degree with attributes and circumstances, adjectives and adverbs, pre- and post modifying 'hows' and 'whens' and 'wheres'. This is apparent if we strip the paragraph down to the basic subject-verb realizations of its main clausal constructions:

> ... I entered the lobby ... and turned toward the escalators ... The escalators rose toward the mezzanine ... They were the free-standing kind ... [An] escalator of daylight ... met the real escalators. ...

If these are the main grammatical agents and actions of this passage then we are safe in saying that the first paragraph of this novel is marked by a preponderance of circumstance items; most of its energy, shall we say, is devoted to naming objects and then elaborating their details through the qualification of nouns and verbs. The perceiving and speaking 'I' establishes itself but then immediately recedes, and it is left to the escalators, as agents of actions, to do whatever else is done here. The actions themselves are more told about than actually shown, with not-especially-dramatic verbs: 'entered', 'turned', 'rose', 'were', 'met'. People and processes are kept in the background. While the appeal here is highly visual, the writer's aim is not really to show things in action but to demonstrate what these things are like as they register upon a wonderfully curious consciousness that takes great delight in describing and thinking about things.

And all the while there is this pretence that the eye is more important than the 'I'. For description is finally the very key to conventional realism; more than any other device, it is what writers use to persuade an audience – which includes that 'other me' of freewriting and all inventive procedures – of an intention to be objective. Naming, elaborated into detailed sensual imagery, is the trick of all tricks when it comes to hiding subjectivity with style. Baker is following a very common kind of pattern when he introduces the person doing the seeing, then slowly withdraws that person as the attributes of the scene start to accumulate. Look at the way John McPhee does the same thing in a highly descriptive paragraph about a trip into the Alaska wilderness:

> There are five of us, four of whom are a state-federal study team. The subject of the study is the river. We pitch tents side by side, two Alpine Draw-Tite tents, and gather and saw firewood: balsam poplar (more often called cottonwood); sticks of willow and alder; a whole young spruce, tip to root, dry now, torn free upriver by the ice of the breakup in spring. Tracks are numerous, coming, going, multidirectional, tracks wherever there is sand, and in gravel if it is fine enough to have taken an impression. Wolf tracks. The pointed pods of moose tracks. Tracks of the barren-ground grizzly. Some of the moose tracks are punctuated with dewclaws. The grizzlies' big toes are on the outside.

There is a 'we' who are here to study the river and then one more, the fifth of 'us', implicitly an 'I', here to do something more. Or something less – if the naming of description is an activity writers engage in not because it's useful, in the way of state-federal studies, but because it's interesting, as are stories. The naming, as you can see, is highly specific, and it quickly escalates into detailed phrasings which assume objectivity as this naming 'I' pretends to get closer to the things it sees by, paradoxically, withdrawing from our attention. First the wood: balsam poplar which can also be named cottonwood; sticks and a whole tree are listed and qualified without a finite verb; then the tracks, which also lose syntactic organisation as they 'leave' an impression, in sand and gravel and on the observer's mind. This is the conceit of power. That mind, its eyes, the 'I' – this name for subjectivity discounts its own activity as the names it assigns to the scene accumulate into an ever more finely delineated picture of the world 'out there'.

This is not to deny that there is a world wholly and truly out there, but only to point out that the very success with which it seems to present itself in strong description is an effect not so much of its own capability to impress but of the writer's power to achieve a vivid impression. Description is the work writers do. Writers describe. When they describe they find and create, not merely present, an impression or theme. The only purpose in examining the ruses used by subjectivity is not to deny objectivity but to attempt to convince you of your own importance in the endeavour to write, your own role to play in the description of your world, your own power to use language to make that world as real as it is. 'The world is what you make it' is an old, tired proverb; its effect is brought back to life when the new folk saying about 'the writer writing' is put into action and effect.

Circumstantial (Over)Description, Step 5

You have a list of things from memory and then a list of things from observation. You have some conception of a narration of an action, as well as some considerations of the character of the actor. Then you have some freewritings about your impression, and a series of looped 'centres' exploring that impression. It is now time to develop your impression into a 'theme'. Take this entrance-way to a significant public place and describe it so that we see it in a way that you want it to be seen. After you have done that, remove the 'I' by doing all you can to foreground the *eye*. Consider this the start – and only the start – to your own story about a place that is important to you. Finally, give it to someone else to read.

In this chapter we have talked about observing and naming, selecting details, the copiousness of observations, and the importance of the writer's impression to the endeavour of description. A scene (or the 'world' of a story) is constructed out of sensory images that 'fit' a narrative action (or plot). Our everyday world is primarily eye-minded, but other senses are important as well when the objective is to involve the reader in the writing. An impression or point of view has to be *explored* in writing before it can be presented to a reader. Freewriting can help you discover what and how you think and feel, and your discovery of this knowledge should convince you that you are entitled to describe the way your world appears to you.

Literary description leaves gaps in a whole situation that readers must fill. This factor of entirety makes literary reading the most participatory of all kinds of reading and writing. The reader of a story has to use his or her imagination to help create a 'world' with the writer, but imagination is what description calls for in other kinds of writing as well. Description is used to create whole worlds for creative writing, literary journals, personal letters, stories and plays, travel accounts, poetry, and memoirs. In other expository modes and in the stricter forms of academic writing, writers do not try to create independent scenes, whole situations, 'worlds'.

Here description, while still imaginative, is more modal – applied to different kinds of writing. To the extent that *involving readers* is part of all writing, insofar as you manage impressions by exploring your subject through naming and detailing your world, then description is indeed an important part of everything you do when you tell about, argue, or analyse your subject.

Eight

Discourse as dialogue: writing on the Internet: e-mail, discussion lists and newsgroups

Once upon a time, before there were personal computers and modems and local area networks and the World Wide Web, when cyberspace was merely an imaginative notion and not yet a virtual place, the information scientist Theodor Nelson foresaw the rise of a great, vast assemblage of interconnected communication systems. This would be the 'docuverse', he called it, a giant text-of-texts. It would expand fantastically like molecular cells, everywhere and forever. It would grow out to absorb and transform writing, *all* writing, assuming every written word into a bodiless circuitry, transfiguring every written text into an electronic ghost of itself. The *logos* would take a new materiality, sacrificing the body of the book for absolute ubiquity and relatedness. Written meaning would be inscribed upon nothing more substantial than electronic air, yet every text that ever was, will now be tied to every text that ever will be.

In the 1990s we are witnessing the genesis of the docuverse. The Internet began as a military strategy in America's nuclear defence programme. It started to grow in universities, developing into research and communications networks such as JANET in the UK and BITNET in the US. And now, with the rise of commercial services like Compuserve, America On Line, Prodigy, MSN and many others, the Internet is quickly becoming a familiar part of everyday life. In two years, 1994 and 1995, worldwide use of the Internet has tripled, to 60 million users. As it quickly – and ever more quickly – infiltrates classroom, workplace and home, the Internet is changing the nature of professional and personal conversations in very noticeable and sometimes profound ways.

At work now, you scroll your computer screen as well as check your pigeonhole for memos from the boss, and soon that old wooden mailbox in the office, like the old wooden card catalogue in the library, will be gone for good. On the factory floor, one or two workers monitor from computer screens the robotic welding arms that do the work at every point on the assembly line. For homework, Professor Blooker has asked you to point your Web browser to Shakespeare's home page. You visit there by keying its URL into Netscape, Mosaic, WebExplorer, Internet Explorer or another software program for access to the World Wide Web (about which more later). An URL – Uniform Resource Locator – is a Web address. Two of Shakespeare's many current addresses are: http://the-tech.mit.edu/Shakespeare/works.html.   and   http://www.Shakespeare.com. You arrive at the Shakespeare site, download the definitions of several archaic words, then mail some observations from your reading to an e-discussion of *Hamlet* on your class's own discussion list.

Now, your homework finished and the work week done, Saturday night is barbecue night in the garden. You experiment your way around the heart-clogging animal fat of charred burger and hotdog with a lime-daiquiri marinade for skinless breast of chicken (free range). Everybody loves it, so you telnet to an FTP site in France and upload your recipe to the 'New Arrivals' subdirectory.

Almost overnight, the Internet seems to have changed everything about writing. The postman, chatty on his daily round, is suddenly the all-day and all-night e-mail with instant delivery and automatic sorting commands. Our desks are now desktops, drawers opening inward with a click rather than outward with a pull. We open Windows on-screen now rather than screens on windows. On-line novels can be fully illustrated or 'graphic' – and if you don't like the ending you can dismiss it and write your own. All of a sudden and all of a piece, our theories and practices of writing must leap into the future. Things have changed and will continue to change for some time, sometimes dramatically and sometimes subtly. How we tell about, analyse and argue our way through life is going to be different now.

E-MAIL: THE FEEL OF THE FORMAT

To date, Africa is the only continent not yet thoroughly networked. E-mail is almost everywhere. It has virtually annihilated the physical distance between point A located anywhere in the world, and points B through Z located everywhere else throughout the rest of the world. In so doing, electronic mail has quickened the rhythms of written correspondence and heightened a sense of immediacy in writing. It has fostered a sense of intimate interaction among people, which is more than a bit deceptive as e-mail is nowhere near as private or as individualised as it seems. E-mail turns individual people into members of vast new communities of readers and writers. As a new writing technology making international communication cheap and easy, it presents us with a great many boundary-breaking philosophical, economic and sociological revelations to think about in relation to our daily lives. These aside, the primary practical effect of e-mail has been to elevate the importance of writing in everyday life while at the same time making writing more like speech. For although we often say that people 'talk' on e-mail we mean of course that they *write*.

Getting On-Line

Writing on the Internet is best approached like a regimen of physical exercise: the best way to get started is not to think about it too very much. 'Just do it', as the runners say.

First, of course, you will need access to the Internet. Electronic mail is the basic building block of communication on the Internet, therefore commercial providers of interactive services usually offer e-mail and USENET access as the key part of their basic service. It should not be difficult, therefore, to get an e-mail account via these increasingly popular businesses, although a commercial provider may not furnish you automatically with access to other basic Internet resources such as File Transfer (FTP), Telnet, and the World Wide Web.

If you are a student, even part-time, in higher education, then it is likely that getting on-line will be a simple matter for you. Most colleges and universities try very hard to keep right in pace with fast-paced developments in educational technology. If you are enrolled at such a school, it is not unlikely that an e-mail account will be provided to you for the asking. Students are very rarely charged for Internet access. If you do not already have an account, inquire at the Computer Centre on campus or in a computer lab in your department or faculty. As with so much else in college life, the college library is often the place to start asking questions.

Never be afraid to ask questions about the Internet. An often-noted incidental affect of the rise of the Internet is a spirit of cooperation among people interested in exploring it. Chances are very good that someone you know is already adept at navigating the Internet, so if you ask around among your friends and acquaintances you will probably find someone very able and more than willing to help you get started.

Once you have an account you will follow the local procedures for logging-on with your password. Currently, the most popular programs for e-mail are Pine, Pegasus, Eudora, and similar 'mailers', each of which acts as an interface between you and the Internet. You will need to learn the basic techniques of running a mail program such as one of these. If you use Windows or an icon-based, 'point and click' software package for the Macintosh, you may already be familiar with the little symbols you will activate with the computer's mouse in order to start your local mail program.

Ask several of your friends for their e-mail addresses. Better yet: give your e-mail address to several friends and ask them to write to you. Note that an e-mail address can be long and complicated in appearance, so it might be a good idea to inscribe the e-mail address of a friend into the address index on your mail program as soon and as accurately as possible. Later, we will consider some interesting possibilities for contacting people far away.

If one of your friends sends you a note, it is the simplest of matters to reply. You simply execute the REPLY command, which is usually the most noticeable and apparent feature of a mail program.

When you initiate the sending of a note on e-mail the system will present you with a template or format for composing the message. It will have a 'header,' a basic set of items with tag lines and prompts that will look something like this (with possible variations):

Date: Sun, 18 Jun 1995 09:23:03 –0500 (CDT)
From: <Your name> <your e-mail address>
To:
Subject:

The date and your name and e-address on the 'From' line are usually provided automatically. You put your correspondent's address on the 'To' line and a short description of the topic on the 'Subject' line. After writing a message you will use a key stroke or two to execute a simple SEND command.

E-mail's primary purpose is one-to-one or one-to-many communication. Now that you have addresses, send an e-mail message to one or several of your friends. Make it a simple, short message of greeting, letting the person know that you're now on-line. As with all e-mail notes, you make plain your purpose in writing by describing it in a word or phrase on the Subject line of the header. If the note you send to a friend does not 'bounce' (return to you almost immediately with a message stating that your mail was undeliverable for a stated reason), then you know that your note has arrived in your friend's account or 'inbox.' Time now to wait for a reply, which will likely be in your inbox the next time you log on.

Writing researchers are busy developing a 'rhetoric of e-mail' that will allow them to describe the practical experience of writing on the Internet. The very first element of that experience may be the feeling you have when you write a note after first announcing its subject by filling in a blank on a template. The factor of the template – the feel of the format, shall we call it – has a major effect upon the form and content of the message in e-mail. Your feel *for* the format of an e-mail note conditions your topic by making it a matter of blank-filling, on the one hand, or acceptance of what you find already there on the blank line. On e-mail you identify your topic by filling in a blank, or by accepting the word or phrase on the Subject line of the note just written to you, when you allow it to serve as the topic of your own new note. When you choose the REPLY key (by entering <y> for 'Yes' at the 'REPLY?' prompt on a mail program), you effectively recycle the same subject for the next round of messages. The feeling to be associated with this very common transaction, the turnaround of the topic, is the feel of the format.

We are defining this 'feel' colloquially, as you may have noticed. It is a 'touch' or an ability, a competence. It can be said to originate in a perception of continuity or flow in speech. When you identify 'what they are talking about' in a set of voices engaging one another in conversation, you are exercising a feel for a format. Intuitively, you have accommodated the swift flow of people's voices engaged in conversation. You adapted yourself to a sensation of the speed involved in the vector of conversation, the impulsive forward tumbling of talk. The feel of the format on e-mail takes its form from your highly developed skill at grasping the topical exchanges of everyday discourse, as these are defamiliarised, initially, by a template, a keyboard, and a blinking cursor.

There is a very quick tempo of dialogic give-and-take in an e-mail conversation, principally because of the typewritten – actually keystroked – nature of an e-conversation. (This has become a common prefix, by the way, the 'e-' that has moved from e[lectronic] '-mail' to many other words.) An e-conversation is fundamentally affected by the keystrokes you use to set up a new note. This makes the feel of the format a bit strange, initially, because we may not be accustomed, even after a decade of familiarity with word processing, to featuring the act of typing as an important part of the meaning we create in writing. The very word 'typing' is actually little used when describing what one does with a keyboard at a computer screen. 'Inputting,' shall we say, is usually thought of as an entering of data, just as typing is thought of as transcribing – something that comes *after* we have discovered and organised our meanings.

E-mail draws upon traditions and conventions of word processing, wherein composing is apt to occur on a keyboard; e-mail may therefore seem strange at first because even more radically than the word processor, it collapses the transcribing stage of a writing process into the composing stage. On e-mail, therefore, your stroking of the keys will at first be tentative and fumbling but very shortly, as you become familiar with composing and responding to messages directly on-line, your every intention will evoke a confident flurry of flying fingertips.

Of all the things the fingers do to set up a new message, the most notable movement attends your quick decision about the topic.

Whether you are responding to or initiating a message, the subject slot on the header speeds up the enterprise. It imports a sensation of speed into every message, and yet it also stimulates the slightest snag in the flow – for it remains the single stroke in the process that will never be habitual. You will always have to think – no matter how quickly – about the topic.

That said, it is true that e-mail correspondents sometimes ignore the Subject line and use the REPLY key merely because it is quicker. Even when this happens, however, the ostensible subject can never be wholly or permanently ignored; sooner or later, as the conversation moves on to other things, a writer notices that the subject has actually changed and revises the topic word or phrase accordingly. It is probably safe to assume that most e-mail conversations develop in exactly this fashion. They follow a twisty-turny line of conversation down a road where the direction signs, in the form of Subject lines, change en route. For reasons to be explained later, e-mail messages are often 'single subject' missives that fail at sticking to topic; they are phrased and shaped to a subject line which they effectively and quickly outgrow.

Whether or not the particular term on a subject slot holds sway over the actual content of the immediate note, the interactive nature of the entire activity of writing on e-mail is always powerful and always quick. On e-mail you are thoroughly, pervasively, fundamentally, always *connected* to other writers. An expectation of a response shapes a statement that may not even be asking explicitly for an answer to a question. On e-mail you don't so much create a new note as respond to a previous one, even when you compose a message from scratch. The COMPOSE feature of the mailer's program is very often usurped by the REPLY key, by your ability to send a message by replying to one, as I have mentioned. Most people send their first few messages this way, by electing to REPLY to a note they have received rather than composing a new note without antecedent. In either case, the Subject line requires that a title be assigned to even the slightest purposes in writing. Although there is nothing to stop a writer from filling in or changing the Subject line after a note has been composed (the lines are very rarely left blank), the topic has to be enunciated at the start of the message. If you do select the COMPOSE feature and originate a new message you will still feel the format, still sense that you are implicated in the many voices and quick flow of conversation, for right away you hear your own voice demanding to know 'What is this message *about*?!'

At first, as you adapt your customary writing habits to these new expectations, the process of give-and-take between writer and reader seems wholly governed by the machine. Soon however, a sort of kinaesthetic competence takes over. Soon after you first try it you will feel like you know what you are doing on e-mail. This may not be wholly a good thing. Writing researchers have found that an initial period of fumbling unfamiliarity on e-mail is actually a very productive condition. Don't be afraid, in other words, of being a bit afraid of e-mail. Initial nervousness in front of the apparent technical complexity of e-mail seems to produce an 'envelope' or window of opportunity. When a person is first finding out about electronic communication the time is ripe, in other words, for learning. While the experience *feels* new, while the technology seems opaque or difficult to access, e-mail challenges writers to accustom themselves to it. Then, when the technical manoeuvres grow familiar, writers often return to older habits of writing and revising or otherwise stop learning about this new medium.

That envelope of opportunity does not last long because, simply put, electronic mail is truly not a very difficult thing to do. The machinery of the network sets up conversational 'turns' in the form of the mailer's template. You 'open' or read one note (or file) at a time; very soon the format of the note is recognisable and very easy to manipulate. This means that it is extremely simple to compose/reply and (re)send the note. It is a smooth process, from start to finish, and the computer emphasises the flow and speed of the process, shaping your written words to the form and features and flow of a verbal conversation. You find yourself thinking that writing is more like speaking than it used to be: the act of composing on e-mail gets blended into the activity of responding.

Because of the speed and flow and conversational nature of this communicative process, the technology of e-mail can be said to encourage quick functional response rather than slow creativity. That encouragement is hidden, as it were, by the fact and feeling of speed, which is itself couched in an attention to the give-and-take of talk. The nature of the medium is highly responsive and its clock is set to turnaround time. Notes are read soon after they are sent; answers are composed and re-sent soon after they are received.

The point to be made in drawing attention to the keyboard and the Subject line and their effects upon electronic writing is simple: like any other rhetorical genre, e-mail has its own characteristic features and conventions. These constrain communication in some ways and in other ways enable it. Because they are rapidly exchanged, e-mail messages are short and sharply pointed, and this calls for certain skills. As with any other kind of writing, these skills are a blend of technical and conceptual competence. To keep up with the brisk interactive flow of this medium you must check your mail often and read quickly or 'scan' to get the point; you must think quickly to be able to compose; and you must type or keystroke quickly to keep the inner voice of your thinking in beat with a rhythm of response that has greatly accelerated the turnaround time of regular or 'snail' mail.

Feeling the Speed

In a moment we will ask you to join a USENET newsgroup or a mailing list. Responding to an e-mail note on a newsgroup should acquaint you with the feel of the format, because you will have to scan notes and quote from them in your response – and learn how to struggle, perhaps, to keep up with a large volume of mail. For now, however, let's do something simple again.

Open your mail program to its inbox and see if any messages have been sent to you. Choose a note and reply to it, using the REPLY key. For the subject, use the same word or phrase that you find already there on the Subject line.

After you have sent the first note, write another note but without using the REPLY key. At the address line, fill in the e-mail address of a friend whom you know to be basically familiar with the Internet. You are going to compose this note from scratch, as they say. At the Subject line, put this phrase: 'Newsgroup query.' In the body of the note (the 'message area,' as it is often called), tell your friend about the main 'extra-curricular' interests in your life.

Outside of your job or your studies, what do you do? What are you interested in? *Il faut avoir une passion*, the French say. 'You must follow your bliss.' What is your passion? your bliss? Do you make and fly kites? Write nature poetry or science fiction? Fire electronic rockets? Train horses? Skydive? Flyfish? Waterski? Do you go in for ballroom dancing? Are you a short-wave radio enthusiast? Do you race motorcycles on the weekends or play saxophone in a rhythm and blues band or wander among market stalls in search of old tables, lamps and chairs? Whatever you care about, create or collect 'after hours', for the love of doing it, tell your friend about it.

Go into some detail about your latest experiences with your *passion*, but write very quickly, and feel free not to proofread. After you have described your interest, ask your friend to recommend a USENET 'newsgroup' to which you may subscribe. It is virtually a certainty: if you are interested in it, there is a newsgroup on the Net already talking about it.

There are thousands of interest groups already on the Internet (18,000 at the time of this writing), and more everyday. Whether or not your friend will know of the right newsgroup (or several of them) for you is another story, of course, about which more in a moment.

You should send the note before you have edited it in any way or for any reason.

E-mail is sometimes said to be diary-like. One of the reasons for this is the high tolerance among friends for simple mistakes on the surface of the text. You write quickly on e-mail as you might in a diary. Errors of spelling and sentence construction and mechanics are not always regarded as cardinal sins by writers on the Internet. This may become less the case – and such errors may assume their traditional importance – as the on-line editing functions of mailing programs are improved. When you first become active on the Internet you may also notice that e-mail correspondents often adopt the quick style of composition an earlier generation recognised as telegraphic 'cable-ese'. Diary- or memo-like elisions abound. People skip pronouns for the sake of speed, forget capitalisation conventions, and sacrifice perfect coherence and cohesion for short, not always precisely punctuated, phrase-like sentences and unindented block-like paragraphs.

Writing researchers call these short passages 'language bits' and regard them as the basic unit in e-mail composition. This feature is also conventional in diary writing, and e-mail is also diary-like, it has been noted, in the 'intimacy' of the medium. E-mail involves a writer not merely in new expectations of speedy topic phrasing, lackadaisical proofreading, and an elliptical style, but also in a feeling of intimacy or privacy between writer and readers. However, precisely because e-mail is conversational without being leisurely, it breeds a curious, almost paradoxical sense of intimacy, a somewhat strange form of togetherness. There is something unfamiliar about the familiarity engendered here. People who have never met each other in person speak to one another on-line as if they know one another well. Electronic communication seems to encourage community, to invite people to want to get to know one another. Writers on the Internet report that e-mail can be warm, familiar, friendly – and yet also, in a new and unusual way, it can feel technical, demanding, restrictive – even at times cold. To find out from an e-mail message that a close friend has died is a very chilly thing to do. Occasionally you may find yourself questioning just how good e-mail is for the communication of serious news. Once again, this is at least in part due to the effect of the Subject line, the feel of the format, which *requires us* to shape, fit and formulate our intentions and opinions and wants and needs, be they simple or grand, commonplace or tragic, to the single word or phrase on the blank space at the start of your message.

There is another, important way in which the intimacy of e-mail is more apparent than real: e-mail is not private. Perhaps naively, we assume this to be a medium that guarantees the privacy we are used to in our traditional postal system, but this is not the case. Every local network has a system operator ('sysop') just as every newsgroup list has an 'owner.' Among others, these people are the human factor in the machinery of Internet. They are authorised and entitled to open files on computer systems, and there are many others who can see what you write on e-mail. Filtering mechanisms and guidelines and rules may or may not provide the truer kinds of intimacy we are familiar with in other kinds of writing; at most, monitoring and self-policing devices are in early and unruly stages of development. Legislation that will regulate the Internet is, for better or worse, on its way. In other words, much of what the Internet will look like, relative to the familiar and highly valued principles, rules, and mores that govern older writing technologies, has yet to be determined and formulated. For the time being, the natural expectation that our on-line writing is private is actually unfounded. Even though e-mail may feel intimate, the wise writer knows that the message he sends out into the world no longer guards its contents from strangers, no longer wraps itself into secrecy in a brown or white paper envelope. System operators and hackers and other people who know how computers work can open files, and e-mail is not private.

NETIQUETTE

Some rules of the electronic road have already been devised, and one of the more positive aspects of your membership in on-line communities is the general openness about conventions and expectations you will find on the Net. One way to find explicit codification of what is expected of you as a writer and speaker, listener and reader in cyberspace, is to search out and read the files called 'Netiquette.'

Until now, an electronic screen meant usually meant one thing to most people: television, and passive viewing. You could slouch on the couch and still get the most of whatever the medium had to offer. Unlike television however, and word processing, e-mail is very highly interactive. Because of this, it is possible that e-mail is having the general effect of making people more mannered, more consciously aware of the DOs and DON'Ts of situations, more concerned about a system of etiquette governing conversation. Indeed, various versions of a 'Netiquette' file have shown up across the Internet.

Such a file consists of a list, sometimes long, of suggestions and guidelines meant to govern individual participation in news, discussion or 'chat' groups, and interactive sessions. It is often to be found alongside the FAQ (Frequently Asked Questions) sheet in the file archives of USENET newsgroups and Listserv mailing lists.

Finding Out About the Rules

One of the more interesting, useful, and considerate features of the Internet is the close attention people give to the conventions of membership and participation in e-groups. On the Net, people take care to tell each other how to do something and how to behave while doing it. Someone once said that all the rules on the Internet come down to one: 'Don't waste computer resources, and don't be rude' (*The Idiot's Guide to the Internet*. Indianapolis, IN: Alpha Books, 1994: 357). Although accurate, this is a bit too concise. As different kinds of writing situations have proliferated on the Net, specific rules and regulations have multiplied. Providers are usually quick to make guidelines readily available, especially because astounding numbers of people are joining the Internet every new day.

America On Line, for instance, posts its 'Rules of the Road' where they can be perused at no cost to the subscriber, in the Members' On-line Support department. If you use a commercial provider like AOL or many others, there will be ample opportunities to download the rules governing conversation in news groups and discussion lists. Generally speaking, then, explicit guidelines are available; they are to be found close to the front end or beginning of any system or service's user shell. It's usually one of the first things you see, in other words, whenever you join or subscribe to a group.

At your university, the best place from which to retrieve a 'Netiquette' file is probably from the nearest Gopher site. Gopher, a program developed for the Macintosh computer at the University of Minnesota, has been very widely adopted among university computer centres because it makes 'cruising' the Internet a matter of following a menu rather than knowing a machine language. If your school or college's computer centre maintains a Gopher site, it is likely that you will find some version or another of 'the rules of the road' for the information highway, such as 'Netiquette,' therein.

You may simply read the file there at the site, or have it sent to you. If you have a Windows gopher client then you can use WS Gopher to send this file to your account. Usually an 'M' command will send a file to any address you specify. If you need help doing this, you might seek out one of the resident experts on the technical support staff of your college's computer centre.

One of the most popular and widely disseminated collections of rules and regulations was put together by Arlene Rinaldi at Florida Atlantic University. If you have a WWW browser (which provides access to the World Wide Web as well as Gopher), you can read this document, 'The Net User Guidelines and Netiquette', in a hypertext format at this URL: http://www.fau.edu/rinaldi/netiquette.html.

Everyday conversation has always had rules of politeness: guidelines, both tacit and explicit, which serve to protect members of speech communities from each other's aggressions and from the intrusion of outsiders. Defensiveness and gate guarding, however, are among the more dispiriting of group behaviours, and despite the 'flaming' (angry *ad hominem* attacks) and 'spamming' (intrusive commercial advertising) that do go on, there is good news about human nature on the Net. Generally speaking, there is not quite enough bad behaviour to gratify the cold heart of the cynic. To the contrary – still speaking generally – there is a noticeable spirit of cooperation abroad, a lively tradition of tolerance and a quick aversion to restrictions. Active participation among members is highly valued in news groups, so politeness has many purposes. A Net-community works the same way as any other community in that its expectations are formalised as conventions. In any kind of community then, when outsiders become insiders they apprehend the rules of behaviour of the group they wish to join. Learning the rules is in many ways the same thing as learning to speak the language of the group – and that ties your participation in a community to the kind of participatory writing we have been studying here.

LANGUAGE BITS AND INFOGLUT

Especially at the present moment when the new technology and its languages and media of interaction are young (as they will be for quite some time to come), writing on the Internet is more technical than other kinds of writing, in this sense: to feel the format you must get to know the machine. The ways you interact with the machine on the Net will indeed become more recognisable and familiar. But until these various interfaces become more like the standardised dashboard on the automobile, i.e. more unobtrusively transparent (or even wholly 'user-friendly', if such is possible), a writer will have to accommodate the Internet by learning to use the computer.

Needless to say, this affects the way we think and talk about writing. To some extent then, any participation in USENET, discussion lists and the World Wide Web involves one in technical talk, or 'techno-rhetoric', as some communication theorists on the electronic frontier like to call it. Even now, however, as near as we yet are to the complicated origins of the docuverse, it is safe to say that just about anyone who wants to write on the Internet can with some effort find out all that they need to know. What makes this possible, as we shall see in gradually greater detail throughout the rest of this chapter, is the World Wide Web.

There are two principal features in the writing that typically takes place on discussion lists and USENET newsgroups. First, when you write you compose in quasi-colloquial 'lexia,' or language 'bits', and then the machinery of the computer and the people on the network do more of the work of writing: developing, clarifying, unifying the meanings that belong to everyone. Second, if you are bookish by disposition and like to read and write in traditional ways, you will have to deal with infoglut.

Infoglut is a term for a condition we must acknowledge sooner rather than later. It denotes a kind of cyberspatial agoraphobia, a more or less natural, all-too-human vulnerability in front of too-much-of-everything. And already on the Net there is too much of everything. As a kind of fear of open spaces, in other words, infoglut preys upon a flaw, if you will, in our innate sense of perceptive balance. It attacks the gyroscopic capabilities of the mind to fix field upon ground, to attend, concentrate, or focus upon that which is most immediately under the nose. It takes form on the Internet and elsewhere as a reflex reaction against gross over-abundance; or conversely, in the face of excess, surfeit, *copia*, a surrendering of attention to regressive distraction. You either turn off the machine and stay away from it, or you surf the Net without purpose or point.

As anyone new to the Net will tell you, *some* surfing for kicks is okay. To cruise around the World Wide Web on Netscape – clicking on the mouse . . . glancing at the next screen . . . pointing to another hotspot . . . clicking on the mouse – is a good way to find out about the Internet and how to use it. But like teenagers driving around in their parents' car, soon enough you feel like there's 'nothing to do'. Infoglut is a serious problem for a writer because, as Sven Berkerts has pointed out, it strains 'durational thinking'. There are few things more powerfully mesmerizing than the speed with which the sights and sounds can change on the World Wide Web. And you are likely to encounter some form or another of infoglut on your first tentative excursions into cyberspace, even on a mere search for news or discussion groups.

According to some students of the new communications

technologies, the greatest challenge to our customary habits of reading and writing on the Internet is the huge volume of information we expose ourselves to simply by venturing onto the Net. Indeed some writers talk about a fundamental redefinition of 'literacy' for the next century as the learned or learnable capability of handling huge amounts of interconnected, unfiltered information. A quick glance at the long catalogues of Listserv lists and USENET groups at Tile.Com or on Netscape shows that currently there are about 18,000 USENET groups alone. Many people report a feeling of being overwhelmed by the sheer load of messages when they first subscribe to mailing lists or visit news sites. How can so many people have so much to say about so many different things? If the mere sight of the lists on USENET seems overpowering, so also will you feel this pain when you turn on your computer and log on to your e-mail account to discover that a hundred, or perhaps even several hundred, new messages have come in overnight on the mailing list you have subscribed to.

Infoglut is serious because it could drive you away from the Net or swallow you up into it. After one or two bad experiences you may never want to learn to write with the new technologies and then shun them altogether; or, after one or two of the wrong kind of good experiences you might get lost in the distraction of amazing details and immerse yourself in the MTV-like flash and noise of Web surfing. In the face of too-much-of-a-good-thing, you must not feel overwhelmed (principally by learning to read Subject lines and using the 'delete' key); you must not let the machine use you (by following distracting links into other subjects instead of concentrating on topical configurations of your own design); and finally and more positively, you should teach yourself to actually make use of the awesome fact of interconnectedness on the Net (by familiarising yourself with the feel of the format).

Unlimited interconnectedness in writing may be potentially overwhelming at first, but if you know how to write on the Internet – which means that you must find out how it feels to write on the Internet – you will use the machine more than it uses you. You will find that the power to make and follow connections can make you see and perform the act of writing in exciting new ways.

Despite the dangers of 'drift' or 'float', the good news here is that the last thing you are on the Internet is alone. Good minds have already set themselves the task of hacking paths and charting courses through the vastness and density of this new domain. Universal filtering programs, web-wide indexes, automatic retrieval, searching, sorting and filing applications – all kinds of powerful devices for making use of the Internet are beginning to appear. Already many of these are distinctly user-friendly. They are maintained by authoritative people: Net pioneers and first generation developers, individual inventors and corporate enterprises, public-spirited innovators and commercial entrepreneurs.

SEARCHING FOR WHAT INTERESTS YOU

There are literally thousands upon thousands of places to find an ongoing discussion on the Internet; therefore an integral part of any writing process on the Net is a capability to make use of the means of accessing things. Different categories of conversation have arisen on different services. On Compuserve, for instance, discussions are called 'forums'. Different commercial providers will have different interfaces, but directly on the Internet conversations take place principally in the form of USENET newsgroups or e-mail discussion lists maintained by a Listserv or Listproc system (a central computer that automatically manages the flow and distribution of messages on a mailing list).

The common element to both kinds of conversation is the posting of notes where other people can see, read and respond to them. On a certain level of scale then this is a very interesting development for everyday writers. What it means is rather profound; what it means is instant publication; it means spontaneous readership. To write to a newsgroup or on a discussion list is to have a public, a real one. To write with pen and paper or typewriter or word processor is to write alone in your room with an imagined audience. To write on-line is to write alone in your room with a real audience.

An on-line audience is, furthermore and perhaps paradoxically, not really an audience – or no longer merely an audience – which is to say that your readers are not going to be *passive*. When people subscribe to a newsgroup on Usenet they visit a site and leave e-mail messages for others to read *and respond to*. This is new. When you write, you will have readers who write back. And this they will do more or less immediately, relative to the turnaround time you might be used to if you are one of those heretofore special writers in possession of a wide, real, anonymous, passive, large readership.

Along with newsgroups there are thousands of mailing lists on the Internet dedicated to thousands of occupations and preoccupations, professions and confessions, jobs and hobbies, diversions and even perversions. Every conceivable human interest has its place here. Contemplate for a moment your own interests. Think upon your passion, muse upon your bliss, and then get ready to be surprised at how many other people in the world, the virtual world now at your fingertips, are as crazy to talk, read and write about it as you are.

Once again, Gopher is a good place to begin searching out a conversation you may want to join. Quite often a local Gopher site will support a directory of newsgroups and mailing lists. The very best place to begin is not with Gopher however, but in the realm of something far more old-fashioned: word of mouth. Look about you in real time and space and ask your friends and colleagues what lists they know about and like.

If word of mouth seems folkloric or old fashioned, and if you are willing to be your own cyber-librarian, as it were, you can be systematic and exhaustive and absolutely up-to-the-minute with everything out there in virtual space. There exists a supra-bibliographic lists of lists, maintained by Listserv, and there are several ways of getting access to it. If you do not want to limit yourself to some speciality or specific topic, you can eschew all selectivity for the closest thing to totality on the Internet by consulting this single giant roll of e-addresses. Almost mythic in proportion, this catalogue contains nothing less than the 'Whole Thing' – every last Listserv discussion list on the Net. You can have it sent to you by sending the message 'list global' to listserv@listserv.net. Be warned, however, that this comprehensive register of lists is very long, long enough to blow out the seams of your allotted space on a server's hard drive. This is a fine way to attract the wrath of your provider and it will put you on less than best terms with the other people sharing your server's hard drive with you.

To save your good name and the integrity of your account you should narrow your search to a specified topic. If you are interested in a specifically academic line of talk, you can send an e-mail note to listserv@kentvm.kent.edu, consisting of this one line command:

'get acadlist readme'. For more (and indeed all) general topics, you can send the command 'lists global /keyword' (where keyword is a term like 'eighteenth century' or 'fifties sitcoms' or 'cats' or whatever) to listserv@listserv.net (or your local listserv address).

Then there is the World Wide Web, the interface of choice now for most people on the Internet. It represents a plateau of sorts, a level of development that seems to have slowed the dizzying rate of change on the Net and attracted attention as a somewhat stable place to dwell a while. Through the WWW you can access Gopher, WAIS, FTP, USENET, telnet and many more of the programs that have been developed. Soon there will be a single Web-wide index that automatically catalogues new sites, but for now there are several different subject indexes. The original and still best known catalogue is The WWW Virtual Library (http://www.w3.org/pub/DataSources/bySubject/Overview.html).

There is a growing 'Searchable Directory of e-Mail Discussion Groups' at http://www.liszt.com. The most complete topical index of Web sites currently available is Yahoo (http://www.yahoo.com), which has a sophisticated search engine. Using one or the other of these – and they are very easy to use – you can find the most current version of a list of discussion groups maintained by Stephanie DaSilva. Currently her list of groups can be found at the FTP site ftp://rtfm.mit.edu/pub/usenet/news.answers/mail/mailing-lists. (You may also want to use Yahoo to have a look at the excellent overview of the WWW, the 'World Wide Web FAQ,' the hypertext file of 'frequently asked questions' maintained by Thomas Boutell and lodged at several sites throughout the world.)

The only program commercially available at the present time that will 'tailor' your subscriptions to mailing lists – automatically searching archives, channelling your messages, and otherwise managing information to your own specifications – is Infomagnet, a program conceived and operated by a private company, the Walter Shelby Group. This company maintains a Web 'Info' site that may contain the most complete of available indexes to discussion lists and USENET groups. You can access their indexes, at no charge, at http://tile.net. With the search tools found at http://tile.net/listserv/, you can comfortably research the comprehensive Listserv list of lists discussed above.

JOINING AN E-MAIL COMMUNITY

A subscription to an e-mail discussion list means that messages are sent to every subscriber's e-mail address. When you join a list your messages wait in rows of files for your next log-in session, at which time you exercise your citizenship in the group by opening, reading, responding, forwarding, saving, deleting, or otherwise organising these messages. Your volume of mail may go up or down depending on how many mailing lists you join and on how busy each list is, for individual lists can go through cycles of intense traffic followed by fallow periods.

Subscribing to a List

Find a discussion list to which you would like to subscribe by visiting the Shelby Group's Info Web site at Tile.com. Get there by pointing your Web browser at http://tile.net. Once there, follow the menus to the Listserv section. Note that the subject categories are alphabetized and that once you have found a list, you can join it through the Tile site itself.

The standard Listserv 'subscribe' command is very simple:

Subscribe <listname> <your name>

When dealing with a listserv address you must leave blank the subject line on the header of the e-note; send this note, therefore, without indicating anything on the subject line.

There are many other commands for managing mail on a list, which you can usually request with a 'help' command sent to the Listserv or Listproc address after you have subscribed. Like most computer programs Listserv and Listproc can seem technically complex to untrained eyes, but the initial acts of subscribing to or unsubscribing from a discussion list are exceedingly simple: be sure that you have the list server's address with perfect accuracy (including 'case-sensitive' capitalised letters); be sure that you have the name of the list exactly right; leave the subject line empty; now, send the Subscribe command followed by your name, being certain that any case sensitive letters are correct and any gaps or spaces in the address are maintained.

Subscription processes follow a standard pattern. A visit to

Tile.com and the subject search 'Jazz' generated a list reference called, appropriately enough, 'JAZZ-L' ('L' for 'list'). This group bills itself as 'the list for jazz lovers'. Getting the address was not difficult, and joining the list was even easier. Within 60 seconds of the instant I sent in my subscription request I received two messages, one indicating in rather technical terms that I had been added to the list and the other a longer file orienting me in a more friendly fashion to the conventions of the list and several important commands.

That second message is worth a close look because it demonstrates a number of points about participatory on-line writing:

> Hello, and welcome to Jazz-L! As one longtime subscriber put it, '. . . This humble salon of ours is unlike anything else on this fair planet. While the ratio of jazz to other discussion may vary, we do manage a consistency and level of chewing satisfaction of which we are quite proud, and this stems from the very fact that, unlike other lists on which one might get chafed for discussing anything even slightly 'off-topic', our laid-back forum and the virtual and personal bonds which we've established have enabled us to achieve something more like a real conversation, with intelligent (or sometimes just silly) tangents diverging and converging just like they would in an actual gathering of like-minded intelligent people from diverse backgrounds.'

Several common tendencies present themselves here. The colloquial, even slangy tone ('chewing' and 'chafed') emphasises informality and invitation. The 'forum' is even labelled as 'laid back'. There is a conscious idea of the nature of conversation and community: tangents are tolerated so long as people are 'like-minded' and 'intelligent.' The mention of diversity affirms the democratic ethos of the Net. Then at this point in the passage something interesting occurs – another voice returns:

> I'll just add that if you prefer your mailing lists to be more on-topic than is often the case on Jazz-L, there are other jazz-based mailing lists out there to suit your tastes. Now on to the boring, administrative stuff. . . .

What follows beyond this point has more to do with the details of signing on and off the list and other technical matters than with anything too administratively fussy. 'I'll just add . . .' has the more important function of reminding the reader that most of the material here is a quotation. The voice of the narrator (actually the 'list owner', as the managers of lists are called, in this case a man with the name of Jacob Haller) begins to speak and then switches to another voice ('longtime subscriber'), all but immediately. This, I would suggest, is a habit of the medium. It is a microcosmic gesture toward the grand design of on-line writing. This is a primary figure, a first trope, an originating pattern of the participatory writing process that *is* on-line discussion.

The process not only admits of but features other perspectives, making them an integral part of *a* voice. When the first voice on JAZZ returns, it is to underscore the main point made by the second voice: for writers on JAZZ, subjects come in clusters; voices can be multiple; topics can be fuzzed; these things happen deliberately or spontaneously – it matters not which – and when they happen it is a good thing. JAZZ is into jazz, in other words, and if you want tighter attention to topics then you're not hip to what happens here.

If composing on-line is more like performing in a jazz ensemble than writing used to be, then the participatory ethos of on-line conversation is not to be described as empirical: letting the tightly focused object of your attention 'speak for itself' as much as possible. What happens on-line is more radically and constantly cooperative and referential: always quoting, paraphrasing, repeating, alluding, speaking of, pointing-to. To a very great extent, all on-line text is intertext. To make proper use of the technology, to let it affect the form and content of the message as it should do, is to capitalise upon new possibilities of interconnectedness. To make proper use of the technology is to fend off infoglut by taking into practical account the factor of connection and relation and reference. To write on-line is to sensibly, bravely, intelligently make use of other voices as you follow your topics where'er they go.

As soon as you have successfully subscribed to a discussion list you should be prepared to receive a lot of information, right away. Within moments of sending your subscription request you will probably see a notice of some kind telling you that you have been successfully subscribed to the list. You may immediately be sent a good deal of other text as well, perhaps the list's FAQ or a routine report of the machine's activity (which is merely a record of the 'output' utilised in getting you subscribed).

Once you are subscribed to a list you will deal with a different address, sending and receiving messages from the site of the list itself rather than the Listserv or Listproc computer which manages the mail. Something the first voice of JAZZ suggests to new members is a commonplace of list-ownership: it is a good idea to create a mail folder for the first informative files you receive from a list you have joined. That way you can refer to the 'boring' administrative commands you will need for the routine commands of the list.If the list is popular and active you will also see actual content messages almost immediately. The first few messages I received when I joined the JAZZ list concerned the Simpsons, the popular American cartoon television show. At first I wondered what this topic, the vegetarianism of Lisa Simpson, had to do with jazz music; then I remembered that in the introductory message I was explicitly warned that JAZZ was a tolerant group, friendly to the prospects of frequent topic drift and open to the whims of its subscribers. I also learned later, after I had asked about it (and being unfamiliar with the television programme) that Lisa Simpson plays a baritone saxophone: 'It all comes around eventually' my correspondent assured me.

When you join a discussion list, the first few messages sent by list members to one another may seem somewhat odd. You have just dropped into a conversation *in medias res*. It is as if you have just overheard two or three strangers on a train talking to one another about something you care about. Your attention piqued, you bend your ear to listen – what exactly are they saying? 'I know about this! Excuse me ... but don't you think? ... Yes I see ... No, I don't agree with that ... What's that again? ...'

And you're off! The first few notes will come to you without an immediate subtext of situation, so it will be up to you to interpret the prior state of the discussion before you enter into and continue it. You are of course already 'into it,' already there in the thick of the actual talk at the very instant you begin to interpret where this conversation 'is coming from'. The first thing you might acknowledge then, about this new mode of writing–responding–writing, is the quickness with which you must figure out your stance. You interpret the cues and signals about where you might fit in; you analyse this conversation to see where it is coming from and where it is going to.

WRITING ON USENET

Perhaps you have divined by now that the word 'subscribe' has two different meanings on the Internet: 'visit,' and 'join.' You visit a USENET group and browse among different discussions; when you *join* a discussion list, messages are sent to you as e-mail. Subscribing to USENET, you visit a group that designates its categorisation with its address: a group that begins with 'alt.' is for the discussion of alternate viewpoints; 'bit' groups collect items of interest from Listserv groups (and some newsgroups are 'gatewayed' with discussion lists, meaning they can be either visited or joined); 'biz' groups discuss business and advertising; 'sci' is for scientific concerns; 'rec' denotes recreational pursuits and hobbies.

On a USENET newsgroup, messages falling into these and other categories are posted for any subscriber to read and respond to. Your interface with USENET is a program – the most common ones are called TRN or RTIN – provided by your Internet service. When you sign up with an Internet service you are provided with the address of a USENET server or program, or you can use one of the many Internet programs now commercially available for Windows or Macintosh. You can find, study, review and order these many different programs at the Web site maintained by Robert Stroud at http://cws.wilmington.net.

Tile.Com maintains a list of USENET sites, as does Netscape. The great advantage of USENET is that it allows you to be more 'read only', as it were. When you go to a USENET site you read current messages, make a contribution – or not – and then go on your way. In on-line parlance, to read but not to write on Net lists and newsgroups is to 'lurk.' Lurking is a lower level of participation than reading-and-writing, yet it does necessitate attention. News sites are often maintained rather carefully; old messages can be removed at frequent intervals depending on the volume of message traffic at the site. Some sites are as slow and sleepy as neighbours chatting on a sunny porch while others are as busy and boisterous as traders on the floor of the stock market. You may have to pay close attention to a particular newsgroup and visit it regularly if you wish to participate actively.

To lurk, surf, cruise or scroll down the long list of USENET sites is to watch the world go by. The names for groups tease, amuse, mock or baffle the imagination, and the very volume of topical interests beggars credence. It's an unending column, and it's extremely *levelling*, when all is said and done – although one sees here (here or nowhere) that nothing human ever will be finally said or utterly done. For there is no unusual topic; no subject is special; not when classification runs as wild as it does here. Again, one can marvel at the abundance, the dense undergrowth, can bewail the exfoliation of verbiage, the babble; or you can celebrate this quickening of public discourse, this enlivening mess, this carnival, this Big Fun, this babble, here where 'no sound is dissonant which tells of Life'.

In front of the name of each newsgroup is a number indicating how many messages are waiting. Since the tally happens to vary so widely from group to group you can instantly see what topics are truly of interest to a general or common readership, as it were, and which attract only dedicated enthusiasts, true connoisseurs, blinkered hobbyists, true kooks, dangerous nuts and loony perverts. Some messages number in the thousands; here people post longer 'articles' and then shorter notes and queries they want to share with the world.

USENET shrinks the world. Not long ago, for instance, you talked about the popular English television programme 'East-Enders' only in the UK. Now rec.arts.tv.uk.eastenders makes anyone anywhere an expert on this close-knit neighbourhood in the East End of London:

[UNIX] (c) Copyright 1991-93 Iain Lea.Reading . . .
Wed, 15 Nov 1995 03:30:32   rec.arts.tv.uk.eastenders
                                          Thread 1 of 26
Lines 13
Re: Nigel gets her   No responses
paul.rhodes@liffe.com   Paul Rhodes at London International
Financial Futures Ex

jrouse@infi.net (John Rouse / Capital Gazette) writes:

>How far behind in the series are you folks? Nigel's married to
>her now, poor sod,

Not *that* Liam's bird. The other one!

>and we in DC are waaaayyy behind the UK.

We can tell :-)

If you have an interest in this television programme and you want to talk about it here, you will need to find your bearings *toute de suite*. Hence you must orient yourself, as you would in any oral conversation you care to join, by translating cues into the sense you need to catch or follow meaning. In this case you are, interestingly enough, tuning into an intercontinental *mis*reading: the topic at hand (see the Subject line: 'Nigel gets *her*') is transforming before your eyes. It is not *that* woman but another (the asterisks providing emphasis as the e-mail version of underlining). For the quoted matter refers only indirectly, at best, to this announced topic. This is the first note in line of twenty-six 'threads', as is indicated in the header (meaning that there are twenty-five other topics to follow). That this note is first in line on this day in this thread means that it could be a new Subject heading. However, the question it addresses has been lifted from a previous posting – that much you can deduce with certainty. Thus what we see here is another more or less characteristic mutation of topics, from who is Nigel's 'her' to the lag time in cable broadcast of the programme in the United States.

Small world that has such mutable topics in it. This transatlantic exchange about 'EastEnders' is a timely example of the much vaunted and ever-growing 'globalism' of contemporary life. It also shows the impact of participatory discourse upon your and my knowledge about other people and places. The world is smaller now, both on- and off-line. In the city, town or neighbourhood where you live, you or someone you know may lose or gain a job because of the internationalisation of vast new markets and services and goods, but the on-line place where you and I read and write is where we are going to experience most immediately the great expansions and contractions of our age. Because information on the Internet is immediate and universally dispersed, knowledge itself is almost always new. USENET taps into a world-wide current of both curiosity and expertise. It *makes* things into data and then data into information and then information into knowledge. It can transform an event, person, place or thing from any particular place into an item of international Net 'news'. On

USENET everything is immediate, new, and everywhere; general information is a kind of global knowledge because somewhere, somebody is learning something.

USENET locates its discussions in electronic 'conference' space, hence the different ways it transforms information into knowledge, and the quality of the talk itself, is not unlike what goes on in the 'small world' inhabited by the academic specialists in the novel of that title by David Lodge. The difference of course is that Lodge's professors converse busily about their interests in the rooms, hallways and lounges of their conference hotels, while USENET reader-writers fly about the world without ever leaving home. On USENET the *things* of the real world cannot be much more rapidly dematerialised, re-encoded and transmitted into virtuality; information cannot get much more superficial and immediate and widely disseminated – and yet there is knowledge. There *is* durational thinking and depth of perspective here in this conversation about 'EastEnders'; attention is being focused and concentration is being brought to bear.

People are talking about what they care about. They are exercising considered opinions. In story, analysis, and argument, they are following their bliss:

Ian.York@brunel.ac.uk (Ian York) writes:
>So does that mean that he's considerably younger than
>Kathy?

After all,

>35 would only make him about 5 years older than Ian, &
>barely older than his daughter-in-law.

So how old do you think Ian is?

Although news notes and items from discussion lists are not really ever written to be submitted to close reading, the merest inspection reveals the ubiquity of quotation in the rhetoric of e-mail discussions. Ian.York@brunel.ac.uk reveals his e-literacy when he de- and then reconstructs the substance of a previous note into a new point of information, a 'query,' as it is often called on the Subject lines of e-mail notes that ask for information. This writer obviously possesses a great deal of content knowledge about the characters from the television show, but he also has the ability to manoeuvre the shaping power of the medium to meet his needs, and that power is largely an ability to *re*-shape previous statements. He achieves new text by remodelling old text and renovating context.

Quotation is made cheap and easy in e-mail by the REPLY mode on the machine, for all you need to do is register 'yes' to the prompt that asks if you would include the original message in your REPLY. The computer then reproduces the note you are responding to, in its entirety. You then choose the words you want to make a part of the new message by discarding all the other words of the original message. In an e-mail note, the > symbol running down the left margin of a new note indicates quoted language. Passages that fit tight to the left margin without this symbol are new:

Mon, 20 Nov 1995 11:57:51   rec.arts.tv.uk.eastenders
Thread 13 of 26
Lines 19
Re: In defence of Nigel!!   3 Responses
shea@trend-analysis.co.uk
                SGB
aim2@aber.ac.uk (aim2) wrote:

>Hi there,
>I have read loads of Nigel-bashing posts recently, accusing
>him of being pathetic, wet etc. Well, Ok maybe he is a bit,
>but its not a crime. As for not coping with his problems –
>IMHO he's done bloody well! I think anyone who has been
>married for a year and then their partner is killed has a
>right to act a bit loopy now and then. Plus, how can he be
>doing such a bad job if Claire wants to stay with him?

>Give poor Nigel a break!

>Janet

Yeah ... shame he gets rewarded by getting killed off by a car bomb in a special terrorist crossover episode next year.

The ease with which quotation is managed on e-mail is the main reason why on-line writing is done in language *bits* – and the main reason why a discourse composed of bits does not lack cohesion. 'Bits', called *lexia* by academic theorists of e-mail rhetoric, look more curt and casual than they actually are. They may not be long and they can be quick, but they are important. In this medium of communication, you indicate your awareness of on-line community when – as a writer – you manage language bits so that your note furthers the cohesion of the 'thread.' By your handling of language bits you signify your feel for the format. You are writing effectively when you can produce notes that are recognisably part of the thread.

This is the case even when you are moving the discussion beyond the topic announced in the subject line and into a new subject. It is considered a flaw of Netiquette – a sign that you are a 'newbie,' unaccustomed to Net codes – to quote long stretches of previous content without intervening to make your new point, merely placing your comments at the very end of a stretch of quoted matter.

The fact that e-mail communication is composed primarily of language bits makes writing on lists and newsgroups primarily a matter of artful intervention. One of the truly revolutionary new writing capabilities of the Internet (containing truly revolutionary implications for domestic and international copyright law) is its immense power as a copying machine. Not only is e-mail a photocopier of unparalleled capabilities, it also allows people – any people – to distribute texts (just about any texts) faster and wider than ever before imagined. Quite literally, you can duplicate and disseminate information as easily as pushing a button.

Legal consequences aside, what matters here is what matters in any older writing technology or technique: your own voice. Even when your point of view is constructed as a 'thread', when your participation in the conversation is woven into the present moment as a point or nexus where messages past meet messages to come, your intentions have all the power they ever had. In any e-mail note you compose, your perspective determines – or should determine – the relationship of new to old information. If you want to be part of the conversation, in other words, you have to indicate your addition; you have to make your sources your own; you have to find your own voice. You do this by marking off your own contribution to the ongoing conversation from that which came before. In the above note the writer, shea@trend-

analysis.co.uk, is able to work a joke on the American audience of
'EastEnders' because he knows, from a previous post, that the
telecast is 'way ahead' in the UK. With his knowledge of a
previous part of the conversation he can pretend to know what
will happen to Nigel ahead of time, as it were, while at the same
time mocking the apparent earnestness of Janet's feeling for Nigel.
On both counts it is the presence, participation, or sound of other
voices within his own voice that makes for the achievement of
'writing'. [S]hea@trend-analysis.co.uk writes by manoeuvring his
voice among other voices, by exploiting with some finesse the
factor of referentiality and the function of quotation. He capitalises
upon the ease with which the networked computer allows him not
only to quote but to select and shape that quotation.

His joke takes hold, eliciting this earnest rejoinder from the next
(North American) correspondent:

> Is Nigel really going to be killed off next year? After all that,
> who will get Clare then?????

Which in turn provokes Janet to come back, this time as a
knowing participant in the joke. Again it is worth noting: her
contribution is enabled by quotation:

> >Is Nigel really going to be killed off next year? After
> >all that, who will get Clare then?????
>
> The Nigel/Debbie/Clare scenario is turning into a tragedy that
> can only be equalled by the long-suffering parrishes [*sic*] on
> Home and Away. What next?
>
> Perhaps Liam could be killed by drowning in a vat of hair
> grease.
>
> Well, it's a thought :)
>
> Janet

The main limitation on a writer on e-mail is that while you can
– and often must – copy and quote from previous messages, you
cannot see that previous message in its entirety. Unlike writing
with hardcopy in front of you, on e-mail you do not see the entire
document to which you are responding and referring. There is

some disagreement among specialists as to whether this makes Internet discourse a writer- or reader-based medium. Whatever the case, e-mail correspondents have constructed some sets of tools or devices for dealing with the quickness of the medium and its limitations. One such set of devices is an elaborate set of 'smilies', figures composed of bits and pieces of punctuation marks. These are meant to mimic facial gestures. The most common of these, the sideways smiling face :), is so widespread as to remind us of how very closely e-mail approximates speech. This admittedly silly symbol attempts to compensate paralinguistically for the absence of oral clues in the writing situation; as a sign for humour, irony, or sarcasm, it gets heavy duty in any e-discussion of topics that people care about. For a list of such smilies, go to http://galway. informatik.uni-kl.de/rec/smilies.html. There is also in circulation a long list of acronyms with the same purpose. Some of these, such as the familiar FYI ('for your information') ASAP ('as soon as possible' and BTW ('by the way') are borrowed from the office conventions of business culture. Others are plainly derived from the fast paced give-and-take of e-mail converse. AFK ('away from keyboard'), BBL ('be back later'), OIC ('oh I see') TIC ('tongue in cheek') and other shorthand referents show a certain ingenuity adapted to a cultural need. Many of these are, like the often used IMHO ('in my humble opinion'), metalinguistic hedges that allow disputants to manage tone by massaging attitudes, as it were, in the conduct of informal arguments.

These conventional devices are conversational gambits which have have arisen out of intensive practical experience with e-mail. Their purpose is to compensate for the limitations of the medium, but they also serve as a means of transferring colloquial skills from speaking to writing. For dedicated users of the Internet (and there is reason to believe that very many people indeed are on their way to becoming such), the interconnectedness of speech and writing on e-mail can be rather profoundly confusing. Some speaker-writers (Mark Hughes, in an e-mail note from the WELL, on p. 39 of the *Harpers* magazine of August, 1995) report that their speech in everyday life is now more halting, considered, and composed. E-mail writers are more aware of themselves *composing* in real time as speakers, their casual speech – now less casual – being influenced by the quick 'one step ahead' style of composition on e-mail. When you compose language on e-mail – quickly but not as quickly as speaking – an interlocutor does not see you, of course. But if a habit of writing starts to become a habit of speaking, then there is an interesting devil's bargain with technology here. On e-mail you write more quickly and with less attention to cohesion and length than older technologies, but your speech then starts to approach the condition of writing.

Smilies and acronyms and other developing uses of language on the Internet offer ways of easing transitions; they further the more or less subconscious transfer of intuitive speech skills from oral conversations to e-mail; they allow people to feel the format that much more freely by encouraging them to write in ways they speak. Like the short, single topic message notes that make up the standard unit of e-mail communication, smilies and acronyms are 'language bits'. As agents of phatic, interpersonal meaning, they help overcome the limitations of the medium and at the same time further a new kind of textual cohesion: a machine-oriented, thread-based, 'net'-necessary, community-owned 'conversation': the scroll.

When you read your e-mail you 'scroll' down the subject headings and then scan individual notes, and then read more carefully the messages you care about. When you write you compose in quasi-colloquial 'lexia,' or language 'bits', and then the machinery of the computer takes over. The e-mail template with its elaborate header and subject line conditions the immediate response of the writer-reader, and the ease of quotation, duplication and distribution of notes on the Internet shapes the larger trends of the medium toward a new relationship between speaking and writing in everyday life.

Writing takes place on e-mail as short messages or 'language bits', lexia, single-topic notes with smilies and acronyms. These and all the rest of the changes and developments that are coming on the Internet, are more useful to readers and other writers as chunks of information in a searchable, connected, cross-referenced network than as anything free standing. Therefore one need neither fear nor resent these changes in writing technology, either as trivial pieces of fragmented meaning or as networked pieces of an awesomely interconnected and hitherto unconceivable whole.

The meaning is in the *scroll*, in the lengthening and expanding cohesion of an archived body of notes and messages formulated in and by language bits. We have seen in this chapter how these aspects of a new technology take some of the old work of writing away from the individual and give it over to other readers on the network – readers who write back. This means that your correspondents on the network now have new work. They prompt you – and you them – to continue – always to continue – reading and thinking and writing. This means that the development, clarification and cohesion of discourse now belongs to the conversation itself, which is growing and changing all of the time.

Nine

Projects, themes & diversions

'Starts with life; makes a text; then a revision literally, a second seeing, an afterthought erasing some but not all of the original while writing something new over the first layer of text.'

Gore Vidal, *Palimpsest*

PRELIMINARY NOTE: THE FREE SOCIETY OF WRITING

We call them 'Projects', etc., not 'Exercises'; because our aim is to stimulate discussion and experiment, perhaps even to promote a measure of self-discovery, rather than to prescribe tasks after the fashion of a schoolteacher setting homework to a submissive class.

Composition can be many things; a liberal art, a loner's sullen craft, a parliament of one, but never a matter of regulations handed down from above. Never a dictatorship; nor yet an anarchy, for there are some rules after all − but they are such governing principles as the governed must discover for themselves, in the free society of writing.

We propose a division of these Projects into three sections, headed *Compositions, Free and Bound*; *Creative Analyses*; and *Rewritings and Interventions*. Although these sections must overlap, in content and procedures, what is envisaged here is a progression from the larger questions of compositional design (e.g. 'What are my intentions?', 'What is expected of me?', 'Are there models for this kind of text?'), through the understanding of texts as linguistic structures ('What patterns do I perceive?', 'What choices are available?', 'What connections must be established?'), and so to a criticism of design and language, a criticism executed by means of rewriting and by what Pope 1995 calls 'interventions'. ('How might this be differently done?', 'How does rewriting change the "meaning" of the text?', 'How might X do this?')

So much for the rationale of the Projects. It need not, however, bind anyone to a set content or a prescribed course. Add or modify whatever you please. And begin where you please; in the free society of writing, all beginnings are points of departure towards the same ends.

A. COMPOSITIONS, FREE AND BOUND

> I read every readable book in the house, and also most of the unreadable ones. I wrote two epic poems ... I wrote cameos of everyone I had ever met. I recorded all I saw, felt, thought. I had myself a time.
>
> Martin Amis, *The Rachel Papers*

Background. Chapters 1 and 2, and also Chapter 7, may be useful as preliminary reading, or for companion reference to the Projects suggested in this section. Those chapters touch on the question of how texts begin, on the role of convention and innovation, on writing for oneself and writing for an audience, on types of textual model, and specifically (in Chapter 7) on composition in a particular genre, that of literary description.

Then why 'free'? Why 'bound'? In 'free' composition, writers ostensibly choose for themselves. In 'bound' compositions, they respond to some form of prescription; they write to order, or, more commonly, they accept the prescriptive influence of models. In the latter respect, a great deal of writing is a *palimpsest*, a writing-over of things that have been written before. Whether any writing can be truly 'free' is a moot point; but let us see.

A1 One supposedly free form of composition is the personal diary. Then try keeping one, daily, for a week or two. Put aside a time, preferably the same time each day, for writing your entries.

Spend no more than 30 minutes.
Write quickly, allowing little or no time for second
thoughts or worries about wording.
Correct nothing.
Edit nothing, 'in' or 'out'.

Attempt, however, something more than simple annotations of
your excursions, encounters and incidental expenses. 'Went to the
park. Met Susie. Bought her a Coke' will not provide you with a
rewarding study. In recording the day's events, record also your
responses to experience, the impetus and flow of your ideas, the
impressions that come upon you suddenly.

In doing this, you are not seeking to please or instruct anyone
else. This is for your own edification. You are having yourself a
time.

Another interesting way of experimenting with the form of the
diary – specifically, of gauging just how 'free' or individualistic a
genre this is – is to find an e-mail partner for a co-diary. There is,
after all, something basically diary-like about an e-mail correspondence with a friend. You are writing quickly – almost to yourself,
as it were. Flow is easily established. Pronouns disappear and
elisions proliferate. In e-mail exchanges of a certain type – frequent
missives to a far off friend or family member, for instance – you find
that you do a lot of talking about yourself.

So choose someone you know. Compatibility is important; this
should be a friend rather than acquaintance. The only technical
consideration is a need to save your messages. This is usually done
automatically, as most programs have a SENT MAIL file to catch
all outgoing files. However, you may want to include your friend's
notes as well, just to have access to the questions that prompt at least
part of your daily entries. It may be a good idea then to 'formalise'
this experiment by dedicating a file to this correspondence. Include
both sets of entries and call it *CO-DIARY.*

Beyond this you need do no more than follow the above
suggestions about time spent on an entry, editing and length, and
the suggestions below about diary *style*. If there is anything
stylistically distinctive about an e-mail 'co-diary', it might be
interesting to compare these novel characteristics with the textual
attributes of a regular diary entry.

Now when you have had time enough, and enough of yourself

to be going on with, attempt a critical assessment of your diary, and in particular ask yourself:

(a) Does the diary have something definable as a 'style'? This is an important question, raising as it does an interesting theoretical matter. Is the notion of 'style' appropriate to any writing as intimate and wholly personal as a diary? Can 'style' exist only in the presence of an audience, a presence 'out there'? In short, is 'style' essentially *societal*? (You will not find answers to these questions; only transient convictions.)

(b) Very well – let us say you perceive a style in your diary. Then is it characterised *negatively*, by omissions and simplifications, or does it appear more positively, with recurrent choices and preferences in vocabulary and sentence-structure? Typical 'omissions' might be the dropping of articles, of personal pronouns, of prepositions, of some conjuncts, of the verb 'to be'. 'Positive' markers might be found in the recurrence of certain words or types of word, or in syntactic preferences – for instance, an inclination to 'front' your adverbials. ('After dinner, went see Simpkins. In strictest confidence told him of heart's dearest wishes. Without laughing, for which grateful, heard me out. Later in evening both got v. drunk.')

(c) Would you then describe your diary style as 'close-knit' (elaborately cohesive, see Chapter 4) or more 'open-textured' (not bothering to demonstrate links between sentences, or to present a pattern, e.g. the 'steps', 'stacks', 'chains' and 'balances' of Chapter 3)?

(d) Assume (this is an assumption you may feel increasingly inclined to question) that your diary must by its nature exclude marks of interpersonal communication – it is, after all, only you, talking *to* you and *for* you. Does it nevertheless convey a feeling of *interpersonality*? Do you appear to house in your own person a dialogic partnership? If so, how do you detect this in your writing?

(e) This is perhaps the same question, in a slightly different perspective. Subjectively, does your diary writing strike you as 'warm' – 'engaged', even 'impassioned' – or 'cold' – 'detached', 'judicious'? (Or indifferently 'tepid'?) Then in what features specifically do you detect this discursive temperature? Trying to answer this question may help you to discover something about your temperament as a writer.

(f) Assume (that assumption again!) that the diary is stylistically 'neutral', written with no external audience in mind, and with no preconceptions of language and form. Do you believe that what you have written bears out that assumption of neutrality? And is it possible that your writing has gradually begun to dictate its own terms – that you have more or less unwittingly shaped a style which then imposes upon you a kind of standard, or 'norm'? And were you, in spite of instructions not to edit or correct, at times challenged by the difficulty of saying something vividly and precisely? In short, does there come a point beyond which, for whatever reason, the personal diary stops being a wholly 'free' form of composition?

Note: It may well strike you that the above questions are all 'loaded', or, as the learned say, *tendentious*. And you will not be wrong. But you are free to resist the tendency. My loaded gun may be your load of old baloney. Think, and shoot, for yourself.

A2 An instructive extension of the diary might be a commonplace book. In classical rhetoric, the *koinos topos* (Gk) or *locus communis* (Lat.) was a succinct observation concerning human nature, behaviour, people, events: e.g. 'Man is a speaking animal', 'Old men should not take young wives', 'Law requires the assent of the people'. An essential feature of these *positions* (a better translation than 'place' for *topos* or *locus*) was that they were public property, so to speak – you did not need any technical expertise to be able to discuss them. That is still the case. The topos, the commonplace, the position to which we are all assumed to have access, is where discourse begins.

In modern practice, the *topoi* often take the form of 'one-liners' – proverbs, popular sayings, maxims, aphorisms. They furnish newspaper editors and essay-writing students with so-called 'topic sentences'. Topical one-liners are also useful to car salesmen ('Safety begins with seat belts') and writers of graffiti ('If you can't stand the heat, stay out of the Sahara'). In an expanded form, however, the commonplace is a segment of text – a few sentences, a short paragraph – representing a 'thought', or the kernel of an idea, and doing so with some elegance and concision. (Remember Alexander Pope's definition of 'Wit' as 'Nature to advantage dress'd, / What oft was thought, but ne'er so well express'd'.) In the past, such felicitous 'thoughts' were regularly transcribed into collections called 'commonplace books', the aim of this being to furnish the collector with materials for conversation or composition.

So, keep a commonplace book. Keep it as you might keep a snapshot collection, or a book of cuttings. Copy down, clip out, paste in, type up, any briefly expressed sentiment, theme, etc., that strikes you as worth keeping on file for future reference. Surf the Net, if you are one of the *wired* (on this see Chapter 8); burrow in broadsheet newspapers and supplements (for sententious pronouncements, the British 'quality' press is hard to beat); keep a pencil handy as you enjoy a novel, a history, a book on current affairs – indeed, any of the varieties of writing casually illustrated in Chapters 1 and 2.

Do this, BUT leave space after each entry for your own response to, and potential development of, the commonplace theme. See yourself as entering into a dialogue, not with a person, but with the *topos* itself. It is an *assertion* which you must *answer*. If the answer leads you to make further assertions, you must 'answer' them, too. (This might lead you to present your 'topic' piece in the form of a dialogue – which is useful practice, if you care to do it in that way.) Write quickly at first. Get the thought onto paper in some kind of shape. 'Fuller' composition – monitored, corrected, edited, 'groomed' – can come later.

Two new kinds of commonplace book

A2.1 Diary/Commonplace
Another interesting hybrid is the combined diary/commonplace book. Start a commonplace book/writer's diary. Get an 'utterance' that originates outside the self. Any pithy thing will do. A song title or theme: 'You light up my life ...' or 'C'mon Baby Light My Fire'; a bona-fide proverb: 'A stitch in time ...', 'Red sky at night, shepherd's delight; red sky in the morning, shepherd's warning' (North American version: 'Red sky in the morning, sailors take warning, red sky at night ... sailor's delight'); or a modified axiom: 'It doesn't hurt to know what you think you're doing.'

For each entry:
(1) Write it out. Change the font on your wordprocessor so that

the letters in the words of this base text signal in some way or another that this is the 'original'.

(2) Talk about what it 'feels like'. Be intuitive and impressionistic. Simply respond. Do not worry about anything technical in the language. What memories, associations, feelings are 'set off' when you read this saying? Be expansive and write a lot.

(3) Talk NOT about what it feels like but what it *does*. Now you can be more technical, precise, systematic. Analyse the construction of the statement. Is this a question, an imperative, a description? How are its elements realised? Parse it. Check transitivity: who is kicking who? (This is the contemporary rhetorician Richard Lanham's favourite stylistic dictum: determine 'who is kicking who?' in a sentence by finding the action/agency/ verb and assigning it an actor/agent/subject. The 'who' form in the object slot is, by the way, Lanham's preference; proper usage prescribes 'whom', but Lanham prefers the more informal subjective case.) What is the focus and theme? Get to know this saying. It helps you think clearly about what is being said, by whom, about what.

(4) What can you do to it? (Do it!) Make a change. Analyse that change. Rewrite it. 'Intervene' in the commonplace by making a change, any change whatsoever. Is this a change that the 'voice' of the commonplace would agree with? Describe that change using the language of stylistic analysis. With the change you have made, are you going with or against the intentions in the original message? Finally, continue revising and rewriting the commonplace by teasing out and following down all the implications of your first change. Then make another change – and another. Which change do you prefer? Why? If none, then make the change that you yourself want or need to make. Repeat the process.

A2.2. *An On-line Commonplace/Diary*

Integrated software packages are becoming ever more highly developed. Therefore the chances are good that you can run your word processing program and web browser at the same time. If this is the case, then cruising the net for useful commonplaces should be an easy and interesting thing to do.

Find the *switch*. Whatever form the command takes or wherever it is to be found on a menu, the switch is the keystroke or button-click on the web browser's menu that will allow you utilise the cut-

and-paste function of your word-processor's editor. All you need to do is start switching back and forth between programs. If you can highlight, cut-and-paste, and move text easily while you are on-line, it will be very easy for you to be able to save your cuttings to a file in your word-processor program.

With such a format as we have recommended – leaving space after each entry for your own comments – it will be very easy for you to engage individual statements in the topical dialogue we propose.

There is something pleasingly anti-anachronistic in the idea of a cyberspatial commonplace book. The schoolboy's commonplace handbook was a repository, into which went the cuttings and parsings, the epigrams, axioms, one-off ripostes, ersatz embellishments and proverbial pieces of high literate culture. It has a tradition long and fine and adaptable enough for it to endure into the brave new world of cyberspace. You yourself can make the changes that bring the commonplace handbook forward into the new age.

This involves, again, your 'feel for the format'. Your feel for the format can make this a very interesting thing to do. You are having a look, as it were, at how your mind works. With the power to make connections made possible by the new writing technology, you can set up and connect a series of observations that show you how you think about things, how you put things together, how you make sense of your world – as a writer. This writer's view of himself writing involves reflexivity as well as reflection: you are going to comment on your commentary on the commonplaces.

On most word processors you can open windows onto other files and other applications; you can open windows upon windows and run numerous programs simultaneously. With this technology you are able to make basic connections at your fingertips; why not experiment with the form and format of the commonplace? Start to regard the commonplace not as a found statement belonging to someone else, but as the initial prompt, the first word, the originating impetus for a new kind of document. If you know how to use html (hypertext markup language) or a program like Webweaver that uses html, you can insert 'hot spots' that link a commonplace to other commonplace statements or commentaries.

But you need not go straight into hypertext; you can do roughly the same thing with the usual capabilities of a word processor. Start with the original saying that you have cut-and-pasted into a file. Now add your comment. Now open a 'summary' box on your comment and say something about HOW you wrote what you did *about* the commonplace. Now find something that someone else has said in the way of commentary on the original commonplace, and comment upon *that*.

You will end up with a set of clustered boxes functioning as your own private reference system. The interesting point to make about this web of connections is how it will redefine 'privacy', 'individuality,' and the uniqueness of perspective. While a home-page, conceived of as a collection of connected commonplaces, reflects your own intuitive sense of 'what goes with what', your own associative preferences for linking bits of the world one to another, the resulting electronic document is emphatically not private. You are not being solipsistic in broadcasting your 'home' to the world. In a world as awesomely interconnected as hyperspace, individuality is now something you collaborate upon. That seems nonsensical, but only in an old-fashioned sense of 'self'. A self that you present to the world in an on-line commonplace/diary indicates the fruition of a postmodern sense of style. You will indicate your individuality on the Internet in the way you connect things. The moment you encounter a commonplace in hyperspace and connect it to another commonplace you have put your mark upon a juncture, a link, a location. You have deepened and broadened the human index, and joined the conversation.

Finally, do not neglect the possibility of generating your own commonplaces. What better source? (The exquisite Lord Foppington, in Vanbrugh's play *The Relapse*, rejects 'the forced products of other men's brains', preferring 'the natural sprouts of his own'). Some quite engaging commonplaces occur to men as they shave, and to women as they do their hair. There are thoughts that strike us as we peer into the bathroom mirror; reflections as we walk in the park or amble home with the shopping; the mind's ceaseless mumbling to itself, overheard in the junctures of the day. Catch at these fugitive notions, and while you still hold them commit them, too, to your commonplace book. Do not fret if the commonplace seems just too commonplace for words. Aim at springing surprises from familiar positions. Have yourself a time. This is one step on the way to becoming a writer.

A3 The next stage is to begin to go public; leave the palisade of writing for your own benefit, and start to address an audience – some person or persons 'out there', in the street, across the other side of town, at the far corner of the next county, somewhere over the rainbow. You do not know these persons from Adam; yet you know them because you *are* Adam. (Your commonplace book may have taught you that.)

Then take the step that leads from a diary, through a commonplace book, to a fully written-up, outward-reaching Journal of Things at Large.

Write commentaries, after the fashion of journalistic 'pieces' or 'columns', on matters of public concern or interest. Write, for example, on:

> the economy
> the state of the nation
> the state of the United Nations
> the magic of Science
> the religion of Sport
> the poetry of Fashion
> the force of the Family
> the family of the Fuzz
> etc.

meaning, Anything in the World as you see it Right Now.

As to length, try for 1,000 words and no more. Impossible? Yes, of course, but this is a valuable discipline; it is better practice to 'write short' than to 'write long' (provided that you are not attempting to summarise Proust or write a Commentary on the Heptateuch).

When you have collected one or two pieces, look through them critically and ask yourself the following questions:

(a) Are they *coherent*? Is it obvious that you are telling a tale, presenting an argument, conveying a message for readers to understand without having to ask themselves, in exasperation or embarrassment, 'What on earth is this person trying to say?'

(b) Are they *cohesive*? This follows from the above. Cohesion is the linguistic testimony to coherence (though there might be some pleasure and instruction in trying to write a cohesively incoherent paragraph). It means, are the 'gaps between sentences' satisfactorily filled, the links that span the text adequately demonstrated? Consult Chapter 4 for reminders on this matter.

(c) On personality: Where do *I* – that is, *you*, the writer – stand? Am 'I' centrally involved in this piece? Or peripheral to it? Or (seemingly) outside it altogether? Are there ways of connoting 'I' without resort to the first person pronoun? (Give some thought to that one; it is a recurrent stylistic problem. Compare the sentences 'I think the moon is made of green cheese'; 'The moon is assuredly made of green cheese'; 'Green cheese, folks, is what that old moon up there is made of')

(d) Consequently, where do *they* – your readers – stand? What is assumed about the readership, its character, preferences, politics, class, education, etc.? In what features of the text is *their* presence implied? What is the apparent attitude of author to reader? (Is the reader my brother, my sister, my respected parent, my elderly relative, my lifelong friend, my colleague, the man next door, the woman of my dreams, the ordinary taxpayer – etc?)

(e) From which follows the corollary question: What is the writer's attitude to his theme, and to the actual business of writing? How can this be inferred from the text – what are the pointers to irony, flippancy, enthusiasm, seemly detachment?

These are *some* of the questions you can ask about your own writing, as something conceived in the public domain. There are other questions, but you will discover them for yourself; these will do to be going on with. Do not overlook the value of studying models. (On this matter, see Chapter 2.)

A4 More 'public' projects. It is unlikely that you are reading this book out of casual interest. You have probably come to it because you are a student of the liberal arts, or 'humanities', and you propose to write about one or other of *the arts*, whether it be literature, or history, or philosophy, or painting, or music, or the theatre, or – to put it briefly – WHATEVER.

Your prospective role and stance may be that of a scholar, preparing a dissertation, writing for a learned journal, composing your ultimately leatherbound *magnum opus* – and that is a trade with its own secrets. On the other hand, you may aspire to the decent status of the columnist or day-to-day essayist, whose writings may be ephemeral but involve, nevertheless, study and skill. Take that stance, for practice' sake, and begin by examining some reputable periodicals and news-sheets, paying close attention to the language and structure of *review* articles and notices: book reviews, theatre and cinema reviews, reviews of operas, of concerts (classical, jazz, 'pop'), of CDs and albums, of TV programmes.

Supposing that you have chosen to study varieties of style and structure in book reviews, what do you consider to be the importance, and usual position in the text, of:

(a) General remarks about the author and his/her work: some placing of this subject in a general field.
(b) An outline of the content of the book – in fiction, of the plot, in non-fiction of the substance of the argument.
(c) An evaluation of the content / the plausibility of the tale / the depth of characterisation / the conduct and persuasiveness of the argument.
(d) A particular critique of language and style (in expositions, descriptions, representations of dialogue).

Most book reviews will cover these matters; some will go on to cover more.

Write, now, (right now), a review of a chosen book/film/ concert/exhibition of paintings/piece of architecture. The world is wide, and relentlessly busy; there is a great deal around us to read, see, hear, appreciate, criticise. Then ask yourself:

(a) What is the impression of 'stance' in this review? Is it warmly involved or coolly detached? Is this what I intended, or is the text speaking against me? (Writers often speak of a strange counter-current in some writings, when things 'come out differently'.) How have I conveyed my (intended) stance? (Reference to Chapter 5, on 'penning', and Chapter 6 on words in appropriate places, may help here.)
(b) In writing this review, have I tried to tell the reader as much as I am able to convey about the book, film, etc.? Or have I used the ostensible matter of the review as a base or starting point for an excursion into an interesting field of enquiry? Is the subject of my piece a book (etc.)? Or is it me writing about a book

(etc.)? Or yet further, is it me writing about me writing about a book (etc.)?

(c) Taking my review(s) as evidence of a general compositional skill (practice, they say, makes perfect), do I discern in them smaller, constituent skills? – for example, the ability to present the essentials of an argument, to analyse a style, describe emotional responses or sensory impressions, summarise a plot? (On plot summaries, see Project B17 (p. 217), in our section *Rewritings and Interventions*).

SUMMARY OF PROJECTS, SECTION A

Keep a diary; start to create a commonplace book; write a journal on social and political themes; write reviews and discussion pieces on the arts. Add to these any other theme that takes your fancy – Tourism and Travel, the World Wide Web, Fashion, Sport, Photography.

Query: 'How can I find something to write about?'
Answer: *Write about anything.*
Query: 'How do I know what I want to write about?'
Answer: *Write about what you want to know.*

Writing is *heuristic*. It enables you to discover things, about the world and about yourself. You will learn nothing by not writing – except how not to write. So write: have yourself a discovery.

The purpose of the Projects suggested in this first section has been to proceed through types of 'free' composition, into the varieties of 'bound', model-governed writing: or from 'private' to 'public' composition. These studies should have raised (by reiteration) at least one important point for discussion: how 'free' can writing really be, and where can a line be drawn between the 'private' and the 'public'? These questions will recur as we turn to consider technical matters.

B. CREATIVE ANALYSES

Still thro' the rattle, parts of speech were rife
Browning, *A Grammarian's Funeral*

The word 'analysis' no doubt suggests some abstract process, dry to the point of aridity; but to analyse phenomena and experience is a necessary human activity, without which we would be bewildered patients in life, lacking understanding and judgement. It can even be a creative art, showing what might be done, offering guidance through the mazes of choice; and that is our purpose here, in the second group of Projects. In the thought and imagination of Browning's dying grammarian, the 'parts of speech', those tarnished classroom counters, were *rife*, like growing plants and living organisms; they were evidence of an invisible world of energy and creativeness. Then let conjunctions, clauses, participles, paragraphs, etc. be similarly *rife* in our creative study of composition.

Background

The Projects are related in the main to the content of Chapters 3–6. The student should also keep certain books at hand, as 'desk volumes'. Acquire, therefore, a guide to English usage; a good desk dictionary; a thesaurus; and a reliable 'reference grammar', that is, one that gives a lucid and fairly comprehensive description of grammatical forms and functions. Some guidance on these matters is given in the Bibliography.

B1 The pattern of the paragraph. Here is a paragraph from a *Guardian* editorial (4 August 1996). The story in the background is that of the Metropolitan Police Commissioner, a Mr Paul Condon, who had given widespread offence with his claim that 'very many of the perpetrators of muggings are young black men'. Commenting on the letter in which these words occur, the *Guardian* editor writes:

First, the wording inflames racial prejudice and is ammunition for the populist right. From the suggestion that most muggers are black, people conclude that most black men are muggers – which is blatantly false. Condon now says that only a small minority are involved. He should have done that originally. Second, crime and unemployment are strongly linked. Afro-Caribbean people are disproportionately poor and out of work – over 60 per cent of young black men in London are jobless, compared to 24 per cent of young white men. Third, it makes it harder to work with ethnic minorities. To his credit, Condon has done much to tackle racial prejudice within police ranks. But the history of racism by members of his police force will take time to overcome. Members of ethnic minorities in London still believe – rightly or wrongly – that the police are prejudiced against them, and an unqualified remark like Condon's is bound to increase tension.

Examine the patterning of this paragraph. Is one pattern followed throughout, or is there any changing or admixture of patterns? What are the executive devices – the types of word or phrase that bring the reader through the text? Is this pattern effective, or could the paragraph be written on a different plan? If you think so, attempt such a rewriting.

B2 Continue the foregoing Project by discussing, analysing, and possibly re-casting the two following examples of 'leader' or 'commentary' composition. In the first, an editor criticises proposals made by a British Home Secretary (Mr Michael Howard) for the stricter control of immigration:

(i) But then let us get this question absolutely into perspective. Yes, there is a mounting refugee problem in the world as a whole. Yes, modern communications make it easier for refugees to travel huge distances to seek asylum and impose inevitable burdens upon the countries which the refugees seek to enter. But no, the dangers of Algeria, Sri Lanka and many others are not imagined. No, it is not good enough to respond to the phenomenon by each nation barring its doors. No, the burdens faced by the 'host' countries cannot be seriously spoken of in the same breath as the burdens faced by those who seek to enter them. No, Britain is not a 'magnet' for the rootless and wretched of the world, as even the most cursory study of European, and in particular of German, responses to such movements of population would prove beyond doubt. No, Britain's laws are not more lax than those of comparable countries. And yes,

Michael Howard is fanning these issues into flame for purely party political reasons. He is playing the race card and as a recent descendant of refugee immigrants he ought to be ashamed of himself – and doubtless would be, if a capacity of embarrassment formed any part of his character.
(*Guardian* 25 October 1995)

In the second, a commentator describes the 'millions of young people who share a few of the prevailing nostrums':

(ii) They are not ideologues: rather the reverse. They are pretty sceptical of, and pretty bored by, conventional politics (because it barely acknowledges their existence in terms they recognise). They are men and, *crucially*, women of education and aspiration who are redefining what living together means, and thus what marriage means, if anything. Their concepts of family life have nothing to do with Pride and Prejudice. They have scant connection with organised religion, or indeed with any multidisciplinary organisation. But they aren't remotely selfish – on the contrary, they throw themselves into causes where something may be accomplished. They care, but not to order. They are individuals, not party hacks.

Compare these extracts, one with another, and compare both with the *Guardian* paragraph cited in B1. Do you perceive similarities, (a) of procedure, in the way the arguments are marshalled, and (b) of 'stance', the writer's general tone and the attitude to the task in hand? If there is a common stance here, how would you define it?

As an experiment, transcribe B2(i) *without* the words 'Yes' and 'No'. What does the experiment tell you about the stylistic function and importance – the *value*, if you will – of those words in this passage?

B3 Here are a dozen sentences, roughly jotted down as preliminary notes for a short piece on Writing and Political Correctness:

1. The demand for PC nags at the modern writer.
2. Some grow very nervous about it.
3. They monitor their own usage anxiously, always fearing to give offence.

4. Others care less for language in particular than for intention in general.
5. Their argument is that ... [supply an argument – briefly].
6. These positions are surely not irreconcilable.
7. Good intention is demonstrated by expressions which are exact and appropriate.
8. But some lapses of particular expression may be excused if good intention is perceived.
9. Something must depend on the reader's good will.
10. A racist/sexist reader can create, by imputation, a sexist/racist writer.
11. The phrase '*raising* consciousness' has a conceivable counterpart in '*attributing* consciousness'.
12. Then in clear cases, censor; in doubtful cases, give the benefit of the doubt.

The first object is to 'write up' this rough material, turning it into a finished presentation. You are not obliged to respect scrupulously the wording of these sentences (they are no more than jottings), nor need you hesitate to supply them with all the apparatus of linkage and paragraph-patterning. If you wish, you are free to interpolate additional sentences, to expand the argument or make smoother, more plausible transitions from point to point.

So, write the piece. Then consider: have you written it as one paragraph?; or two?; or more than two? Use this small incidental enquiry as an aid to answering the question 'What is a paragraph?' – which you may now wish to re-phrase as 'What are the circumstances that demand, or justify, or create the concept of, a paragraph?'

Try making several drafts of the piece, noting the grammatical forms – in particular the linking and highlighting devices – that become prominent or semantically relevant as different versions take shape.

B4 Coherence, cohesion, sentence-variation. The editorial from which B2(i) is taken begins with the following paragraph:

Muggings are scary crimes; they're on the increase, and police have a poor record in clearing them up. If Operation Eagle Eye – launched yesterday by the Metropolitan Police Commissioner Paul Condon – proves successful at stopping street crime in

London, it could be extended to the rest of the country. What a shame then that Condon's strategy should be undermined by his unapologetic behaviour yesterday over his recent insensitive race remarks, and by Home Secretary Michael Howard's desire to play populist politics in the run-up to the Tory Party conference.

Count the sentences in that paragraph. Surprisingly, perhaps, there are only three. (But four if the two independent clauses of the first sentence are reckoned separately.) The word-tally, sentence by sentence, gradually increases: in the first sentence 19 (4 + 15); in the second 28; and in the third, 34. Think about this in connection with paragraph structure. Are some paragraphs naturally shaped on a principle of increasing weight? (for 'weight', see p. 87).

The third sentence in that extract begins 'What a shame then'. What about *then*, then? What is it doing, this *then*, just there and just then? Would the text be in any way defective if it were omitted altogether?

Experiment with the deletion of *then* and the possible insertion of *therefore* or *so* or *consequently*, or *in that case*, or *given that possibility*. Do these make better connectives than *then*, or worse, or does it matter little in this context? (Argue the choice; it is always necessary to know WHY). Do any of these suggested substitutes appear to require some re-wording of the surrounding text, or some change in word-order? (Work out the best wording in each case.)

B5 In Projects A3, reference is made to the possibility of writing 'a cohesively incoherent paragraph.' Here is an example:

Once there was a British government. It lived in an alley at the bottom of a coal mine. There, every evening the Grand Duke and his retinue passed pompously by, accompanied by forty septuagenarian cornet players. They grew troublesome in winter because of the frost getting into the pipes. But the law was passed all the same. Then the moon rose backward over the House of Parliament, while three princes of the blood royal were being turned into frogs.

As a passage, that makes no coherent sense – because the apparent content keeps changing – and yet is written as though it did. It is *topically incoherent*, a schizophrenic discourse, but it is *textually cohesive*, furnished with pointers to connection and continuity. The principal marks here are the words introducing sentences: *Once . . . It . . . There . . . They . . . But* [+ *all the same*] . . . *Then*.

It would be quite easy to use those same simple tokens of connectedness in a semantically coherent passage:

> Once there was a neighbourhood movie-house. It stood near the meat and vegetable market, on one of the town's shabbier corners. There, on Saturday nights, old films would be shown to the market traders and their families. They could be restive if the movies were in French, because very few of them spoke any foreign languages. But as a rule the show was greatly enjoyed, particularly if the film starred Douglas Fairbanks. Then the house would settle down in a mood of warm appreciation, while boys cuddled their girls on the back rows.

That text combines topical coherence, an evident continuity of content, with textual cohesion, a demonstration of narrative links and turns. This is what we normally expect from simple narrative or passages of exposition.

'Normally', however, does not mean 'invariably'. One might compose a topically coherent narrative (one that makes sense) which is not a cohesive text (one that shows how sense is to be made). Take this sample:

> Summer was a good time. The boys bought pup tents and trudged off into the wilderness. The fish jumped high and handsome, snapping up the proffered bait, whatever it was. Canoes were desired and bikes were a must. The little ice-cream man kept a bottomless bucket of Chocolate Ripple. The sun was still up at half past nine at night. School was out for weeks and weeks and weeks.

If that paragraph has a pattern, it is the design of the Stack (see p. 48). Other patterns – Step, Chain, Balance – normally require some marks of linkages between sentences. Not that the sentences all begin with the Subject element, in the form of a noun or noun phrase; the regularity of this conveys a feeling, at least, of cohesiveness. But note that the ordering of the sentences can be freely changed. (Try it.) *Position* (see p. 91) is not a critical factor here, though it is true that repositioning a sentence can change the scheme of prominence in the text, and so affect the reader's interpretation of it.

NOW – for a challenge –

1. Use your powers of invention to write a 'cohesively incoherent' paragraph. Go ahead, fantasise. It can be a piece of crazy narrative, a wayward description, a deranged argument. [Here a point for reflection: How often, on examination, does that confident public argument – the editorial column or the political speech – turn out to be cohesively incoherent?]

2. Then invent a narrative/description/argument which is both topically coherent *and* textually cohesive.

3. Then try writing a text which is non-cohesive but topically coherent (like the passage above beginning 'Summer was a good time').

For general discussion: What is the importance of *cohesion*, (a) in argument or in the discussion of social/political/philosophical topics, and (b) in fiction, in oratory, or in any form of 'affective' rhetoric that is, language designed to appeal to the emotions?

A further Project, for 'free' composition: Write a story, the stylistic feature of which is to be a fluctuating state of cohesion and cohesiveness, a wandering in and out of connectedness and consequence. Write the story in the first person. Your narrator is a teenager/a shop assistant/a busy, bothered mother of four/a senior citizen. Include speech and dialogue, if any, in the run of the text, without quotation marks (e.g. I'm working in my garden. Hullo, how are you? The sky's as blue as the Virgin's gown. As if I would speak to the likes of him, or ever have done). A thousand words, or fifteen hundred at the most. Plot? You're on your own, my friend. Do you want us to do *all* the work for you?

B6 More about sentence connection: the gap-filling game. Here is a text of peculiar incoherence – 'peculiar' in that it clearly relates to the same topic throughout, yet appears to contradict itself, abruptly, at almost every juncture:

The piece was a success. It was a distinguished failure. Reviews were uniformly hostile. The show closed after three weeks. The backer had a drink problem. There was some consolation for the writer. Very few people got to see this play. Everyone was talking about it. It was a triumph.

The trick is, to convert this into a textually coherent and topically cohesive text, without changing the wording and order of the constituent sentences, other than by inserting into each sentence an appropriately connective word or phrase. Choose from the following list:

> however, nevertheless, in a way, yet, consequently, therefore, taking one thing with another, thus, as a result, all in all, furthermore, moreover, after all, all the same, of sorts, of a kind, in that respect, on the other hand, by contrast, actually, though, unfortunately, in the event, admittedly, then, but for that matter, surprisingly, to everyone's astonishment.

When you have solved the problem once, try again with a different set of connectors. Does a different overall sense emerge?

B7   More on connectors and the 'flow' of the text. I am (let us say) a social historian, and I sit down to write a piece on the mood of Britain in the year 1914, at the outbreak of the First World War. I begin with some disconnected jottings of things as they occur to me:

> Aug. 1914 − overheated patriotism − finished by Christmas − Bank Holiday mood − straw boaters − recruitment queues − Germany v. strong − 4 yrs fighting − Somme, Yprès &c − Armistice at last − irony of 'over by Christmas'.

On this basis I begin to shape a text:

> At the outbreak of war in 1914, the mood in Britain was one of almost imbecile enthusiasm. It would all be over by Christmas. An August Bank Holiday feeling was in the air. Men in straw boaters waited patiently in line at the recruiting centres. Germany was not easily defeated. Four years of bitter fighting followed. Few of the August volunteers would survive Mons, the Somme, Yprès, Loos, Passchendaele. The Kaiser's heroically stubborn armies at last laid down their arms. It was not over by Christmas.

I am not hugely impressed with this as a text. It does not read well; it is what students sometimes call 'jerky'. I need to unjerk it, to work in some smoother transitions. I revise, therefore:

> At the outbreak of war in 1914, the mood in Britain was one of almost imbecile enthusiasm. There was an August Bank Holiday feeling in the air, among those men in straw boaters waiting patiently in line at the recruiting centres. It would all be over by Christmas, everyone said. But Germany was not to be so easily defeated. Four years of bitter fighting were to follow, and few of those August volunteers would survive Mons, the Somme, Ypres, Loos, Passchendaele. At length the Kaiser's heroically stubborn armies laid down their arms; but it was certainly not over by Christmas.

This revision involves more than the insertion of some helpful connectives. One or two linking phrases there certainly are, e.g. the 'at length' that bridges an awkward gap between sentences towards the end of the text; and there are some subtler touches of cohesion, such as the change from the definite article in 'the August volunteers' (or from no article at all, in 'Men'), to the demonstrative *those* of 'those August volunteers', 'those men'. This not only helps to promote the cohesion of the text; it also indicates a perspective, the viewing position of the writer pointing at the features he is describing. This also applies to other changes which 'reframe' the piece and give it narrative dimensions of time, consequence and focus. For instance, the position of one sentence has been moved. [Find out where this has happened, and think about the motive and effectiveness of this change.] A reporting tag, 'everyone said', has been introduced. [Why?] An element of 'modality' in the verbs shapes the closing phase of the narrative: 'was not to be', 'were to follow', 'would survive'. Near the beginning of the piece, an existential sentence ('There was an August Bank Holiday feeling in the air' ... etc.) replaces the simple declarative form of the original ('An August Bank Holiday feeling was in the air'). [Query: How does this change the temporal perspective of the piece?] All these changes in some way mould the narrative and direct the reader's view of things; the account now has some shading, like a picture, replacing the flat linearity of a diagram.

It could be left at that, but we might be tempted to take the transformation a stage further, in the direction of a definable *stance*. One more rewriting, then, with nods and grimaces encoded:

At the outbreak of war in 1914, the mood in Britain was one of nearly imbecile enthusiasm. There was an August Bank Holiday feeling in the air, among those men waiting patiently in line at the recruiting centres, hoping to be off to France before it was too late. Well, it would be all over by Christmas, wouldn't it? So the talk went. But how many of these eager volunteers would survive Mons, the Somme, Yprès, Loos, Passchendaele? Germany was not to be so easily defeated. Only after four years of bitter fighting would the Kaiser's heroically stubborn armies at last lay down their arms. Over by Christmas? Which Christmas?

Examine that, with a view to showing where and how the 'stance' comes in? How would you define the stance? Could you rewrite the piece, conveying a different stance?

Now attempt to tell a brief socio-historical tale on your own account. If a prompt is needed, try one of these: 'America on the Eve of the Civil War'; 'The Armada'; 'The Flight of *Enola Gay*'; 'Nightingale in the Crimea'; 'The Shooting of John Lennon'.

Preferred length, 100–150 words. Write it as one paragraph; or, if you prefer, as two short paragraphs; or even as two short paragraphs with a brief coda, e.g:

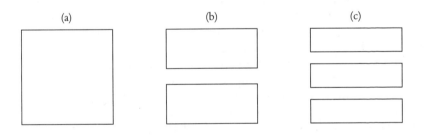

The shape of (a) is that of continuous exposition; of (b), that of theme and counter-theme; of (c) that of syllogistic argument, i.e. thesis–antithesis–synthesis.

B8 Sentences: length, 'weight', type, position. Sentences should be organised for the convenience of the reader, but are as often framed for the writer's comfort. A sequence of short, simple sentences might be symptomatic of an attempt to reduce the complexity of the material by breaking it down into manageable segments. Equally, a massing of complex, multi-clause sentences could be an essay in plausibility, the creation of a pattern that conveniently smooths over or 'recesses' incidental details. Memory – 'now what was it I wanted to say?' – commonly directs the front-weighting of a sentence; on the other hand, the management of a rather heavy grammatical Subject can often dictate the use of an extraposition (see p. 103).

The following is an editorial paragraph from a British Sunday newspaper (*Observer*, 12 November 1995). The editorial concerns the alleged inadequacy of a government obsessed by questions of financial 'cuts', in public spending or in tax. The penultimate paragraph, consisting of three sentences, reads:

> When Social Security Secretary Peter Lilley is moved to complain about the 'devastating' cuts demanded by the Treasury, while consenting to the abolition of the single-parent premium, it is clear that the Government has lost all sense of proportion. Hugh Colver, the former Tory communications chief, reinforced this point when he quit, protesting that in his job: 'You have to be a zealot, a political zealot, and it tends to reduce the level of debate.' It is a telling indication of the Tories' priorities that Michael Heseltine, in his expensive new guise as Deputy Prime Minister, has nothing more important to do than launch yet another attack on bureaucratic waste.

Look at the first and third sentences. They are complex; but in each case the stem of the sentence is an extraposition. In the third sentence, the motive for extraposing is to shunt to the end of the construction a quite unwieldy grammatical Subject. (Check this by rewriting the sentence with the Subject up front: 'That Michael Heseltine, in his expensive new guise as Deputy Prime Minister, has nothing more important to do than launch yet another attack on bureaucratic waste, is a telling indication of the Tories' priorities.' The 'telling' indication in that case 'tells' rather less when one has already been 'told' what it is.)

In the first sentence of this editorial paragraph, the extraposition comes in the final clause: 'it is clear that the Government has lost all sense of proportion'. The whole sentence would have been heavily end-weighted if the writer had begun it with this extraposition and continued into a sequence of subordinate clauses: 'It is clear that the Government has lost all sense of proportion when Social Secretary Peter Lilley is moved to complain about "devastating" cuts demanded by the Treasury, while consenting to the abolition of the single-parent premium.' The 'fronting' of the subordinate clauses distributes the weight of the sentences, and, moreover, highlights a content, a *theme* (as opposed to a grammatical Subject).

But the second sentence? Try this experiment: copy the paragraph as it stands, BUT place the second sentence in a new position, at the end. The question is, whether this shift of position makes an appreciable difference. (One difference is, of course, that the phrase 'this point' acquires a new antecedent, or backward-pointing reference.)

NOW: Rewrite this paragraph with shorter sentences. You might, for example, begin like this:

> Peter Lilley complains about the cuts demanded by the Treasury. He calls them 'devastating'. Yet he consents . . . etc.

OR: Rewrite the paragraph as one sentence. (It can be done – just about.)

Seek out some short excerpts of editorial writing that can be subjected to this kind of testing and experimentation. Fix an appreciative but beady eye on long sentences that appear to run smoothly, so smoothly; they are often tripping so smoothly up the garden path.

Write alternative editorial paragraphs on the topics supplied by your newspaper columnists. The object of this exercise should be the 'penning' of sentences – the choice of sentence-types, length, complexity, highlighting.

B9 It can be a useful aid to understanding the grammatical and stylistic resources of English – an aid to 'penning' – to compose texts at will, and then re-compose them with more or fewer, longer or shorter sentences, noting how the necessary acts of separating or conjoining are achieved. Here are two examples:

> Jack got up early. He ate a hearty breakfast of cereals, fried eggs, bacon and toast. This was going to be a busy morning. First he had to work through some important notes. Then he had to write a long report. Finally, he and Gillian were to go up the hill to fetch some water.

Rewrite this in two sentences. The first sentence of the revision should incorporate the first three of the original. The second should incorporate the remaining three. An easy way of incorporating the first three sentences would be simply to link them by means of the conjunctions 'and', and 'because': 'Jack got up early and ate a hearty breakfast of cereals, fried eggs, bacon and toast, because this was going to be a busy morning.' But you might attempt a more ambitious mode of combination.

The next example is obviously a spoof (but say, what kind of text is it spoofing?):

> Whatever the perceived shortcomings of the Government at a time when the most progressive administration would be undeservedly vulnerable to negative criticism, the fact remains that during the present parliamentary session little if any attempt has been made to address the problem of fixing in the minds of our rulers, by whatever means, some principles of decent English usage. No one would suggest, presumably, that persons heard using the phrase 'feel-good factor' should be subject to on-the-spot fines or a re-educative session in the pillory, but something must certainly be done when such locutions occur in the highest places of government, not to say in the innermost chamber of Downing Street.

There are two sentences in this purposefully pompous patch of prose. Try cutting it up. In doing that, you may feel obliged to alter the vocabulary a good deal.

NOTE: Reading tabloid editorials can provide good instruction in short-sentence writing. Take the passage above, then, and rewrite it as a tabloid text.

B10 An important aspect of 'positioning' (see p. 91) is the effective placing of sentences shorter than the norm of the text. In a paragraph concisely presenting an argument, it may be effective to place a short sentence at the beginning, or somewhere in mid-flow, or at the end. The short sentence at the beginning becomes a 'topic' sentence:

> Libraries are of supreme educational importance. Many a person whose formal education has been rudimentary or unsatisfactory has found in the resources of a good local library a lifelong

nourishment of mind and personality. It is a cliché that books are windows onto the world, but that saying is no less true for being hackneyed; when good parents take their children into the Public Library they are blessing them with the possibility of seeing things that lie beyond the bounds of their immediate experience.

In that passage, the short sentence ('Libraries are of supreme educational importance') introduces the argument, as its 'topic'. In the following, the short sentence has a slightly different role:

To walk the bookshelves, stopping and sampling, enjoying the great, colourful, gently pungent stacks as one might savour the offerings of a street market, is to look upon realms of possibility just a little farther than the borders of one's own neighbourhood. Books are windows onto the world, truly. It is just this quality of exciting the senses and the expectations together, of cajoling with the prospect of a treat for the mind, relished in advance as one handles, ogles, even *inhales* the books, that makes a library a sensuous experience, a little like shopping, and also a mental experience, a little like travel.

There, the short sentence 'Books are windows onto the world, truly' concludes the first part of the paragraph and makes the transition to the second. In this final example, the short sentence comes at the end, closing the argument:

Dr Johnson once observed that if a boy were set down in a library, with its great profusion of choice, he would quickly find the level of his own interest, ignoring all that seemed unappealing or unsuitable. That is probably true, if we recall our own early visits to a library, perhaps unguided by any adult presence, when a title, a binding, a typeface, an illustration, the possibility of what Alice called 'pictures or conversations' steered us towards choices that by and by grew into preferences. Thus a taste is formed.

In these three examples, the short sentence is a rhetorical tool, a species of demonstrative gesture – introducing, progressing, concluding. A further quality of the short sentence is, of course, to vary the rhythms of the writing, and even to temper its visual impact.

Experiment with the possibility of fluctuating sentence length in paragraphs you compose on topics of your own choice: perhaps

Libraries, as above, or Travel, or Baseball, or Music in Education, or The Ghost Story, or – as always – WHATEVER and ETC.

For fun, try writing paragraphs accommodating one or more of the following short sentences:

> The truth is not so simple.
> Would that this were so.
> Meanwhile, what is to be done?
> A stitch in time saves nine.
> The result has been catastrophic.
> To this there is apparently no answer.
> Experience is a hard school.
> Peace is not always a dove.
> Seldom have so many been so wrong.
> Time will tell.
> Today's hope is tomorrow's has-been.

That kind of sentence belongs to the family of the one-liner – the cliché, the proverb, the catch-phrase, the gnomic utterance. A political speech will usually sprout one or two, the minds of politicians being carpeted and wallpapered with quick-fit phrases.

B11 Clause elements, the syntactic order of. Here is an extract from a thriller, *The Li-Lo Man*, by Ivan Foaming. Seething stuff, this is. Hopefully with admiration note how we swing into action:

> Suddenly his brain reeled. Crazily backward and forward through his mind surged a dark incomprehension. Of what was happening to him he had no notion. Onto the cold terrazzo, as if drunk and disabled, crashed the British agent, while through the mists of gathering unconsciousness came a voice hatefully sneering, 'So, Commander Lance Long, alias Agent Eleven, for all your cleverly laid plans you have failed. A fool you are, and die you surely shall.' Unmistakable were those lilting l-sounds. The Li-Lo man, Long's colleagues at the London Lodge called this sinisterly lisping oriental, by all accounts a graduate *magna cum laude* of the Harvard Law School, whose vile machinations it was Long's present mission to frustrate. Most assuredly he it was, thought Lance, as vainly he struggled to fight off the effects of the deadly drug that was rendering temporarily but inconveniently useless his prowess in karate.

One can see immediately that Ivan Foaming has a penchant for pre-posing. Work through this passage clause by clause, looking for examples of 'fronting', e.g. a fronted Adverbial; a fronted Verb, or a Subject Verb inversion; a fronted Subject Complement; an inversion of Object and Object Complement. In some cases there is more than one example to be found.

THEN: Assume the stylistic identity of Ivan Foaming and write the next paragraph of *The Li-Lo Man*. (We suggest that Lance Long is flung into a tankful of sharks, but paralyses them with a powerful repellent released when his cummerbund is soaked in water.)

Such fooling will help you to develop some skill in working changes in the usual order of clause elements, but this is in general a resource to be used seriously and circumspectly. Practise with pairs of sentences, noting how a change of phrase-order in the second sentence has (a) a sentence-connecting function, and (b) a rhetorical 'heightening' effect. For instance:

(a) 'People are looking for indications of a final peace settle-ment in Bosnia.'
(b) 'There are some, certainly, although ...' etc.

The transition from (a) to (b) in that case is fairly muted. Or it might read:

(b) 'Certainly there are some, although ...'

The fronting of the Adverbial has the 'heightening' effect men-tioned above. Or the reading could even be:

(c) 'Some there are, certainly, although ...'

Which is the most demonstrative of the three suggested readings?

Adverbials are often fronted, either to facilitate sentence-connection, or to get an awkwardly intrusive phrase out of the way, particularly when a sentence contains several Adverbials. The usual purpose of fronting an Object or a Complement is rhetori-cal, the equivalent of emphatic gesture.

B12 'Highlighters'. Consult Chapter 5, pp. 102 for some guid-ance to the clause-forms here called 'highlighters', i.e. existential, extrapositional and cleft constructions. Then look at the passage below:

Though our early days are supposedly free from irksome constraints, it is in childhood that most of us acquire disciplines that control our lives in later years. There are, it is true, some people who in all their days never seem to have undergone anything describable as 'training'. What they have always preferred to do is improvise their way – 'wing it', as the saying goes – around any challenge life might present, any duty it can impose. It is a sad fact that such people are seldom found out in their faking. Yet there is surely no satisfaction to be had from doing a shabby job and getting away with it.

That passage is packed with highlighters. The suggested task is to write it without them, reconstructing each sentence so as to avoid, if possible, existential constructions, extrapositions, and cleft forms. [Note: Since the category 'cleft sentence' is not recognised by all grammarians, it might be useful to consult Quirk *et al.* 1985, or Greenbaum and Quirk 1990, under this heading.]

Our second paragraph is another piece of admonition – this time without highlighters:

Our beautiful beach is unfortunately not the safest of places for bathing. Often the waves are steep and rough – *olas bravas*, as the Spaniards say – and come pounding savagely into the shallows. A man was drowned in this bay, in less than three feet of water, only a few weeks ago. In such circumstances, ignoring the red warning flag seems the height of folly. Yet some people go swimming every day, whatever the mood of the sea.

Now the suggested task is to rewrite the passage *with* as many highlighters as can be accommodated without making the text read stiltedly. Then evaluate your rewritten text against the original and try to decide which you prefer.

B13 Participle clauses. For a reminder, the *-ing* and *-ed* constructions in the following sentences are participle (subordinate) clauses. They are italicised:

Smiling amiably, she threw a jug of water over the speaker.
Having dried his hair, he resumed his speech.
He launched into a thunderous peroration *while adjusting his dress.*

Released from the necessity of being serious, the audience laughed their heads off.

Be sure that you understand the distinction between a participle *clause* and the use of the participles in verb *phrases* (e.g. she /was smiling/amiably). Then proceed to study this further episode from *The Li-Lo Man* by Ivan Foaming. In this extract, Commander Lance Long, RN (Agent Eleven) expresses himself rather pointedly:

'Hally' Tosis, the fat blue-collar terrorist, leered foully at Long, and brandished a wicked-looking blade. 'Ok, smartass,' he breathed mephitically, 'let's see you get outa this one.' Long's brain was an ice-cold calculating machine. He slowly finished his double-strength Punt y Mes and carefully removed his special edition Balkan Sobranie cigarette from the gold-banded mother-of-pearl holder that contained his emergency laser beam micro-generator. Then he launched himself feet first at his opponent before the loathsomely obese henchman of hate could guess his intention. 'What the . . .?' muttered the fleshy Trade Union thug, and 'a-aargh!' as a foot slammed into his stomach, precisely twenty-seven millimetres below the navel. He spun around in convenient time for a second foot to be planted in his *gluteus maximus*, not quite as precisely albeit no less forcibly. The heels of Long's hand-tooled Italian brushed leather pumps concealed syringes loaded with enough dioxys-quamaline to incapacitate an elephant. When he was sure that the deadly drug had done its work, Long gently relieved the corpulent socialist of his scimitar. 'Guess I needled him', he murmured.

Now that episode *might* have begun: 'Leering foully at Long, and brandishing a wicked-looking blade, the fat blue-collar terrorist "Hally" Tosis breathed mephitically . . . etc.' Or the text's penultimate sentence *might* have begun: 'Having made sure that the drug had done its work . . .'; or 'First making sure . . .' Or the end of the narrative *might* have read: 'Long waited for the deadly drug to take effect. That done, and gently relieving the corpulent socialist of his scimitar, he murmured "Guess I needled him".' But would *might* be *right*? There are several junctures in the text at which participles are possible (perhaps with some alterations in the sequence and combination of clauses). Try it; but at the same time try to be brutally true to the chilled-out fighting spirit of Commander Lance Long, RN. Perhaps Agent Eleven needs no participles.

B14 Order of clauses in complex sentences: 'branching'. A recurrent stylistic option is the possibility of rewriting a sentence patterned A+B+B+B, where A is the main clause and B etc. a sequence of subordinate clauses, in the form of B+B+B+A. The construction in which the main clause leads is called 'right branching': the stem of the sentence comes first, and the other parts branch off from that. Thus:

> Mary had a little lamb, because her parents believed that children should learn to keep pets and be allowed to take them everywhere, even though schoolteachers might object to additional bodies taking up space in the classroom.

Correspondingly, sentence-constructions in which a series of subordinate clauses comes before the main clause are 'left-branching':

> Because her parents believed that children should learn to keep pets and be allowed to take them everywhere, even though schoolteachers might object to additional bodies taking up space in the classroom, Mary had a little lamb.

Right branching says 'this is the message and here follows the commentary'; left-branching says 'consider the commentary and expect the message'. Either way may conform to the stylistic pattern of a particular text.

Compose right- and left-branching sentences with the following as stem (main) clauses:

> Adolf Hitler was a non-smoker.
> Women drive more carefully than men.
> The average politician is only an average liar.
> The advertiser rules modern society.
> Professors are an undervalued race.

'Branch' material may be chosen, if you so wish, from the following list:

Being, so to speak, remote, unfriended, melancholy, slow
Despite what journalists commonly argue
Because women are in the social ascendant
Unlike some dictators who had been noted for their vices
Although men are allegedly more skilful
Compared with a writer filling out his tax return
Blinding us all with brilliant images
Whatever the man in the street might think
Brought up from infancy to consider others
Though he perpetrated worse monstrosities

In the following text the complex sentences are mainly left-branching:

When all is said and done, and whatever objections may be raised to the behaviour of certain royal persons, the monarchy in Britain is not yet a doomed undertaking. Despite the insistence of the Press, avidly supported, it must be said, by the general public, on turning the affairs of the royal family into the Windsor Show, or Disney-on-Thames, the Court of St James still manages to retain, and express in the sight of the world, a degree of dignity. Furthermore, as a result of the respect which people abroad sometimes inexplicably show for this 1,000-year-old institution, the British monarchy is a not unimportant element in the economy of the country.

Query: Could this somewhat pompous, heavy-breathing piece be improved by making each sentence right-branching? OR – experiment with this – would a combination of right- and left-branching structures offer a better stylistic option? (Answering this should involve two, perhaps more, rewritings of the piece.)

WRITE: A counter-argument, 'Monarchy is Dead', in the same style.

Parenthetical clauses – those which interrupt a large structure in the manner exemplified by this very sentence – are another kind of branching. Call it 'mid-branching'. The mid-branch says 'here is the message, but oh, by the way, before I forget, let me just say...' Now spot the mid-branches in the following:

The old Trollopean serenity of the Church of England – an

institution once described as the Tory Party at prayer – has been disturbed by the Synod's resolution to allow the ordination of women as priests. This decision, taken after a long and troubled debate, may not have immediately obvious consequences in parishes up and down the land. With time, however, the changing character of the priesthood – and there are those who argue that it must change to match social realities – will become apparent in congregations everywhere.

An obvious feature of this is that the parentheses or mid-branches can be deleted without affecting the sense or continuity of the text. They are, in effect, afterthoughts, or reflections occurring by the way. One of them, the participle clause ['taken after . . .'] in the second sentence might as well be re-positioned as a left branch. The others can only be repositioned by more drastic means, e.g. by taking them out of their sentence context, as mid-branches, and writing them as independent sentences (e.g. 'The Church of England as an institution has been described as the Tory Party at prayer. Its old Trollopean serenity, however . . .'). Another possibility might be the total re-ordering of a sentence: 'The Synod's resolution to allow the ordination of women as priests has disturbed the old Trollopean serenity of the Church of England, an institution once described as the Tory Party at prayer.' But this changes the focus and 'highlighting' of the sentence.

WRITE: Versions, with and without mid-branches, of a short text on Drugs in Sport, or Teachers' Pay, or Jury Service, or Literary Prizes, or – you guessed it – WHATEVER.

B15 An omnium gatherum. The following passage exploits different kinds of subordinate and non-finite clauses, different constructions, different arrangements of elements in clauses and of clauses in sentences:

There are few expressions more likely to daunt the hearts of honest householders than the words 'planning permission'. 'Planning permission' is the tyrannical modern equivalent of the squire's bullies or the bailiff's men. Gone are the days when the secure citizen could look out of his front window and declare himself monarch, more or less, of all he surveyed. For all he knows, there are other surveyors, right there at the bottom of his garden, measuring the ground for a finger-lickin' fish-'n'-chip restaurant, with coloured lights. That the neighbourhood can easily dispense with a fish-'n'-chip restaurant – can, for that matter survive without a Rotarians' Club House – is neither here nor there. It is planning permission that counts, and planning permission is what these invaders have mysteriously acquired. Very different is the case of the common man who simply wishes to extend his own property with a games room and workshop to the SW elevation. Though the neighbours may raise no objection, even welcoming the opportunity to do something of the sort on their own account, and given that the proposed construction accords with the architectural style of the locality, he will nevertheless be forbidden to put up so much as a Wendy House, a discreet rest room, or a shed for his motor mower. To do any of that he will require planning permission, and planning permission is what he will receive, if he is to receive it at all, only after several weeks, possibly stretching into months, of corresponding with some faceless administrator at County Hall.

First, propose a paragraphing for this; there is at least one point at which the text might be conveniently divided.

Next, to grasp something of its syntactic variety, attempt a little parsing. Work through the text and identify (if you can do so more or less readily) the type and function of each clause. Do not worry if you cannot do this with the finesse and certitude of a skilled grammarian. In any piece of writing there are stretches of text which the non-grammarian may find difficult to characterise exactly. Rounding up these mavericks is what reference grammars are for – so make use of your reference grammar. What is important is to recognise the *function* of each 'stretch of text'. Ask: what do such constructions do in general, and what is this one doing at this point in this text?

Now, as a revision exercise, consider the 'penning' of this text. Does the piece handle its content adequately? Is it coherent and cohesive? Is each sentence well positioned in the unfolding sequence? Are the sentences appropriately weighted and highlighted? What stance does it appear to present, and is this stance successfully conveyed?

Finally, if you feel you might 'pen' this more effectively, go ahead and try the game. As an aid to the cultivation of what might be called a 'grammatical consciousness', try to identify your syntactic resources, even as you are instinctively calling upon them. (Writers do not do this as a rule, but it is a technical exercise, like realising fingerings and phrasings as one plays a piece of piano music).

B16 A little about vocabulary. The general background is Chapter 6. Take a project on finding fit places for funny words. Here is what purports to be a description of a Buckingham Palace reception:

> One of the Queen's occasional chores is to eyeball some new envoy, come to present his credentials at the court of St James. These do's generally pass off pleasantly enough, with Her Majesty doing the needful to put her visitors graciously at ease. This is an art in which she has an unrivalled competence. Before you can say *Corps Diplomatique* she has those stuffed shirts yacking away ninety to the dozen – albeit with due observance of the forms and courtesies appropriate to a royal occasion. Nothing out of line, natch. Nothing tacky.

A lot of these words are out of place. An old-time rhetorician would have said of this passage that it wants *decorum*. The idiom veers crazily between the up-tight and the low-down. You are to correct this by writing a decorous text, one of sustained formality. Nothing stiff, OK? Nothing nerdish.

B17 For an exercise in comparable vein, consider the problem of idiomatic decorum in the writing of plot summaries. Here are some misguided attempts at jaunty plot-summaries of classic literary works:

> *Moby Dick*: Little could Captain Ahab, one-legged paranoid skipper of the ill-fated schooner *Pequod*, have guessed, or cared, whither his relentless pursuit of the hostile white whale Moby Dick would lead him and his motley crew of international vagrants. Only one man would live to tell how . . . etc.
> *Pride and Prejudice*: Vivacious Elizabeth, second sister of the cash-strapped Bennett brood, catches the eye of Fitzwilliam

Darcy, a cool dude who is providentially loaded. At first, sparks
fly when they . . . etc.
Hamlet: Convinced by a supernatural apparition that his uncle
has killed his father in order to marry his mother and take over
the state of Denmark, worried Prince Hamlet desperately needs
space to clear his head and get his act together. Meanwhile,
however, he mistakenly kills old Polonius, incorrigibly nosy
father of the luscious Ophelia. She, cruelly spurned by the
demented Prince and concerned at the death of her Dad, goes
crazy and tops herself. Consequently, her brother Laertes, also
insane with grief . . . etc.

These summaries are, let us say, the work of that old literary
reprobate, ANON. A feature of Anon's style is his love of
adjectives and noun phrases. List them, beginning with *one-legged
paranoid skipper*. What makes Anon produce so many of these? Are
you similarly given to adjectives? (They tend to grow on you, like
impetigo.) And while we are at it, how would *you* – in all
seriousness – briefly encapsulate the character of Captain Ahab, or
Elizabeth Bennett, or Prince Hamlet?
   Some of Anon's words and phrases call for a little work with a
thesaurus. Try looking up 'cash-strapped', for example. It probably
will not be found in your thesaurus, so look up 'indigent' instead,
and see if that, or any one of the accompanying scatter of words,
would make a better fit than 'cash-strapped'. For further thesaurus
work, look at 'brood', 'loaded', 'motley', 'nosy', 'vagrants', 'cool',
'dude', 'space', and at the phrases 'clear his head', 'get his act
together' and 'tops herself'. Most of these will not be in the
thesaurus, or even in your desk dictionary. Assign them to *sets* of
the kind described in Chapter 6 ('loaded', for example, belongs to
the same synonymic set as 'rich', 'affluent', 'wealthy' and 'well-
to-do'; 'cool' is a hyponym of 'temperament', etc). Assess the
stylistic range of these sets – asking yourself what word is likely to
figure to useful effect in what kind of context.
   Now do a little work with some model texts. That is, study the
plot summaries you will find in encyclopaedias or 'Companions to
Literature'. Try to define their conventions. Assess the skill of their
writers in dealing succinctly with potentially complicated material.
Then write your own summary of a chosen work (book, play, film,
opera). Do some parsing. Then study your own use of vocabulary

in summating, describing and evaluating. In particular, consider how syntax and vocabulary may *mesh* – work *together* – in (a) describing settings and characters, and (b) denoting actions and consequences.

C. REWRITINGS AND INTERVENTIONS

... if from this story I wanted to produce a novel, I would demonstrate once again that it is impossible to write except by making a palimpsest of a rediscovered manuscript – without ever succeeding in eluding the Anxiety of Influence.

Umberto Eco, *The Island of the Day Before*

What Eco means by 'the Anxiety of Influence' is the feeling that it is impossible to be entirely original or totally unprecedented. We cannot 'invent' in that sense. We are influenced by what has gone before – including, it may be, our own writing.

Accordingly, some of the projects in this section involve what Rob Pope (1995) calls 'interventions'; you are invited to re-fashion texts in various ways. Others invite you to attempt an original invention – knowing that you will run up against the truth of Eco's dictum. Others again are quite straightforward rewritings.

C1 To begin with, try rewriting this:

Well may we hope that 2001 will see the establishment of peace all round the world. Sure, the peace process is going fine (well, up to a point) in Northern Ireland and Bosnia, but there are plenty more war-torn places – might I mention Indonesia? and what about Rwanda? – where the peace dove has definitely not landed on anyone's roof. Power to the peacemakers, then. Their task is a hard one because, you know, nationalism rules everywhere and its grip is hard. As long as traditional notions of national – or tribal – grievance persist, making peace is going to be a tough assignment.

Is this not exquisitely bad? Very well, rewrite in the style (as you perceive it) of one of the following:

Her Majesty the Queen
A Prime Minister or a President

The editor of a national broadsheet newspaper
The editor of a tabloid
A preacher (in his Sunday sermon)
An agony aunt (in her New Year column)
An astrologer (ditto)

C2 *Textual Intervention*

To begin. How to begin? This has always been and will always be a fundamental question for the writer, especially the student writing to learn. You are in an English class, or perhaps a Philosophy, Art History, Media Studies or other course in the Humanities curriculum. You have this peculiar feeling that you don't know quite what to *do* with a particular piece of writing. This is a recurring experience: a professor asks you to analyse, critique or interpret this or that passage of writing from an important book . . . how do you begin?

Textual Intervention is a method for entering into texts by changing them. You write by re-writing. Its first assumption is that interpretation is not separable from writing, and both activities are very highly participatory. To write is to interpret; these endeavours call upon your energetic involvement in language and ideas. Textual Intervention is a technique of participation, then, and as such it is a good way of 'tricking' a piece of writing into existence. It gets you to 'play' with the origins of an idea in such a way that you start a new writing almost without knowing that you have done so.

It is a good way to *begin* to *do* things with, and to, the many different kinds of reading you do in everyday life. Although it was developed for literary analysis it need not be limited to any one kind of writing. It is even good for magazine adverts and other kinds of multi-modal combinations of text and imagery, such as the increasingly familiar graphic novel or the Home Page on the World Wide Web. It is more complex than freewriting or other basic invention exercises for getting started with writing, because it not only gets you started – it keeps you going. It is a way of beginning a new conversation by continuing a prior one. As a way of stepping into an ongoing conversation, as a method of writing through *re*-writing, it is as much concerned with revision and style as it is with the discovery of ideas and arguments. It is interpretive *and* creative; it asks you to combine critical analysis with original insight.

Developed by the linguistic critic and educator Rob Pope, Textual Intervention consists in a series of 'things to do'. These steps are well defined and intuitive, and tightly focused upon the intention to generate new material out of old information.

(1) Make a change, any change, in the 'base text'
The change can be grand or small, highly serious or scandalously outrageous. You can rearrange one tiny word or substitute an entirely different point of view. This first move can run the gamut of sophistication: take any single stylistic choice discussed in Chapters 3, 4, 5 or 6 and apply it systematically to the language of the target text; or be more anarchic: like a vandal with a can of paint you can scratch, rub or cut out the original words and spray in the new ones.

(2) Describe the change as with, against, or alternative to the base text
How does the original text 'want to be read'? Where is its *centre*? Is the change you made consistent with this intention? In making this change, are you doing something that the original writing would want you to do? If yes, then your change does nothing dramatic or drastic to the idea or intention, so we say it goes *with* the intended meaning. If not, if you changed the way the text reads so that it now reads against itself, as it were, then your change is *against* or counter to the original. Finally, if your change is neither for nor against the intent of the original – if it's just different – then you are working alongside the base text, or alternatively.

(3) Describe the change using any vocabulary you choose
Creating Texts offers you a good vocabulary for describing stylistic effect. The middle chapters give you terms for understanding what you have done with your change. Parse out the difference you have made. Ask that elemental question about transitivity: 'who is kicking who?' What is the grammatical subject of the new version, and what action is being performed, upon whom or what? Talk to yourself about this, and anyone you may be working with; tell as much as you can about the change(s) you have made.

(4) Discuss the difference(s) as preferences
You may have noted that as soon as you make one change in a text, others follow. You began by wondering what it would be like if the

text were different. Now the text *is* different – because of you. As with any change of any kind, your action has consequences. Now you must take responsibility for the change and all its implications. About that first change: is it something you really want? Does it lead to a new situation that you really want to be part of? Why or why not? If not, what in fact DO you want the text to do? Now change it again – and again and again – so that it accords with your wishes. The principle is ethical: 'Every difference is a preference.' The change you make expresses a desire that things be different. If this is not your preference, then it is someone else's. Imagine the kind of man or woman who would wish that change. Describe that person. Spin out the implications of your first move; if you discover that this difference is not your preference, change things again in the base text, so that you can say 'I did this' or 'I would do this'.

(5) Discuss your own preference(s) – and make more changes to accommodate it
Here begins the process of more extensive re-writing. To claim a preference is to take on further responsibilities and duties. What more needs to happen to the text and the world it describes? Where would you go and what would you do to find out about this?

(6) List possibilities for further reading: sources and resources
Who or what can help you explain your preferences? At this point arises the 'conversational' – and indeed the scholarly – nature of the enterprise. You are now heavily invested in a thorough re-writing of the base text; indeed, things have progressed to such an extent that you are writing rather than *re*-writing. And all such writing involves some kind of research, reference and citation. Who can help you make your case? Who has made similar changes, expressed like preferences? What body of prior statements do you want or need to tap into? Which bibliographies and indexes and other kinds of reference works, traditionally bound and now also on-line, will you use? What 'system of (p)references', to use Pope's interesting phrase, have you already entered into?

C3 In a TV review (*Guardian* 16 October 1995), Stuart Jeffries remarks: 'It was a philosopher – was it Sartre or Ken Dodd? – who proposed that happiness was just a story we tell about the past.' Ken Dodd, for those who may never have heard of him, is not a philosopher but a comedian in the British vaudeville tradition, with a gift for a mawkish lyric. L. P. Hartley begins one of his novels with the words: 'The past is a foreign country; they do things differently there.' Paul McCartney famously confessed 'Oh, I believe in yesterday'. Taking up any of these prompts or person-ages, write a piece on 'The Illusion of Happiness'. (Your piece may be an anecdote, an essay, a dialogue, or even a short story if you are so inclined.).

C4 Look up Mr Kolkhov in Chapter 5. (He sneezes in the park.) Write a story outlining the consequences of his sneeze. Follow this scheme:

- Kolkhov sneezes. He is the bearer of a bacillus.
- The effect of the bacillus is: to drive people crazy; to make them confuse left and right; to turn their bottoms blue. (Choose one)
- The elaborated consequences of Kolkhov's sneezing are: _____ _____ >
- The resolution of the problem is: _____ _____ >

From this exercise, see if you can frame any guideline principles, for your own reference, governing (a) the framing of narrative, and (b) the balance, in narrative, of description and dialogue.

C5 'These few precepts': Polonius, in *Hamlet*, Act I, Scene 3, gives his son Laertes a few words of advice on his going-off to college. Look up the speech, and then attempt to re-cast it parodically in one of the following (imaginary) styles: (Do it *in prose*):

Al Capone
The coach of the Duluth Dinosaurs (American gridiron)
The manager of Giggleswick United (British soccer)
Mr Micawber
Presidential candidate Newty B. Frutti
Liberal Democrat (British) Spokesman Alastair Beanfeast
Tearful evangelist Hiram Claptrap
Jasper Quip, the Comical Columnist

Do not protest that you never met Al Capone, or that you do not know how Newty Frutti would speak. You have met Capone in a dozen old films, and you may be listening to Frutti every day. Remember – the palimpsest.

C6 Choose a piece of non-fictional prose, some 400 words in length. (Broadsheet newspaper editorials are often useful for this purpose). Re-cast it as dialogue – duologue in the first instance, but if you wish, and can see creative possibilities, make it a three- or even four-person exchange. Use the dialogue form to put a 'spin' on the original – for instance, to project, through one participant, a stance of irony or scepticism. The completed piece might take the likeness of a TV studio discussion of some current issue (crime and punishment, owners and players, single parents, women priests, or even the economy – stupid).

C7 If Jane Austen were alive and keeping bad company today, how might she begin an up-dated *Pride and Prejudice*?

> 'Well, lookee here', said Ma B., 'there's a new kid on the block.'
> 'So?' said Mr B.
> 'Whaddya mean, *so*? Listen Benny, Benny sweetie, this guy's *loaded*.'
> 'So?' said Mr B. again.
>   ? ? ? ? ? ? ? ?

If Charles Dickens were alive and well and under the influence of Bourbon, how might he set about telling the story of *Oliver Twist*?

> I have to say this, pardon my not being polite and all, but that workhouse was a *bummer*, yes sir, a real bummer, no other word for it. I am talking about the food, all right, and about what you might jestingly call the *accommodations*, all right, but mostly, folks, I guess I am talking about the *personnel*, inclusive of this beadle, this Bumble freak. In fact, mostly of this Bumble jerk, who, I kid you not, is a right royal pain in the butt.
>   ? ? ? ? ? ? ?

Choose one of those 'beginnings' and continue, in the same stylistic vein, for a page or so. (Ma B. is looking for a rich husband for her girls Marilu and Dee-Dee; Olly Twist is going to ask for a second helping of hash browns.)

OR, as an alternative project: Make up your own 'as if', e.g. 'If Mark Twain/Louisa M. Alcott/Lewis Carroll/William Faulkner were alive and . . . how would . . . begin?

Bibliography

(In documentation format of the Modern Language Association.)

GENERAL

ARISTOTLE. *Rhetoric and Poetics*. New York: Modern Library,1984.
Together with Plato's *Phaedrus* and *Gorgias*, a key document establishing the defining assumptions about *rhetoric* in the Western tradition (see Nash, *Rhetoric*, below).

CRYSTAL, DAVID. *A Dictionary of Linguistics and Phonetics*. 3rd edn. Oxford: Basil Blackwell, 1991.

LEITH, DICK AND GEORGE MYERS. *The Power of Address: Explorations in Rhetoric*. London and New York: Routledge, 1989.
Rhetoric is presented as a continuing, vital tradition of practical language use.

MCARTHUR, TOM. Ed. *The Oxford Companion to the English Language*. Oxford: Oxford University Press, 1992.

NASH, WALTER. *Rhetoric: The Wit of Persuasion*. Oxford: Blackwell, 1989.
A contemporary defence of rhetoric: our common experience of persuasive intention in everyday language is connected to the formal 'designs' of literary, commercial, religious and political speech.

LANGUAGE STUDY AND COMPOSITION STUDIES

ADAMS, KATHERINE H. and JOHN L. ADAMS. Eds. *Teaching Advanced Composition: Why and How*. Portsmouth, New Hampshire: Heinemann Boynton/Cook, 1991.

A diverse and up-to-date collection of essays exploring numerous perspectives upon the teaching of advanced composition, including the rhetorical/linguistic/literary approach of *Creating Texts*.

BARTON, ELLEN. 'Contesting Language.' *College English* 57.4 (April 1995): 481–97.

An insightful review essay exploring the problems and possibilities involved in a confrontational meeting of linguistics and English studies at the junction of composition theory and teaching.

CLIFFORD, JOHN and JOHN SCHILB. *Writing Theory and Critical Theory*. New York: MLA, 1994.

A useful collection of perspectives with several essays that argue for the centrality of language study and different modes of stylistic analysis in composition.

COE, RICHARD M. 'An Apology for Form; Or, Who Took the Form Out of the Process?' *College English* 49.1: 13–28.

An argument for a 'grammar of transitions' in composition studies, by the author of a very widely used advanced composition textbook.

FABB, NIGEL and ALAN DURANT. *Literary Studies in Action*. London: Routledge, 1990.

A *tour de force* of 'things to do' to encourage participatory writing and re-writing in the study of literary and other texts.

FAIGLEY, LESTER. *Fragments of Rationality: Postmodernity and the Subject of Composition*. Pittsburgh and London: University of Pittsburgh Press, 1992: 80–110.

Interesting chapters on the role of linguistics in composition studies, and on the philosophy and conduct of a computer-writing classroom.

HANNAY, MIKE and J. LACHLAN MACKENZIE. *Effective Writing in English: A Resource Guide*. Groningen: Martinus Nijhoff, 1996.

MONTGOMERY, MARTIN, ALAN DURANT, NIGEL FABB, TOM FURNISS and SARA MILLS. *Ways of Reading: Advanced Reading Skills for Students of English Literature*. London and New York: Routledge, 1992.

Another compendium of participatory (reading–writing) activities.

PARKER, FRANK and KIM SYDOW CAMPBELL. 'Linguistics and Writing: A Reassessment.' *College Composition and Communication* 44.3 (October 1993): 295–314.

A pragmatic argument for language study in composition studies.

POPE, ROB. *Textual Intervention: Critical and Creative Strategies for Literary Studies*. London: Routledge, 1995.

An energetic synthesis of critical theory and creative writing pedagogy, focused upon the active participation of reader-writers in sequenced, highly developed and very interesting interpretive projects.

SULLIVAN, FRANCIS J. 'Critical Theory and Systemic Linguistics: Textualizing the Contact Zone.' *JAC* 15.3 (1995): 410–34.

An argument for the recognition of the importance of systemic language study to contemporary writing instruction, consistent with the assumptions about linguistics and writing pedagogy underlying *Creating Texts*.

GRAMMAR

BIRCH, DAVID. *Language, Literature and Critical Practice*. London: Routledge, 1989.
Combines discourse analysis and critical theory to argue that 'grammar has meaning': interpretation and writing are always grounded in particular institutions; these call for specific skills and concepts which condition language use.

BROWN, GILLIAN and GEORGE YULE. *Discourse Analysis*. Cambridge: University of Cambridge Press, 1983.
Comprehensive introductory handbook to pragmatic analysis.

DONNELLY, COLLEEN. *Linguistics for Writers*. Albany, NY: State University of New York Press, 1994.

GREENBAUM, SIDNEY. *A College Grammar of English*. London and New York: Longman 1989.

GREENBAUM, SIDNEY and RANDOLPH QUIRK. *A Student's Grammar of the English Language*. London: Longman, 1990.

HALLIDAY, M.A.K. and RUQAIYA HASAN. *Cohesion in English*. London: Longman, 1976.

HAYNES, JOHN. *Introducing Stylistics*. London: Unwin Hyman, 1989.
A thorough and highly accessible introduction to stylistic textual analysis.

KOLLN, MARTHA. *Rhetorical Grammar: Grammatical Choices, Rhetorical Effects*. Boston and London: Allyn and Bacon, 1996.
Like *Creating Texts*, a textbook that utilises 'grammatical meaning' in a writing process that emphasises revision.

LYONS, JOHN. *Language and Linguistics: An Introduction.*Cambridge: Cambridge University Press, 1990 (1981).

NASH, WALTER. *English Usage: A Guide to First Principles*. London: Routledge and Kegan Paul, 1986.
An introduction to issues and instances of usage organized principally around an avoidance of 'the usage trap'.

———. *Our Experience of Language*. London: Batsford, 1971.

———. *An Uncommon Tongue*. Oxford: Blackwell, 1992.

QUIRK, RANDOLPH, *et al. A Comprehensive Grammar of the English Language*. London: Longman, 1985.

SCHOLES, ROBERT, NANCY R. COMLEY and GREGORY L. ULMER. *Text Book:*

An Introduction to Literary Language. 2nd edn. New York: St Martin's Press, 1995.

A textbook guide to linguistic and other kinds of analysis directed toward an appreciation of the ideological power of language.

SIMPSON, PAUL. *Language, Ideology and Point of View.* London: Routledge, 1993.

A learned yet accessible introduction to recent theories of perspective in linguistics.

SHEPHERD, VALERIE. *Literature About Language.* London: Routledge, 1994.

A study of literary language use celebrating the 'talent for narration' that creatively defines, and is constrained and defined by, 'community'.

WALES, KATIE. *A Dictionary of Stylistics.* London: Longman,1989.

WILLIAMS, JOSEPH. 3rd edn. *Style: Ten Lessons in Clarity and Grace.* New York: Harper Collins, 1994.

Perhaps the most widely used textbook of its kind: a rhetoric aimed at developing the writer's ability to manipulate a linguistic and grammatical repertoire of stylistic choices.

THE LEXICON

CARTER, RONALD. *Vocabulary: Applied Linguistic Perspectives.*London: Unwin Hyman, 1987.

CARTER, RONALD, and WALTER NASH. *Seeing Through Language: A Guide to Styles of English Writing.* Oxford: Basil Blackwell, 1990.

ROGET, P.M. *Thesaurus of English Woods and Phrases.* Ed. SUSAN M. LLOYD. London: Longman, 1982.

NEW RHETORICS

BAZERMAN, CHARLES. 'A Relationship between Reading and Writing: The Conversational Model.' *College English* 41 (1980): 656–61.

One of the first elucidations of a 'community' model of writing-as-participation.

BRODKEY, LINDA. *Academic Writing as Social Practice.* Philadelphia: Temple University Press, 1987.

A notable study of academic writing using ethnographic and socio-linguistic approaches to the study of discourse.

BRUFFEE, KENNETH A. 'Collaborative Learning and the "Conversation of Mankind."' *College English* 46 (1984): 635–52.

An influential argument for an understanding of 'community' in writing.

———. 'Social Construction, Language, and the Authority of Knowledge: A Bibliographical Essay.' *College English* 48.8: 773–90.

An important reading list of sources in the "community" model.

BURKE, KENNETH. *A Rhetoric of Motives*. 1950. Berkeley: University of California Press, 1969.

ELBOW, PETER. *Embracing Contraries: Explorations in Learning and Teaching*. New York: Oxford University Press, 1986.

ENOS, THERESA and STUART C. BROWN, eds. *Defining the New Rhetorics*. Sage Series in Written Communication, Vol.7. Newbury Park, New Jersey and London: Sage Publications, 1993.

A variety of perspectives on the implications for writers and teachers of new, wider, cross-disciplinary re-definitions of traditional rhetoric.

FREIRE, PAULO. *Pedagogy of the Oppressed*. New York: Herder and Herder, 1970.

An important work in a theory of 'participatory' learning, especially relevant for the distinction between 'banking' and 'problem posing' models of education.

HARRIS, JOSEPH. 'The Idea of Community in the Study of Writing.' *College Composition and Communication* 40: 1 (February 1989): 11–22.

The first noted critique of 'community' as a model for writing.

LANHAM, RICHARD. *Style: An Anti-Textbook*. New Haven: Yale University Press, 1974.

MURRAY, DONALD M. 'Teaching the Other Self: The Writer's First Reader.' *College Composition and Communication* 33.2 (1982): 140–7.

An experienced teacher talks about writers talking to themselves.

MYERS, GREG. 'Reality, Consensus, and Reform in the Rhetoric of Composition Teaching.' *College English* 48:2 (February 1986): 154–74.

NASH, WALTER. Ed. *The Writing Scholar: Studies in Academic Discourse*. Written Communication Annual, 3. Newbury Park, California: Sage, 1990.

PERELMAN, CHAIM. *The New Rhetoric and the Humanities: Essays on Rhetoric and Its Applications*.Dordrecht, Holland: D. Reidel Publishing Company, 1979. Synthese Library, Volume 140.

———. *The Realm of Rhetoric*. Notre Dame: University of Notre Dame Press, 1982.

TRIMBUR, JOHN. 'Consensus and Difference in Collaborative Learning.' *College English* 51.6 (October 1989): 602–16.

WRITING IN THE NEW TECHNOLOGIES

BOLTER, JAY DAVID. *Writing Space: the Computer, Hypertext, and the History of Writing*. Hillsdale, NJ: Erlbaum, 1991.
Widely read account of the ways in which the new technologies are redefining writing practices.

COCHRAN-SMITH, MARILYN, and CYNTHIA L. PARIS and JESSICA L. KAHN. *Learning to Write Differently: Beginning Writers and Word Processing*. Norwood, New Jersey: Ablex, 1991.

CRUMP, ERIC, and NICK CARBONE. *The English Student's Guide to the Internet*. New York: Houghton and Mifflin, 1996.
A much-anticipated guide to writing on the Internet by two noted pioneers in educational applications of electronic writing.

HALEY-JAMES, SHIRLEY. 'Entries from a New E-Mail User's Handbook.' *Computers and Composition, 10* (1993): 5–10.
A journal-like account of the sensations encountered in the writer's first encounter with intercontinental electronic communication.

HAWISHER, GAIL E. and CHARLES MORAN. 'Electronic Mail and the Writing Instructor.' *College English* 55.6 (1993): 627–43.

HOLDSTEIN, DEBORAH and CYNTHIA L. SELFE. Eds. *Computers and Writing: Theory, Research, Practice*. New York: MLA, 1990.

HOLT, PATRIK O'BRIAN, and NOEL WILLIAMS. *Computers and Writing: State of the Art*. Oxford: Intellect; Boston: Kluwer Academic Publishing, 1992.

LANDOW, GEORGE P. *Hypertext: the Convergence of Contemporary Critical Theory and Technology*. Baltimore: Johns Hopkins University Press, 1992.
The most comprehensive example to date of the new marriage between traditional and postmodern methods of literary scholarship and networked computer applications.

LANHAM, RICHARD A. *The Electronic Word: Democracy, Technology, and the Arts*. Chicago: University of Chicago Press, 1993.
A popular exploration of the future of writing and the Humanities in the new technological age.

MORAN, CHARLES. 'Notes Towards a Rhetoric of E-Mail.' *Computers and Composition* 12.1 (1995): 15–21.
Identifies the main elements in a prospective academic understanding of e-mail's distinctive generic traits.

TUMAN, MYRON. *Word Perfect: Literacy in the Computer Age*. Pittsburgh: University of Pittsburgh Press, 1992.
A study in the tradition of Marshall McLuhan's ambivalent analysis of technological effect upon literacy and learning.

WILLIAMS, NOEL. *The Computer, the Writer and the Learner*. Springer-Verlag, 1991.

WILLIAMS, NOEL and PATRIK HOLT. Eds. *Computers and Writing: Models and Tools*. Norwood, New Jersey: Ablex, 1989.

LITERARY AUTHORS &c CITED

MARTIN AMIS *The Rachel Papers*: Penguin 1984.
NICHOLSON BAKER *The Mezzanine* London: Granta 1989.
A. L. BARKER *The Gooseboy* London: Arrow Books 1989.
NIGEL BARLEY *The Innocent Anthropologist* Harmondsworth: Penguin 1986.
ROY BLOUNT 'You can move your lips', in *Now, Where Were We?* New York: Ballantyne Books 1978, repr. 1979.
RAY BRADBURY '1999: Ylla' in *Treasury of Great Short Stories* London: Octopus Books 1984.
A. S. BYATT *Angels and Insects* Chatto & Windus, 1992.
RAYMOND CHANDLER *Farewell My Lovely* London: Penguin reprinted 1986.
G. K. CHESTERTON 'In Defence of Rash Vows' first pub. in *The Defendant* (1901), here in *Chesterton's Stories Essays and Poems*, ed. Maisie Ward. London: Dent, Everyman's Library 1935, reprinted 1965.
UMBERTO ECO *The Island of the Day Before* Secker & Warburg 1995.
GEORGE ELIOT *The Mill on the Floss* London: Collins Fontana Books 1979.
E. M. FORSTER *A Passage to India* London: Penguin Modern Classics reprinted 1979.
L. P. HARTLEY *The Go-Between* London: Penguin 1958.
ERNEST HEMINGWAY *The Old Man and the Sea* London: Triad/Panther 1976.
EVAN HUNTER (see ALBERT LEVINE).
P. D. JAMES *Original Sin* London: Faber & Faber, 1994.
PAUL JENNINGS 'Shamblers and Neatpots' in *I Must Have Imagined It* London: Michael Joseph 1977.
JAMES JOYCE *Dubliners* London: Penguin repr. 1976.
ALBERT LEVINE *Penguin English Reader* for extracts from H. Eysenck's *Uses and Abuses of Psychology* and *Sense and Nonsense in Psychology*; and from Evan Hunter's *The Blackboard Jungle*. London: Penguin 1971.
BRONISLAW MALINOWSKI *A Scientific Theory of Culture* New York: Galaxy Books 1960, 2nd pr. 1961.
JOHN MCPHEE *Coming into the Country* New York: Farrar, Strauss and Giroux, 1976.
WALTER NASH *Language in Popular Fiction* London: Routledge 1990.
ANDREW O'HAGAN *The Missing* London: Picador 1995.
MICHAEL ONDAATJE *In the Skin of a Lion* London: Picador 1988.

RANDOLPH QUIRK and GABRIELLE STEIN *English in Use* London: Longman 1990.

SIMON SCHAMA *Citizens. A Chronicle of the French Revolution.* London: Penguin 1989.

HOWARD SCHOTT *Playing the Harpsichord* London: Faber & Faber 1971, repr. 1979.

MICHAEL STAPLETON *The Cambridge Guide to English Literature* Cambridge: University Press 1983.

JAMES THURBER 'The Watchers of the Night', in *Lanterns and Lances* London: Penguin 1963.

BEN TRAVERS *Five plays* London: Penguin 1979.

GORE VIDAL *Palimpsest* Abacus, 1996.

VIRGINIA WOOLF 'Lappin and Lapinova', in *A Haunted House and Other Stories* London: Hogarth Press 1943.

Other sources:

The Health of the Nation HMSO pamphlet, n.d.

Edinburgh University Regulations for the Degree of Bachelor of Education. Edinburgh 1980.

Index A – Topics and names

In reference to topics, the instruction *see also* indicates a collateral topic, e.g. *anaphora – cataphora*; and *see further* an included or extended topic, e.g. *adjunct > adverbial*.

acronyms, in e-mail, 179
adjuncts, grammatical
  continuity, 70
  instrumental, 71
  manner, 70
  space, 70
  time, 70, 78
  (*see further* adverbial)
adverbial, element in clause
  structure, 99 (*see further* place
  adverbial)
'affective' text type, 35, 36, 201
  (*see also* 'fictive', 'objective' text
  types)
anaphora, anaphoric, 50, 52, 75,
  78, 79 (*see also* cataphora,
  cohesion, connectors, deixis,
  pro-forms in sentence-
  connection)
'anti-clockwise', mode in
  composition, 6, 13, 19 (*see
  further* 'three-ring circus')
antonym, 124 (*see further* set)
'appropriateness' in writing, 4, 33

Austen, Jane, *Pride and Prejudice*
  cited, 86, 217, 224

Baker, Nicholson, *The Mezzanine*
  cited, 132, 137, 144
Barker, A.L., *The Gooseboy* cited,
  83, 84
Barley, Nigel, *The Innocent
  Anthropologist* cited, 53
'beginning' and 'textual
  intervention', 220
beginnings of texts, examples of,
  9–11
Berkerts, Sven, 163
'blockages' (verbal), 110–11
Blount, Roy Jr., 'You Can Move
  Your Lips' cited, 10, 13
boilerplate (stereotyped prose), 52,
  72, 111
Boutell, Thomas (maintains
  hypertext file), 167
Bradbury, Ray, 'February 1999:
  Ylla' cited, 11, 14
branching (in sentence

construction), 213–14
Byatt, A.S., *Angels and Insects* cited, 39, 40

'cable-ese' (in e-mail), 158
Carter, R.A., 'Linguistics and Literary Irony' cited, 9 (nr. 1)
Vocabulary cited, 114–15
cataphora, cataphoric, 75 (*see also* anaphora, cohesion, deixis, pro-forms in sentence-connection)
'categorisation' (of e-mail group interests), 172
'centre of gravity' (in *freewriting*), 143, 144
Chandler, Raymond, *Farewell My Lovely* cited, 46
Chesterton, G.K., 'A Defence Of Rash Vows' cited, 10, 12, 13
cleft sentence, 103–5
'clockwise' mode of composition, 6, 14, 19, 20, 31, 64 (*see further* 'anti-clockwise', 'three-ring circus')
coherence, 49, 198–202
cohesion, 20, 24
    close cohesion, 76
    remote cohesion, 35
    textual cohesion, 200–1
collocation, 126–7
'columnar' text, 42, 43
commonplace book, 186
complex sentence, 91, 107 (*see also* multi-clause sentence)
compound sentence, 107 (*see also* simple sentence, multi-clause sentence)
conjunctions
    co-ordinating, 62, 63
    subordinating, 62, 64
conjuncts, 64–7
connectors, 67–71, 202, 203 (*see also* adjuncts, conjuncts, cohesion, deixis; place

adverbials, 'flow')
Conrad, Joseph, 108
'conventional' entry to composition, *see* 'three-ring circus'
Coward, Noel, 'The Stately Homes of England' cited, 34
creative analyses, 195
'creative' entry to composition, *see* 'three-ring circus'
creativity (process of), 134
'cruise', 'cruising' (on the Internet), 172 (*see also* 'lurk', 'scroll', 'surf')
cyberspace, 144, 160

DaSilva, Stephanie (maintains list of discussion groups), 167
decorum (compositional texture), 127
'default option' (declarative sentence as), 16, 31
deixis, deictic, 20–1, 24, 53 (*see further* anaphora, cataphora, cohesion, connectors, endophoric reference, exophoric reference, linkers)
dependency (subordination), 107, 108
description, literary 129–48
diary, as personal text 4, 183
    'co-diary' (e-mail), 184
    'diary/commonplace' (e-mail), 187, 188
Dickens, Charles, *David Copperfield* cited, 37
Dickinson, Emily, cited, 36
discourse, 83–6
discourse as dialogue (e-mail), 144–81
discourse functions (declarative, interrogative, imperative), 96–7
'displacement activity', 15

'docuverse' ('text of texts'), 144
dramatisation (in literary description), 134
'durational thinking', 163, 175

e-mail, 149, 150, 151
  and conventions of word-processing, 154
  is interactive, 160
  intimate but not private, 159
  'kinaesthetic competence' in, 156
  not difficult to operate, 156
  resemblance to diary, 158
  'rhetoric of', 153
e-mail community, joining, 168
e-mail groups (forums, lists), 160, 161, 164, 165
e-prefix, 154
East Enders (British TV series), 173, 174, 178
Edinburgh University Calendar cited, 39
Eliot, George, *The Mill on the Floss* cited, 44
endophoric reference (in texts), 74, 79, 81 (*see also* cohesion)
'end-weighting' of sentences, 106
enthymeme (rhetorical syllogism), 60
enumerative pattern (in paragraph structure), 22, 23, 28, 71
'escapes' from verbal blocks, 111, 112–13 (*see also* 'prompts')
existential sentences, 102–3 (*see further* highlighters)
exophoric refernece (in texts), 74, 79 (*see also* coherence, cohesion)
exposition, 23
'extensional repertoire', *see* strategies of textual continuity
extraposition, 103–4 (*see further* highlighters)

'eye-minded' (perceptual dominance), 135, 147
Eysenck, H., *Uses and Abuses of Psychology* cited, 20
  Sense and Nonsense in Psychology cited, 22, 23

FAQ ('Frequently Asked Questions') on Internet, 160, 170
  hypertext file of, 167
fiction as writer–reader dialogue, 80
'fictive' text type, 35, 37 (*see also* 'affective', 'objective' text types)
finite verb, 108 (*see also* non-finite clause forms)
'flaming' (abusive e-mail), 162 (*see also* Netiquette, 'spamming')
'flow', 'fluidity' (property of freewriting), 139, 140
focus (selection of detail) in descriptive writing, 136
focusing (syntactic highlighting), 104, 106
format, 'feel of', in e-mail, 151, 152, 189
'free' and 'bound' compositions, 183
freewriting, 139, 140, 141, 142, 143
fronting (syntactic; also pre-posing), 90, 210
front-weighting, 88
functional styles, 6, 9, 31, 34
functions of writing, 5

genre-stance, in lexicon, 120–3
Guardian (daily newspaper and supplements) cited, 49, 78, 117, 117–19, 195, 197

Hartley, L.P., *The Go-Between*

cited, 33, 37
'header' (e-mail), 152
hedges, stylistic/semantic, 20, 21, 26, 69
    metalinguistic (in e-mail), 179
    (*see also* linkers)
Hemingway, Ernest, *The Old Man and the Sea* cited, 63
highlighters ('marked' sentence forms), 102–7
    stylistic potential of, 105, 210–11
Hughes, Mark (reference to e-mail note), 179
Hunter, Evan, *The Blackboard Jungle* cited, 31, 38
hyperonym, 125 (*see further* set)
hypertext (Internet), 167
    hypertext mark-up language, 189
hyponym, 125 (*see further* set)

indirect object (grammatical), *see* simple sentence
'inductive (topic-inducing) sentence', 13
infinitive clause, *see* non-finite clause forms
infoglut (portmanteau: 'information' + 'glut'), 162, 163, 170, 176
innovative (entry to composition), *see* 'three-ring circus'
'inputting' (in e-communications), 154
interconnectedness (in e-writing), 164
interface (Internet access program), 167, 172
Internet, writing on, 144–81
    access to (for students), 152
    Idiot's Guide, 160
    influence on writing technique, 150

'logging on', 152
Netiquette, 160
resources, 151
'interruptive' terms, *see* strategies of textual continuity
intertext, 170

James, Henry, 108
James, P.A.D., *Original Sin* cited, 83, 85, 92
Jennings, P., 'Shamblers and Neatpots' cited, 27–8
Johnson, Dr, *Lives of the English Poets* cited, 10

Kipling, Rudyard, *Just-So Stories* cited, 86

'language bits' (lexia; basic units of e-writing), 158, 176
    and *infoglut*, 162, 163, 177, 180
Lanham, Richard, cited, 188
'lexia', *see* 'language bits'
lexical variation, 113
lexicon, lexis, of a text, 21
    lexical items, 53, 113
    lexicon and stance, 94
    retrieving lexical items, 115
'linear' text, 42, 91, 95, 108 (*see also* 'columnar' text)
linkers (connecting devices in texts), 20, 21, 52, 53, 59, 61, 64 (*see also* conjuncts, hedges, pro-forms in sentence-connection)
lists, 'homogeneous' and 'miscellaneous', 29
Lodge, David, 175
'looping' (in freewriting), 142
'lurk/ing' (non-interactive use of Internet), 172 (*see also* 'cruise', scroll, 'surf')

Malinowski, Bronislaw, *A Scientific Theory of Culture* cited, 55 'marked' forms, 89–90 (*see also* focusing, fronting, front-weighting; highlighters; postponed theme)

'masquerades' (of discourse function), 98

'maverick' (in lexicon), 120, 121, 122, 123

McPhee, John, *Coming into the Country* cited, 145

Melville, Herman, *Moby Dick* cited, 39, 40, 217

meronym, 125 (*see further* set)

models of writing, 19–38

multi-clause sentence, 107–9

names, stylistic value of, 119, 120, 121, 122, 123

Nash, Walter, *Language in Popular Fiction* cited, 9 (nr. 2), 13

Netiquette, 160–2

'nodal nouns', 25

non-finite clause forms, 108, 109

object (grammatical), *see* simple sentence

object complement (grammatical), *see* simple sentence

'objective' text type, 35–6 (*see also* 'affective', 'fictive' text types)

Observer newspaper, cited, 118, 119, 205

O'Hagan, Andrew, *Missing* cited, 79

Ondaatje, Michael, *In the Skin of a Lion* cited, 50–1

'On-line', access to Internet, 151–2

on-line audience, 165

on-line community, 160

on-line text as intertext, 170

paragraphs, 39–57, 195–201

'editing' and 'monitoring', 41–2, 55

'mixed' patterning, 55–6

predictive value of patterns, 51

structural patterns: Balance, 54–5; Chain, 52, 54; Stack, 48, 51; Step, 42, 43, 47, 51

paralinguistic cues (in e-mail), 179

parsing (analysing sentences), 82, 86–7, 96, 216

punctuation as parsing, 88

participation (as function of writing), 129–48

participle clause, *see* non-finite clause forms

penning (composing sentences), 82, 86–95, 216

'notions' of

content, 86, 95

pattern, 86, 89, 95

position, 86, 91, 95, 204

stance, 86, 89, 93, 95, 98, 105

weight, 86, 87, 95, 204, 205

'person, convention and society' (influences in writing), 5–6 (*see further* 'three-ring circus')

Pevsner, N., *The Buildings of England* cited, 34

phatic communion, 180

Pinter, Harold, *The Caretaker* cited, 47

place adverbial (space adjunct) in paragraph structure, 43, 44, 45, 48 (*see also* adjuncts, simple sentence)

point of view, in descriptions, 137, 147

in e-discussion, 177

Pope, Rob, *Textual Intervention* cited, 183, 219

positioning of conjuncts and disjuncts, 65–6

of non-declarative sentence forms, 98

postponed theme, 94

Practical Boat Owner magazine, cited, 118 (ext. D)

predictive value of compositional patterns, 51–2

pre-posing, *see* fronting

'presentation' in speech, 90 (*see also* postponed theme)

pro-forms in sentence-connection, 76 (*see further* anaphora, deixis)

'prompts' (for removing verbal blocks), 111, 112 (*see also* 'escapes')

'query' (in e-conversation), 175

Quirk, R., and Stein, G., *English in Use* cited, 10 (nr. 6)

reference ('referential meaning'), 32

register (text variety)
  and the lexicon, 115–24
  and sentence connection, 77–81

'register bound' writing, 123

repertoire of connectors, *see* strategies of textual continuity

rewritings and interventions, 219–25

rhetorical questions (in 'affective' prose), 31–2

Rinaldi, Arlene (and rules of Netiquette), 161

Roget, P.M., *Thesaurus* cited, 116

Schama, Simon, *Citizens* cited, 23, 24, 26, 28

Schott, Howard, *Playing the Harpsichord* cited, 10 (nr. 5)

scroll/ing, e-mail, 180 (*see also* 'cruise', 'lurk', surf)

sentence connectors, 58–81
  positioning of connectors, 65–6
  (*see also* strategies of textual continuity)

sentence length, 92–3, 204 (*see also* penning, 'notions' of weight)

sentence types (discursive/ semantic)
  declarative, 16, 58
  directive, 16
  exclamatory, 16
  interrogative, 16, 98

set (lexical), 111, 124–8, 218 (*see further* antonym, hyperonym, hyponym, meronym, synonym)

short sentence (compositional value of), 92–3

simple sentence, 86–7
  compositional scope of, 100–2
  constituents of,
    adverbial, 99
    direct object, 99
    indirect object, 100
    object complement, 100
    predicate, 99
    subject, 99
    subject complement, 99
    verb, 99

'smilies' ('paralinguistic' cue in e-mail), 179

societal purposes of writing, 4
  attitudes to writing, 7, 182–3
  frame of story, 14
  role of the writer, 7

'spamming' (e-mail advertising), 162

speed, in e-communication, 156, 157–8

stance (authorial tone), 15, 93, 94, 99, 105, 106, 197, 203, 204
  genre-stance, 120
  in e-mail, 171
  in literary reviewing, 193
  (*see also* 'affective', 'fictive', 'objective' text types; penning)

Stapleton, Michael, *The Cambridge Guide to English Literature* cited, 11 (nr. 9)

strategies of textual continuity
    cohesive, 74–7
    enumerative, 71–2
    extensional, 72–3
    interruptive, 73–4
Stroud, Robert, (maintains Web
    site), 172
style borrowing (register
    borrowing), 35
subject (grammatical), *see* simple
    sentence
subject complement
    (grammatical), *see* simple
    sentence
subordination, *see* dependency
'surf/ing' (Internet), 163, 172 (*see
    also* 'cruise', 'lurk', scroll)
synonym, 124 (*see further* set)
synthesis and analysis (in
    composition), 87
    (*see further* penning, parsing)
sysop ('system operator', Internet),
    159

techno-talk (in stylistic varieties),
    120, 121, 122, 123
text, as accumulation of sentences,
    58
    'connective themes' in, 77
    continuity of, 71
    (*see also* coherence, cohesion,
        'columnar' text, connectors,
        'linear' text, strategies of
        textual continuity)

'textual intervention' (R. Pope),
    technique of, 220–2
texture, compositional, 127 (*see
    also* register, style borrowing)
Thesaurus, using, 116, 124, 218
    (*see also* Roget, P.M.)
'thread' (of discourse, in Internet
    parlance), 173, 174, 177
'three-ring circus', approaches to
    composition, 7, 8
Thurber, James, 'The Watchers of
    the Night' cited, 10, 12, 13
topic (statement and
    development in expository
    prose), 24–5
    topic in e-mail, 153, 155
    topic sentence, 13, 49, 50, 51,
        207
    (*see also* 'thread')
topical index of Web sites, 167
Travers, Ben, *A Cuckoo in the Nest*
    cited, 44

variety, stylistic, 115–24 (*see also*
    register)
verbless adjectival clause, 108
vocabulary, 27
    active and passive, 114
    core vocabulary, 114–15
    peripheral vocabulary, 114, 115
    (*see further* lexicon)

Woolf, Virginia, 'Lappin and
    Lapinova' cited, 79–80, 83

Index B

List of interfaces, networks, packages, programs, providers, and other Internet services described in Chapter 8.

America On Line (service provider) 149

BITNET (communications network) 144

CompuServe (service provider) 149

Eudora ('mailer') 152

FTP (File Transfer Program) 151, 167

Gopher (file retrieval program) 161, 166

Infomagnet (Walker Shelby Group's Web 'Info' site) 167

JANET (research communications network) 144

Listproc (e-mail message management program) 165, 168, 171
Listserv (discussion group listings) 160, 164, 168, 171

Mosaic (access program) 150
MSN (service provider) 149

Netscape (access program) 150, 163

Pegasus ('mailer') 152

Pine ('mailer') 152
Prodigy (service provider) 149

RTIN (interface with USENET) 172

Telnet 151, 167
Tile.Com (subscription to lists) 164, 168, 172
TRN (interface with USENET) 172

URL (Uniform Resource Locator; Web address) 150, 161, 167, 168
USENET 151, 157, 158, 160, 162, 163, 164, 167, 168, 172, 173, 174

WAIS 167
WebExplorer (access and retrieval program) 150
World Wide Web ('interface of choice') 150, 151, 161, 162, 163, 167
WWW FAQ (Frequently Asked Questions; hypertext file) 167
WWW Virtual Library 167

Yahoo (topical index) 167